Modern European History

A Garland Series of Outstanding Dissertations

MODERN EUROPEAN HISTORY

Profit-sharing and Industrial Co-partnership in British Industry, 1880–1920

Class Conflict or Class Collaboration?

Jihang Park

Garland Publishing, Inc.
New York and London 1987

Library of Congress Cataloging-in-Publication Data

Park, Jihang.
Profit-sharing and industrial co-partnership in British industry, 1880–1920.

(Modern European history)
Bibliography: p.
Includes index.
1. Profit-sharing—Great Britain—History. 2. Industrial management—Great Britain—History. 3. Great Britain—Industries—History. 4. Trade-unions—Great Britain—History. I. Title. II. Series.
HD3025.A4P37 1987 331.2′164 87-25851
ISBN 0-8240-7827-6 (alk. paper)

All volumes in this series are printed on acid-free, 250-year-life paper.

Printed in the United States of America

Profit-sharing and Industrial Co-partnership in British Industry, 1880-1920: Class Conflict or Class Collaboration?

For my mother and father,

without whose prayers and support,

I could not have endured.

Contents

List of Tables

Acknowledgements

I am indebted to many people for their help throughout this long enterprise. My most immediate debt is to the members of my Ph.D. committee, Professors Bernard Semmel, Richard Kuisel, and Gary Marker, all of whom have generously given me guidance, advice, and support. Professors William R. Taylor, Fred Weinstein, and John Williams not only read the manuscript but offered me invaluable aid and useful suggestions.

Paul Chase and Chiarella Esposito made numerous contributions, including but not limited to their assistance on the computer. I must express my deep appreciation to John Martin who edited most of the manuscript and added substantially to its readability. I am also grateful to Howard Gospel, Jo Melling, and Susan Pennybacker for their help during my research in England. Jeff Kossak's encouragement and support were also extremely important helping me persevere. Finally, with great admiration, I would like to express my deepest gratitude to Professor Eric Hobsbawm, who taught me to be proud of being a historian.

My research in England was financed by the Social Science Research Council, to which I am most grateful.

Author's Note

In this book, the symbol for the British pound (£) is rendered as L.

Introduction

Ever since the idea of profit-sharing and industrial co-partnership took hold in Europe in the mid-nineteenth century, they have had a significant role to play in industrial economy. Almost from the start, profit-sharing and co-partnership were touted as a panacea to the chronic problems of labor disputes and declining productivity. By giving the worker positive motivation and by binding his interest to that of the employer, profit-sharing and co-partnership were thought to permit the greatest possible productivity and stability in labor-management relations. Although, after a time, such enthusiasm somewhat diminished, they were still seen as a most practicable solution. They also continued to be thought of as an extremely desirable element in future industrial organization; indeed they were called the "best remedy that the wit of man so far has devised."

This optimistic assessment has persisted for more than a century--indeed, since the Second World War, France, Great Britain, and West Germany, among others, have passed legislation to promote profit-sharing and industrial participation. In France and Germany, this has been done by statutory enforcement; in Britain, by such typical inducements as tax benefits.

While 'co-partnership' has been replaced by such terms as 'codetermination,' 'employee co-ownership,' and 'workshop democracy,' the present day system strikingly resembles the earlier one. Here, then, is an important reason for an in-depth historical study of profit-sharing and co-partnership, which are today receiving more and more attention in both the industrial and industrializing nations. Profit-sharing was an arrangement by which the employer and the employee agreed to share whatever profits remained according to a proportion fixed in advance, after all the expenses, such as dividends, salaries and wages, and reinvestment, were met. Co-partnership, on the other hand, was a system under which the employee received his bonus in company stock and thereby became a shareholder. In theory, at least, he assumed shareholder rights and responsibilities, finally reaching the board room and thus sharing control. However, for practical purposes, the two terms were interchangeable. The present dissertation also refers to them interchangeably unless a specific argument concerning their differences is made.

In the present dissertation, I discuss (a) the economic and industrial circumstances in Britain under which profit-sharing and co-partnership came into being, (b) the merits and drawbacks of the system as both advocates and opponents saw them, (c) the motivations of employers in introducing profit-sharing schemes, and (d) the implementing of such notable schemes as that of Lever Brothers, a multinational corporation based in Britain. Finally, I assess the role of profit-sharing and co-partnership in the development of modern management practices and industrial relations.

Both contemporary and historical evaluations of profit-sharing have considered it basically a means of control in the workplace as well as in greater society, achieved through giving the worker a stake in the existing social and economic structure. It has also been seen as a management strategy for alienating trade unions from their members--this being a response to the fact that these unions ostensibly adopted socialist policies in the years after 1889. Not surprisingly, then, profit-sharing was proclaimed the best antidote to socialism.

The anti-union factor in the profit-sharing movement, however, has been overemphasized. While profit-sharing originally included a strong anti-union motive and tried to bind the employee's interest to that of the employer, it must be understood that as economic and industrial circumstances changed, so did employer motives and the profit-sharing rationale. Anti-union motives had largely disappeared from the scene by the first decade of the twentieth century, when profit-sharing was employed as a more progressive strategy for greater industrial efficiency and better industrial relations based upon the recognition of trade unionism. This change in employers' attitude derived from their realization that trade unions had come to stay. They also understood that repression was neither the most workable nor the most desirable policy towards labor. At the same time, since the British economy began to worsen generally after 1880, the rationale for profit-sharing was that of techinique whereby to achieve greater efficiency and greater productivity.

This changing attitude reflects the development in management practices that was taking place in the years after 1880. In this period, faced with the declining position of the British economy, progressive employers set about devising ways of utilizing their labor and materials. They also developed new methods of organization and control. This thrust towards greater efficiency proceeded in two distinct directions: scientific management and industrial welfare. Although retrospectively profit-sharing has been simply labeled as a welfare program, it was a function of these two moves towards efficiency and devolved from the premises of both Taylorism and industrial welfare. Profit-sharing resembled Taylorism in its emphasis on incentive wages: it was believed that profit-sharing would improve productivity and thus increase profits as a result of the workers' greater diligence and enthusiasm under the bonus system.

At the same time, unlike Taylorism, which treated the woreker merely as a factor of production, profit-sharing was thouhgt capable of producing a contented workforce through its inclusive "human touch" policy. Many profit-sharing schemes recognized the importance of human dimension and thus provided for (a) the setting up of various works committees; (b) the participation of employees in low level management.

The present study therefore places greater emphasis on profit-sharing as a means for achieving greater industrial efficiency than it does on profit-sharing as a means for achieving contol. The concern with social disorder may have attracted the attention of politicians and concerned individuals in the upper classes, but it was a lesser matter to practical employers. The above argument is the unifying theme throughout this study, and it is specifically discussed in chapters I, VI, and IX.

Another important question dealt with in the present dissertation is the relationship between profit-sharing and trade unionism, which is of particular significance, both because of contemporary understanding and the traditional historical evaluation of the system. If it has been simplistically argued that employers conceived of profit-sharing merely as a weapon with which to fight the unions, it has been just as simplistically argued that the unions played a significant role in deterring the progress of the profit-sharing movement. A closer examination, however, demonstrates that there was no such thing as uniform hostility among trade unionists. Most of the "respectable" old trade union leaders, such as Thomas Burt, warmly welcomed profit-sharing schemes and were actively engaged in promoting the movemet, while the leaders of the new unions that sprang up after 1889 raised vociferous opposition. At the same time, the socialists and the more articulate section of the working class totally disapproved of profit-sharing on the grounds that all profit-making was wrong in and of itself.

However, it is important to bear in mind that a considerable number of union leaders either found no contradiction between trade unions and profit-sharing or, if they did find such contradiction, allowed later experience to alter their thinking. By and large, the British trade unions never seriously considered undertaking a revolutionary transformation of society, and appear to have willingly accepted whatever extra benefits came their way under the existing circumstances. This observation is unfolded in chapters III and V.

Bearing on the question of the union relationship to profit-sharing is the issue of the rank and file's perception of the system. That perception was diverse, depending on the degree of labor organization, the nature of the industry, the strength and make-up of the union involved and its leadership, and the previous history of industrial relations in each industry and each firm. To make things more difficult, it is hard to find the voice of the rank and file. However, the two case studies explored in this dissertation, Lever Brothers and the South Metropolitan Gas Company, apart from other scattered evidene, demonstrate an unmistakable rank and file enthusiasm and show the workers' appreciation of profit-sharing's material benefits. Significantly, when their right to participate in the schemes and to receive financial benefits was hampered by the unions, the rank and file quickly challenged their union leadership. Indeed, they went so far as to sue their union--as the case of Lever Brothers' employees demonstrated.

This sharply contradicts the notion of militant rank and file militancy versus moderate union leadership that has been habitually held by historians and sociologists. On the contrary, it was generally the leadership that pressed for bitter resistance to profit-sharing. These are the themes of chapters III, V, VII, and VIII, the last two being case studies that show worker responses in real terms.

It is true that profit-sharing and co-partnership were often touted as the best solution to indutrial ills. It is not true that the idea was universally popular: the number of schemes instituted during the period under consideration, 1880-1920, remained in a minority. Indeed, profit-sharing is still in a minority apart from those nations where the system is imposed by law. This crucial fact needs to be explained and the present study finds the answer is twofold: human and structural. The most important element was human: the opposition of employers and managers. Most of them viewed profit-sharing and co-partnership simply as an expropriation of capitalist property to the benefit of the workers. Although the advocates of profit-sharing argued that the system would enhance worker productivity and that the worker would therefore improve output in proportion to increased shares under the system, the employer perception was hard to change.

At the same time, the structure of modern industry often hampered the expansion of profit-sharing and co-partnership. First, there were certain industries and occupations in which profit-sharing could not be applied, or if it could, in which it would not produce the desired effect and therefore remain unattractive. Nationalized industries and self-employing occupations were not generally amenable to profit-sharing. Second, there were also industries in which the work was irregular and seasonal and whose very nature, then, made it impossible to establish any coherent system based on regular wages or length of service. Finally, there were industries in which the cost of labor was such a comparatively minor part of the total cost that any attempt to reduce it through ruling out profit-sharing was unnecessary. Generally speaking, profit-sharing is most likely to work in an industry where the ratio of the labor cost to the total cost is high. The above argument is made in chapters IV and IX.

Chapters VI and VII demonstrate the specific practices of profit-sharing schemes in representative companies. I chose the South Metropolitan Gas Company because it was the most conspicuous example of profit-sharing being introduced as a result of conflict between capital and labor. In relation to South Metropolitan, I discuss profit-sharing schemes in the gas industry as a whole--for profit-sharing most prospered in this industry. By its very nature, the gas industry enjoyed advantages in promoting the system. I discuss the nature of the industry, the organization of labor, and the general and particular situation of the gas industry with respect to the practice of profit-sharing. I also examine the scheme of Lever Brothers, the largest soap manufacturing company in England. The Lever scheme was advertised as an example of modern management, ostensibly opposed to paternalism or philanthropy, and emphatically pursuing efficiency. William Lever, later Lord Leverhulme, proclaimed that it was "strictly business," and the sole goal of his scheme was eficiency. However, many elements of philanthropy and paternalism can be discerned in this particular scheme, and it provides a most interesting picture, particularly as contrasted with the South Metropolitan scheme.

In the last chapter, I attempt to draw some

conclusions based on the findings and the discussions of the preceding sections. The concept of profit-sharing must be looked at in the context of the development of modern management. Above all, it represents an employer strategy to establish more efficient and more systematic management practices in response to rapidly changing economic circumstances in the late nineteenth and the early twentieth centuries. Profit-sharig employers were progressive in the sense that they realized that a low wage economy and the stifling of labor organization were no longer the best way to achieve productivity and profits. They were also shrewd enough to realize that "agreeable control is better than enforced control," and therefore replaced coercion and repression with tactics that were often subtle and inventive.

By providing the worker with greater wages under a bonus system than he would have received elsewhere, and by setting up various works committees and consultation committees, profit-sharing promoted a gradual integration of employees into business. To be sure the degree of such integration was considerably limited in most cases. Profit-sharing, however, was a policy of giving before being forced to give, and represented an attitude vividly summed up by Henry Ford: "The employer must meet the employee half-way, and always be there a little ahead of time."

Chapter 1. Economic and Political Circumstances

The changing language of profit-sharing speaks for the history of its fluctuating popularity in British society. In their early stages, profit-sharing and co-partnership were praised as the panacea to the problems that Britain had to confront both internally and externally. Then they came to be thought of as one stage in the development of industrial organization. Even so, it was still considered a most desirable step towards the final goal of complete co-operation between capital and labor.

In spite of the extravagant claims of its early advocates, profit-sharing could not solve all industrial difficulties. Many of these problems had their roots deep in the industrial system, which no single device could expect to eradicate. Thus it was admitted that profit-sharing was "no panacea." It would not make bad people good, nor a bad business a good one: it had not produced "a body of spotless angels." However, it was still thought that profit-sharing would make "decent folks better and it did make a good business a better one," and still was believed to be the "best remedy that the wit of man so far has devised."[1]

These vicissitudes made one contemporary observer

realize how curious it was that "some remedies for our industrial ills come to the front at one period then sink almost into neglect only to be resuscitated at a later stage in history." This tendency had been "particularly noticeable in the case of various forms of co-partnership."[2] Nevertheless, interest in profit-sharing has persisted more than a century since it appeared on the industrial scene, perhaps longer than the interest in any other plan of industrial organization that has come to light.

While profit-sharing emerged in the mid-nineteenth century, it did not attract much attention until the last decades of the century. It was ardently advocated by economists and social reformers but largely ignored by employers and vigorously opposed by certain sections of the labor movement. Finally the movement never became as widespread as expected, yet gained momentum from time to time. It was never a powerful force, but it maintained its modest position for over a century and gradually widened its scope. In the 1960s and 1970s it gained renewed interest: a number of major European countries, including France, West Germany, and Britain, passed legislation to promote profit-sharing and industrial partnership: in France and Germany, this has been done by compulsory enforcement; in Britain and the U.S., by such financial inducements as tax benefits.

The pioneer profit-sharing scheme appeared in

France in 1842: in Britain, the first plan was embarked on in 1865, but this newly devised system did not receive much attention until 1889-90, when it suddenly took hold with the power of the idea whose time has come. No fewer than 83 schemes were started in 1889-92: thereafter, it gained great momentum during two more periods: the years 1912-14 and 1919-20. as the table below demonstrates. Interestingly, these three high points coincided with periods of grave industrial unrest, as the 1920 report of the Ministry of Labour on profit-sharing and co-partnership noted. Why such a sudden enthusiasm? The answer lay in the economic and political circumstances of the time.

Table 1.1 The Number of Profit-sharing Schemes Started, 1865-1920

Year	Total number of schemes started	number per year
1865-1888	66	2.8
1889-1892	83	20.8
1893-1911	132	6.9
1912-1914	51	17
1915-1918	18	4.5
1919-1920	89	44.5

Source: Ministry of Labour, _Report on Profit-sharing and Labour Co-partnership in the U.K._, Cd. 544 (1920), pp.9-10.

The last quarter of the nineteenth century was a period in which Britain encountered the gravest economic difficulties in its modern history. The decline of her economy and trade became evident through reduced profit margins and through increasing foreign competition, particularly from Germany and America in the last quarter of the nineteenth century. It was obvious that Britain was losing its claim to the title of "the workshop of the world."

This worsening economic climate was accompanied by an upsurge in labor unrest which picked up momentum from the socialist unions of 1889-90 and from syndicalism in the years after 1910.[3] This mounting labor militancy terminated the tranquil decades of collaboration that had followed the end of the Chartist movement. Labor's challenge took two forms: (a) organization and collective resistance, which resulted in a rapid increase of trade union membership and strikes during this period; and (b) informal and spontaneous struggle over job performance on what Carter Goodrich called the "frontier of control."[4] In 1889, the number of strikes reached 1,211, involving 337,000 workers, tripled from that of the previous year. The year 1890 saw 1,040 strikes and 393,000 workers idle through those strikes.[5] A survey of industrial disputes during the period 1900-3 shows that conflict over managerial prerogatives arising from changes in working arrangements became increasingly common. This was so because between 1880-1914, workers began to learn what Hobsbawm refers to as "the rules of the game," while employers were losing the advantages they had enjoyed owing to the workers' ignorance.[6]

Thus, the years 1880-1920 saw a vigorous struggle for control between employers and workers, as such historians as Richard Price point out.[7] According to them, the struggle for control by the workers represented a grave challenge to the existing modes of capitalist relations. Understandably, the elimination of industrial waste and the promotion of industrial harmony were conceived of as imperative if Britain was to survive, let alone to retain her position in the world economy.

The journal of the Amalgamated Society of Engineers described the capitalist position as akin to that of the man who found himself "between the devil and the deep sea: the devil in the form of strongly organized labor faces them on the one hand, whilst on the other, is the deep sea of nationalization."[8] Socialism had begun to permeate the labor movement in the 1880s and influenced the politicization of the working class in the 1890s. The Trade Union Congress was regularly passing a resolution for nationalization of land and mines since 1893. Although much of it remained rhetoric, the general mood of the time seemed to indicate the undermining of the existing structure of society. The early twentieth century was to witness another revolutionary movement, syndicalism. Syndicalism, among others, appeared so great a threat that Edward Walls, a director of Lever Brothers, declared that "the utter reign into which Syndicalism and Guild Socialism would lead us make State Socialism seem innocuous by contrast."[9]

The question of the time was considered on two assumptions: "either the existing wage system continue, modified to face the present day conditions, or the existing capitalist organization of industry be abolished--with the wage system also."[10] Figures like George Livesey, the chairman of South Metropolitan Gas Company who was a staunch anti-socialist and a strong supporter of profit-sharing, declared that the wage system had failed:

> If the wage-hire system has not failed, why are capital and labor at war? Capital and labor are so interdependent, and indispensible to each other, and have such a real identity of interest that the undoubted fact of their antagonism indicates something radically wrong in the system of payment by wages.11

Other individuals such as William Lever, the owner of the largest soap manufacturing firm in England, Lever Brothers, held an unbroken belief in the wage system and believed in its economic strength. After all, "the wage system has stood the test of the time," Lever repeatedly asserted; it was "a convenient system, logical and practicable, and an ideal system because it is the most workable."[12] Those who believed in the wage system, however, admitted the need for modification to make it even more workable.

Profit-sharing was considered in this context: it appeared as a new ideal wage system within the boundaries of capitalism. Basically, profit-sharing was an attempt to retain the capitalist system through modification. It never touched the basic frame of capitalism. Profit-sharing would simply add some change by giving a greater stake and a larger share of profits to workers while preserving the merits of the capitalist system intact and keeping efficiency of financial and technical control. Profit-sharing regarded the entire profits of industry as morally and economically the property of the capitalist, unlike a socialist claim which regarded it as the property of the manual workers. Even radical supporters such as G. J. Holyoake, a secularist and a leader of the cooperative movement, were not so much anti-capitalist as anti-socialist and contended that labor, whether "labor of hand or brain," ought to receive a dividend, in addition to wages or salaries, up to a 10 percent limit. Such an arrangement would "satisfy labor for two centuries to come."[13]

Although some viewed profit-sharing as "the third way between capitalism and socalism" as de Gaulle was to describe it years later in the 1960s, or as the combination of "the best points of both Socialism and Individualism," it was a perfect substitute for the threat of socialism to a majority of proponents. It seemed a "definite constructive policy" that could meet socialism.[14] A vigorous campaign for maintaining the existing structure of capital, management, and labor was conducted. Sir Benjamin Browne, a prominent engineering employer, preached:

> It is absolutely self-evident that nothing is more injurious to the interest of the working classes than to worry, frighten or interrupt the only man who finds the capital, organizes the industry, and gets the orders--the only man in fact who can give employment.[15]

Sir Christopher Furness, later Lord Furness, a captain of industry and twice Liberal MP from the Hartlepools, boasted himself as such a man. He often referred to the service he rendered to his employees, namely to find work for 40,000 or 50,000 men whom he employed in the giant Furness combine and to pay them over L 60,000 every week.[16] William Lever preached what might be termed a "management theory of value" as an alternative for the labor theory of value, placing management at the core of production.[17]

Their political economy understandably stressed the importance of competition and the priority of production to distribution. Socialism was a misfortune, it was argued, for the whole country and particularly for the working class because socialism, without proper stimulus of individual reward, would bring about less prosperity. At the same time, to increase the size of the pudding was more important than to quarrel over the portion each of capital and labor would take. Socialism was not the best way to make the poor richer, George Livesey asserted, for "it is very easy to make the rich poor, but it does not follow that thereby you will make the poor richer."[18]

This reasoning received powerful support from the main stream political economists including J. S. Mill and Alfred Marshall. Mill proclaimed that every restriction of competition was "an evil, and every extension of it, even if for the time injuriously affecting some class of laborers, is always an ultimate good." To be protected against competition was to be protected "in idleness, in mental dullness."[19]

To Marshall as well, competition was absolutely essential for progress. His ideal engine of progress was the small business with its captain of industry, always pressing forward with initiative and enterprise, whereas socialism meant management by a governmental department. He believed that, unless the total production of wealth was increased, the portion returning to labor would remain as little as ever. To him, socialism could not guarantee greater wealth. Marshall admitted the merits of labor organization and the efficiency of trade unions on wages and other working conditions. But such an organization did not increase the amount of bread and butter of the world; all it did was "to take away from other factors of production and other classes of society."[20]

Importantly, profit-sharing was not merely a preventive: it was a more aggressive policy of incorporation. A prominent businessman asserted that "In democratic capitalism such as ours, one way to broaden the capitalist system is to see that more people have a stake in it."[21] It is not surprising, therefore, to find that the Anti-Socialist Union took profit-sharing as the most promising device to fight Socialism. "There is no stronger rampart against the assaults of Socialism," declared a writer of the Anti-Socialist Union, "than arrangements which will allow the workers to participate in the profits of the business in which they were engaged." The goal was converting the "have nots" to the "haves."[22] Thomas A. Brassey, a prominent captain of industry who practiced profit-sharing in a mine he owned in Sardinia and once served as the vice-president of the Labour Co-partnership Association, asserted that had the South Wales mines been administered in past years on the profit-sharing principles, "Keir Hardie or any of his type would not be members of Parliament for South Wales."[23]

If profit-sharing impressed the general public and politicians, who were alarmed at the industrial turbulence in the years after 1889, it also inspired practical employers who felt an urgent need for efficiency caused by severe labor conflict. The declining economy pressed employers to turn to the innovation of technology and reorganization on the one hand, and on the other, to tighter control over the workforce through more calculated methods of manipulation. Naturally, these employer strategies provoked stronger worker resistance than ever. The tightening of employer control and worker resistance were indeed simultaneous and reciprocal. While a new supervisory system, a new payment system and workshop reorganization were initiated in the period after 1880, the reinforcement of employer control simultaneously inspired militancy and radicalism among the workers. Thus, the struggle between employer and worker over control was severe in the years 1880-1920.

Among the most severely criticized worker resistance was the restriction of output. This practice stemmed largely from the doctrine that "there is only a fixed amount of employement to be had, and therefore the less any worker does, the more there will be for others to do."[24] Restricted output did not, however, result simply from a workers' sympathy with his fellow men. It was also a challenge to economic disparity in the capitalist system. Emile Pouget, the syndicalist leader and advocate of sabotage, was reported to have recommended that the working class follow this policy: "bad wages, bad labor," or "an unfair day's work for an unfair day's wages."[25]

Understandably, this practice was vigorously attacked by employers. A building employer in Coventry asserted: "I am of opinion that the men have so long been encouraged by trade unions to do less that they cannot now perform the same amount of work as they formerly could."[26] Restricted output, however, was not confined to skilled workers or union workers. Edward Cadbury, a Quaker chocolate manufacturer in Bournville who conducted various industrial and social surveys, discovered that even young, largely unorganized girls assigned to piecework practiced systematic output restriction.[27] Hence the urgent industrywide need to eliminate such deliberate waste and inefficiency. One aim of Frederick W. Taylor's scientific management was precisely that of remedying the evil of output restriction.

Appropriately, this period coincided with that of the beginning of modern management. Although the genesis of modern management can be traced back to the early days of the industrial revolution, as Sidney Pollard points out, the decades after 1880 saw the existence of systematic management and an increasing desire for a scientific approach to management.[28] On the whole, British employers were late in perceiving the need for effective management. The idea of comprehensively managing the worker had captured the attention of only a few exceptional employers in the years up to 1914. As late as 1891, an employer expressed his disapproval of "managing the men," for he believed that the men knew "what their work is and how to do it." They were no slaves, he said, to be driven by whips to work and duty, but men "with minds and conscience, able to and willing to do a fair day's work for a fair day's pay."[29] This was in sharp contrast to the scientific management movement that was taking hold in America around the same time.

However, the indifference of British industry to the question of management had begun to disappear by the last decades of the nineteenth century. A small number of shrewd and progressive employers began to seek a more effective approach for coordinating resources and workforce. Gradually, systematic supervision, the recruiting of a professional management staff, and the incentive wage system became accepted elements of efficient industrial operation.[30] Piecework and the premium bonus system attracted much attention and became a popular form of payment, particularly in the engineering industries, where foreign competition was most keenly felt.

This efficiency movement has been labelled as scientific management or Taylorism, taking its name from the founder of the movement, Frederick W. Taylor. Scientific management was the outgrowth of the works management movement and the pioneering work of Frederick Taylor at the Midvale and Bethlehem Steel Companies in the 1880s and 1890s. Far from being a totally new system, it was in large part derived from old ideas, the most notable of which were the time study and the incentive system.[31]

Its basic idea was to increase the material benefits of both employer and employee, achieving this through wage incentive plans for the worker and increased output for the employer.

Its value, however, supposedly did not stop there: it was also said to be the best means to overcome class conflict at the factory. This would be done as "both sides take their eyes off the division of the surplus until this surplus becomes so large that it is unnecessary to quarrel over how it shall be divided."[32] Under the influence of scientific management, piecework and the subcontracting system lost favor and were replaced to a considerable degree by management-designed incentive payments. In the most progressive and larger firms, meanwhile, a centralized system for the selection and training of workers was being established.[33]

To be sure, the development of systematic management in British industry went only so far. This was traceable not only to the structure of industry but to human factors as well. For the most part, systematic management was limited only to the newer, larger, and more progressive industries and firms. In the majority of companies, the traditional practices persisted due to the small size and the uncertainty of the market. At the same time, the climate of employer sentiment remained hostile to Taylorism. Very few employers read Taylor and even those exceptional ones who did, disagreed on the ground that it was inhuman and simply another form of speed-up.[34] And there was the opposition of organized labor which viewed it simply as a new means of exploitation. To sum up, then, there were reasons for the unpopularity of scientific management in Britain: (a) the unsuitability of the small firm; (b) the opposition of those employers who felt the system was inhuman; and (c) the opposition of organized labor, which viewed it simply as a new means of exploitation.

The slow spread of the premium bonus system can be seen from the fact that the Amalgamated Society of Engineers, the union most affected, had less than 10 percent of its employed members working under the bonus system in 1909.[35] As late as 1917, the president of the Institute of Mechanical Engineers was exposing the archaic practices of the British engineering industry as follows:

> Except in a few cases, workshop organization here has not received the attention given in America or Germany. There are still shops without definite planning of the process of the work...and without standard shapes of tools of a tool-room;...where men drift about in search of tools or tackles; where machinery is obsolete and light is so bad that good work cannot be done.36

Thus, scholars such as Craig Littler argue that the British thrust towards scientific management did not really gather full force until the 1930s. Gordon and others make the same argument as to the serious introduction of Taylorism into American industry.[37] However, it is important to recognize that the last years of the nineteenth century clearly began to see this unprecedented and significant departure in managerial practice, limited as it may have been.

The development of modern management was by no means restricted to scientific management; an equally important development was industrial welfare. Welfare work was hardly an innovation of this period: it went back at least as far as Robert Owen and such followers as Titus Salt. These early welfare approaches, however, derived in essence from paternalism and tended to be conducted on a communal basis. In the closing years of the nineteenth century, another type of employer was converted to welfarism; his motives were understandably quite different and welfare work was relocated to the workplace. Thus, William Lever, a leading welfarist employer, asserted that welfare work was not a question of canteens, model villages, free libraries and so on but was much more a question of "wages and hours, of ventilation in the factory, of cubic air space, of heating and lighting and sanitation."[38]

Industrial welfare was neither a homogeneous nor an integrated movement. Unlike Taylorism, which encompassed a definite set of practices, such as incentive wages, welfare work would include any number of programs: old age pension, free library, canteen. skill training, and profit-sharing...all these were conceived of as welfare programs. Thus there was no clear definition of welfare, and Daniel Nelson points out the extreme range of provisions that were identified as belonging to it.[39]

Like Taylorism, welfare work was also a response to the business man's demand for a more systematic approach to labor problems, and aimed at reducing the cost of production by improving the worker's performance and reducing labor resistance by improving his living and working conditions. The new generation of welfarist employers shared a high regard for efficiency. They agreed with Edward Cadbury's assertion that business efficiency and the welfare of the employees were "but different sides of the same problem."

> A business could best avoid waste and loss, by making the well-being and development of the employee at least of equal consideration to the rate of per cent paid as dividend on capital. The highest function of a business was the development and perfecting of the health and character of the employee.40

Leading welfarist employers, such as William Lever, preached that welfare work coalesced with the "truest and highest form of enlightened self-interest": "Enlightened self-interest required that we pay the fullest regard to the interest and welfare of those around us, whose welfare we must bind with our own, and with whom we must share our prosperity."[41] With this goal in mind, Lever launched what he called prosperity-sharing, a version of profit-sharing, and then transformed it into co-partnership.

Other employers who hardly listened to the preaching of the leading welfarists had begun to discover the value of welfare work on their own. One such employer not only practiced profit-sharing, he also paid higher wages than the district rate for shorter working hours and provided paid holidays. He asserted that good treatment of employees was a major factor in the striking success of his business, which expanded seven fold in three years. Yet he was not motivated by any humanitarian concern and frankly declared, "You know I do not believe in philanthropy in business."[42] Perhaps the difference between the early paternalistic welfare employers and the employers of the later period is that the early employers had no desire to prove that welfare provided a return in the way of the usual investment, whereas the new generation "scientifically" calculated the effects of welfare measures.

Again, the limits of welfare work ought to be noted. It was prevalent mainly in larger and more profitable sectors of industry. The larger and more profitable companies not only had the resources to establish a welfare program but recognized the necessity effectively coordinating workplace and workforce. Their understanding of the need for efficiency helped them create a more progressive management. Undoubtedly, welfare work was not confined only to the Quaker firms, as the conventional studies on welfare work tend to argue.[43] Nevertheless, the number of firms which provided any form of systematic welfare remained considerably small. It was only during the First World War that welfare work was extended and elaborated through encouragement from the government.[44]

If principles and approaches of these two movements differed, they nevertheless met at one point in reality. As discussed above, both scientific management and industrial welfare were a response to the labor question. They aimed at achieving the maximum efficiency and the greatest material benefits for both the employer and the employee. One particular form of scientific management was to take care that every worker was in a position to render his or her services in the most efficient manner, and in order to secure it, perfect physical health, an untroubled mind, and a cheerful disposition were sought for. The famous welfare works, such as Cadbury's Bournville, aimed at the same result. The careful selection and training of workers as well as the avoidance of fatigue were commonly found in Bournville and indeed at any factory adopting Taylorism.[45]

This was the point where welfare and scientific management most conspicuously intersected.

However, the similarity of the two stopped there. For the proponents of scientific management, the incentive wage was the answer to labor unrest; the proponents of industrial welfare, by contrast, looked at the non-material side of worker function and worker grievance. Like most engineers of the period, Frederick Taylor considered welfare work a "joke." He was interested in the worker's welfare not from a humanitarian standpoint but as a matter of economy: "just as a man objects to having a horse abused for he becomes less efficient."[46] Ultimately, Taylor's view of industrial relations derived from his belief in the efficacy of the incentive wage: "No self-respecting workman wants to be given things, every man wants to earn things."[47]

Welfare employers, on the other hand, viewed scientific management as simply another form of the speed-up and objected to its effect on the worker's moral and physical condition. Aware of the importance of the human factor in industry, employers like Seebohm Rowntree, another progressive and benevolent Quaker employer who conducted the famous survey on poverty in York, asserted that "Business has a soul; it is not a sordid mechanical thing but a living and worthy part of the social organization."[48] Thus, they endeavored to establish a rational and humane policy in employer-employee relations rather than simply relying on incentive wages.

Profit-sharing and co-partnership reflected these moves toward systematic management, and demonstrated major principles of these two distinctive movements. Profit-sharing admittedly resembled Taylorism in its emphasis on trying to solve labor problems through incentive wages. Many practical employers indeed saw profit-sharing as a corporate bonus scheme and a system of payment by results, as we shall see in chapter VI. But it was very different from Taylorism in its insistence on treating the worker as a human being rather than as a mere factor of production. Thus, it was to introduce into industry the personal touch and help establish fully human labor-management relationship. The function of profit-sharing was, then, first to make the worker's income greater than it would have been otherwise, and second, to buy his human interest and enthusiasm through the policy of incorporation. Profit-sharing was a modified form of efficiency movement with a human face. Taylor's fundamental motivation, as was discussed, derived from a desire to increase production. The welfarist employers on the other hand paid more concern to the labor turmoil and tried to overcome it.

Further discussion on profit-sharing as both incentive system and a welfare program will be found in chapter VI, which deals with employers' motivations behind adopting profit-sharing. Here, it is only necessary to note that profit-sharing reflects the response to labor challenge that was threatening the existing capitalist system with increasing intensity, and the abrupt thrust towards efficiency in industry that characterized the years from 1880 to 1920.

Notes to Chapter I

1. Labour Co-partnership, June 1906, p.83, Nov. 1913, p. 162: Labour Co-partnership Association, Report, 1905-6, p.14; William Lever, "Prosperity-sharing; Rejoinder," Economic Review, 11 (July 1901), p.321.

2. H. Sanderson Furniss, "Co-partnership and Labour Unrest," Economic Review, 23 (Jan. 1913), p.61.

3. Labor unrest was not a peculiar phenomenon in Britain in this period: it was found in all industrialized nations and thus, it was argued that the country which first found a soution to it would dominate the industrial world. See James Bowie, Sharing Profits with Employees (London: Sir Isaac Pitnam, 1922), p.144.

4. Carter Goodrich, The Frontier of Control (London: G. Bell, 1920).

5. James Cronin, Industrial Conflict in Modern Britain (London: Croom Helm, 1980), pp. 206-211.

6. Keith Burgess, The Challenge of Labour (London: Croom Helm, 1980), p.84; Eric Hobsbawm, "Custom, Wages, and Work-load" in Labouring Men (Garden City, N.Y.: Doubleday, 1967), p.413.

7. Richard Price, Masters, Unions, and Men: Work Control in Building and the Rise of Labour 1830-1914 (Cambridge: Cambridge Univ. Press, 1980), especially pp.6-11, and chapter 7; Price, "The Labour Process and Labour History," Social History, 8, (Jan. 1983), pp.57-75; Jo Melling, "Employers, Industrial Welfare, and the Struggle for Workplace Control in British Industry, 1880-1920" in Managerial Strategies and Industrial Relations ed. Howard Gospel and Craig Littler (London: Heineman, 1983), pp.56-81.

8. Amalgamated Engineers Journal, Aug. 1912, p.27.

9.
William Wallace, _Prescription for Partnership_ (London: Sir Isaac Pitman, 1959), p.257. British syndicalism has been largely underestimated. However, according to recent studies, syndicalism, of all forms of socialism, had the greatest impact on the British working class in the early twentieth century. Moreover, allowing that what counts is not the concrete achievement of the movement but the impact of the general atmosphere, syndicalism clearly appears to have been a very vital force in the working class movement in the pre war era. See Bob Holton, _British Syndicalism, 1900-1914_ (London: Pluto, 1976), especially chapters 4, 9, and pp.202-212; Joseph White, "1910-1914 Reconsidered" in _Social Conflict and the Political Order in Modern Britain_ ed. J. Cronin and J. Schneer (New Brunswick, N.J.: Ruters Univ. Press, 1982), pp.84-5, 92-3.

10.
L. Maccasey, "National Wage Position," _Nineteenth Century_, 81 (Nov. 1920), p.760.

11.
George Livesey, "The Failure of the Wages System of Payment and the Remedy--Profit-sharing," Institute of Gas Engineers, _Transactions_ (1892), p.35.

12.
Progress, Dec. 1912.

13.
Labour Co-partnership, Dec. 1901, p. 87.

14.
Economist, May 3, 1980, p.84; _Parliamentary Debates_, 5th series, vol 34, p.115, Feb. 15, 1912.

15.
Benjamin Browne, _Selected Papers on Social and Economic Questions_ (Cambridge: Cambridge Univ. Press), p.221.

16.
Clarion, Oct. 8, 1908.

17.
William Lever, _The six-hour Day and Other Industrial Questions_ (London: George Allen and Unwin, 1918), p.313. Benjamin Browne stated the labor theory of value as "just like saying that all the credit of a cup of

tea is due to the hot water and nothing at all to the dried leaf." Selected Papers, p.158.

18.
South Metropolitan Gas Company, Co-partnership, 1908, p.194. Socialism was absolutely disregarded by advocates of the system. Robert Cecil, for one, maintaind that state socialism would make the employer more impersonal than he was now. "The question is to devise a plan to humanize the existing conditions of things, and make the workman feel that he is more than a machine." Labour Co-partnership, Dec. 1912. p.182.

19.
John S. Mill, Principles of Political Economy, Collected Works vol. 3 (Toronto: University of Toronto Press, 1965), p.795.

20.
Pigou's reasoning followed a close line to Marshall's. Like Marshall, Pigou was also concerned primarily with production than distribution. He pointed out that the only means to raise the aggregate amount of real wages were, first, a transfer from other sections to the working class, and second, an increase in the size of the whole heap. Plainly he saw no other way. Pigou was against the first method which he saw as a simple confiscation of the rich. A. Marshall, Poverty and Wages, Three Lectures by Alfred Marshall on Henry George's Economic Ideas (London: 1885), p.6; A. C. Pigou, Alfred Marshall and Current Thought (London: Macmillan, 1953), p.59; Pigou, Limiting Factors in Wage Rates and how they can be improved by Altering Distribution or Increasing Production (London: Labour Co-partnership Association, 1920), pp.6-8.

21.
P. S. Narashimhan, "Profit-sharing: A Review," International Labour Review, 62 (Dec. 1950), p.477.

22.
Anti-Socialist, April 3, 1909.

23.
Times, Dec. 11, 1912, 10d. In an attempt to pursuade the working class, even the similarity of socialism and co-partnership was presented. Both were forms of collectivism, it was argued, and co-partnership indeed "sprang from socialism and therefore socialism is its parent; like socialism, co-partnership aimes at the common ownership of business; the difference lies in that whereas socialism employes compulsory collectivism, co-partnership advocates voluntary collectivism." Labour Co-partnership, May 1913, p.56.

24.
E. H. Phelps Brown and M. H. Browne, A Century of Pay (London: Macmillan, 1968), p.86. This alarming problem was vividly exposed by Edwin Pratt's articles on restriction of output in the Times in 1900-1. Pratt's articles were later published as book: Trade Unionism and British Industry (London: John Murry, 1904).

25.
Quoted in S. B. Mathewson, Restriction of Output Among Unorganized Workers (London: 1931; rpt. Arcturus, 1969), p.xxix.

26.
Quoted by Thomas Bushill, Royal Commission on Labour, Sitting as a Whole, Minutes of Evidence Cd. 7063-i (1893), Q. 6010. One trade union official indeed estimated the difference in value between limited output and output of efficient working to be at least 30 percent. See Quarterly Review, "Profit-sharing and Co-partnership," 202 (1905), p.62.

27.
Craig Littler, The Development of the Labour Process in Capitalist Societies (London: Heinemann, 1982), pp.83-4.

28.
Sidney Pollard, for instance, finds a prototype of the early industrial management in the Boulton and Watt partnership in Soho, which was established in the 1770s. Pollard, The Genesis of Modern Management (London: Edward Arnold, 1963), pp.122-137, 175-9.

29.
Institution of Gas Engineers, Transactions, 1908, p.72.

30.
In certain industries, especially public utilities--gas, elctric, and poer--the duties and qualifications of foremen, superintendents, and managers, their training and reruiting, their promotion and remuneration, were frequently discussed. See L. H. Jenks, "Early Phases of the Management Movement", Administrative Science Quarterly, 5 (Dec. 1960), p.426.

31.
D. Nelson, and S. Campbell, "Taylorism vs Welfare work in American Industry: H. L. Gantt and the Bancrofts", Business History Review, 46 (spring 1972), pp.2-3.

32.
Lyndall Urwick and E. F. L. Brech, _The Making of Scientific Management_ vol.1 _Thirteen Pioneers_ (London: Management Publishers Trust, 1945-9), p.35.

33.
For the development of systematic management, see A. Fox, "Mangerial Ideology and Labour Relations", _British Journal of Industrial Relations_, 4 (Nov. 1966), pp.366-78; Howard Gospel, "The Development of Management Organization in Industrial Relations", in _Industrial Relations and Management_ ed. K. Thurley and S. Wood (Cambridge: Cambridge Uiv. Press, 1983); L. H. Jenks, "Early Phases"; C. Littler, _The Development of the Labour Process_; L. Urwick and E. F. L. Brech, _The Making of Scientific Management_, vol. 2 _Management in British Industry_ (London: Management Publishers Trust, 1945-9); Daniel Nelson, _Managers and Workers_ (Madison: Univ. of Wisconsin Press, 1975).

34.
Edward Cadbury, "Some Principles of Industrial Organization: the Case for and against Scientific Management," _Sociological Review_, 7 (April 1914) and the subsequent discussion, ibid.; William Lever, _Six-hour Day and Other Industrial Questions_ (London: George Allen and Unwin, 1918), p.251; Littler, _The Development_, pp.94-5; Urwick and Brech, _The Making_ vol. 2, p.89.

35.
Littler, _The Development_, p.85.

36.
Quoted in Sidney Webb, _The Works Manager Today_ (London: 1918; rpt. N.Y.: Arno, 1979), p.134.

37.
Littler, _The Development_, chapters 7 and 8; R. Edwards, D. Gordon, and M. Reich, _Segmented Work, Divided Workers: The Historical Transformation of Labor in the U.S._ (Cambridge: Cambridge Univ. Press, 1984), pp.145-6.

38.
William Lever asserted that welfare work must concentrate on safety, sanitation, and working conditions within the factory. _The Six-hour Day and Other Industrial Questions_(London: George Allen and Unwin, 1918), p.183.

39.
Nelson and Campbell,"Taylorism vs Welfare Work," pp.2-3.

40.
A. H. Mackmurdo, _Pressing Questions_ (London: John

Lane, 1913), p.43; Labour Co-partnership, Aug. 1910, p.122.

41. The Second Viscount Leverhulme, Viscount Leverhulme by His Son (London: George Allen, 1927), p.243.

42. Thomas Bushill, Profit-sharing and the Labour Questions (London: Methuen, 1893), p.103.

43. See John Child, "Quaker Employers and Industrial Relations", Sociological Rev. 12 (Nov. 1964); Littler, The Development; Jo Melling, "British Employers and the Development of Industrial Welfare", Disser. Univ. of Glasgow, 1980; Melling, "Employers, Industrial Welfare, and the Struggle for Work-place Control in British Industry", in Managerial Strategies and Industrial Relations (London: Heinemann, 1983).

44. Although welfare employers did not accept Taylorism and the followers of Taylorism disliked welfarism, and the two principles were clearly contradictory to each other, more and more practical businessmen were embracing both during the period concerned. Up to the first World War, there were probably fewer than one hundred welfare officers in British industry. By the mid-1920s, there were around one thousand firms with welfare managers, and among them were an increasing number of men. Gospel, "The Development of Management Organization", pp.102-3; Nelson and Campbell, "Taylorism vs Welfare Work", pp.15-6.

45. Webb, The Works Manager, pp.138-9; A. Shadwell, "The Welfare of Factory Workers", Edinburgh Review, 224 (Oct. 1916), p.371.

46. Quoted in Nelson and Campbell, "Taylorism vs Welfare Work", p.5; Nelson, Frederic W. Taylor and the Rise of Scientific Management, (Madison: Univ. of Wisconsin, 1980), p.45.

47. Quoted in Nelson, Managers and Workers, p.108.

48. Preface to O. Sheldon, The Philosophy of Management (London: 1924; rpt. Sir Isaac Pitman, 1965), p.iii.

Chapter II. The Advocacy of Profit-sharing

I. The Pioneer Profit-sharing Schemes

Before discussing the advocacy of profit-sharing, we should examine the prototypical profit-sharing system, the one that established a working model and inspired the subsequent development of the movement. Profit-sharing was devised not by visionary theorists but by a practical employer, the Frenchman Edme-Jean Leclaire.[1]

Maison Leclaire, Paris

Leclaire, the father of profit-sharing, was born in 1801, the son of a poor village shoemaker. At the age of ten, he was put to work in the fields. Later he became a mason's apprentice. In 1818, he was apprenticed to a house-painter; ten years later, when only 26 years old, he started his own business, a house painting firm. His extraordinary ability, energy, and determination brought succeed; his firm, Maison Leclaire in Paris, had two hundred workers at the inauguration of his profit-sharing plan in 1842.

When he first became an employer, Leclaire followed the common practice of the time, paying the lowest possible wages and dismissing workers arbitrarily. However, he soon became aware of the difficulties of living in "close and hourly contact with people whose interest and feelings were hostile" to him.[2] Some permanent relationship with his men seemed desirable. He first tried to reach them by raising wages and, to a certain degree, succeeded. But the question of active supervision remained. As soon as his back was turned, the men slackened their pace and at the end of the day barely two-thirds of the assigned work was finished. Thus, he inferred that the surest way of increasing labor productivity would be to scale the workers' remuneration to the value of their work. He therefore decided to distribute a portion of any increased profits resulting from improved productivity to those whom he considered deserving.

However, Leclaire was animated not merely by a desire for economic gain: he also genuinely cared about his workers' well-being. Originally a laborer, and always a sincere Christian, Leclaire had long been concerned with the welfare of the working class. He felt particular sympathy for older workers, who, after serving an master for many years, were often ruthlessly discharged by a new employer and left without any means of subsistence. Leclaire called for better work and larger profits mainly to provide the workman and his wife with the means whereby to live in comfort during their old age. With this end in view and also with an eye to greater business efficiency, he developed the profit-sharing scheme.

The outline of the scheme was as follows: at the end of the year, interest of 5 percent on the capital invested and a salary for Leclaire would first be taken out of the net profits; then, the remaining surplus would be divided among those entitled to participate, himself included. Leclaire remained the absolute monarch in running the system: only he had a right to choose the participants, no one had a right to see the company books without his consent; and absolute managerial authority was his alone. At the outset of the scheme, Leclaire declared: "No one will imagine that on the day when the association is established everybody will be free to do as he pleases. No, gentleman,...I am the master of my own business."[3]

Understandably, the men were at first suspicious and remained so until Leclaire summoned 44 workers entitled to share at the end of the first year and flung down upon the table a bag containing 12,256 francs in gold--11 pounds per man--their share of the profits of the preceding year. Thereupon the suspicion turned into enthusiasm. The next year, 1843, 82 workers were entitled to share and the amount to be divided was more than half as much again as in the previous year. The scheme worked almost exactly as Leclaire had thought it would. His best workers doubled their exertions and received a sum amounting to more than a third of their regular wages as a bonus.

Leclaire modified the details of his plan in 1867 to enable the system to survive his death. Besides himself, there were now two other partners in the concern--another unlimited partner and a provident society, which was composed of all the other employees, whose liability was limited. Each of the three partners had a capital of 100,000 francs invested in the business. Leclaire and the other unlimited partner, Defournaux, received salary as practical managers and divided one-half of the net profits. The other half went to the workers, two-fifths of which was paid to the provident society. The other three-fifths was distributed among the individual members. However, Leclaire still reserved the right to decide who would share in the distribution and to what degree.

The effects of the scheme appeared splendid, both morally and economically. The bonus ranged from 12 percent to 18 percent on regular wages, averaging 15 percent, a substantial addition to the income of the workers. In addition to the bonus, a generous pension was also provided under the system. When the worker retired, he received from the mutual fund a pension of L 40 per annum for the rest of his life if he was 50 years old or over and had worked at least for 20 years for the firm. Since L 40 represented a sum more than half as large as the regular wages paid per annum, it can be seen that a certain retirement comfort was guaranteed to Leclaire's workers. The scheme seems to have been beneficial to Leclaire as well. When he died, Lecliare left L 48,000. He always declared that, had it not been for profit-sharing, he could not have accumulated so much "even by fraudulent means."[4]

Equally impressive was the scheme's effect on worker ethics. The work of Maison Leclaire was performed not in workshops but in scattered sites all around Paris, and thus required considerable supervision. Yet after the scheme was instituted, less supervision was necessary and better work was reported. Leclaire himself testified to the improvement in the habits and behavior of his workers, not only at work and in their relations with him but at other times and in other relations. The Paris painters in general were notorious for drinking and for being unmanageable. At the time of the scheme's inauguration, the number of painters of Maison Leclaire who laid off on Mondays and drank excessively was about 40 percent. After the scheme came into existence, however, the laying off drastically diminished and for the years between 1873 and 1883, the percentage did not reach even 1 percent, according to R. Marquet, one of the managing directors who replaced Leclaire after his death in 1872.[5]

Perhaps the most remarkable result of the profit-sharing plan was the profound loyalty demonstrated by Leclaire's employees. This did not disappear even after Leclaire's death. In 1876 when a general strike took place in the Paris building industry, painters at Maison Leclaire did not join it.

The experience of Maison Leclaire was widely discussed and admired among social reformers and economists in Britain. J. S. Mill, for one, had publicized Leclaire's experiment in detail in his *Principles*. However, it took the British more than two decades to inaugurate their first profit-sharing system, that of Henry Briggs and Son.

The British Counterpart: Henry Briggs and Son

Briggs's scheme was started in 1865 in more turbulent circumstances than its French counterpart: whereas Leclaire had no real labor trouble at the time of the scheme's inception, the Briggs collieries had suffered from serious labor disputes for years. Labor relations in the West Riding mining industry represented a continuing struggle between the employers' organization and the West Yorkshire Miners' Union. Henry Briggs, then chairman of the employers' organization, became the chief object of the workers' resentment. This was exacerbated by disputes at his own pits, Whitwood collieries, which employed some 1,200 regular workers. In the ten years before 1865, lost days through strikes amounted to the diiminishing total of one and a half years at the Briggs colliery.[6]

Determined to break the union at any cost, Briggs embarked on a program of replacing unionists by non-union workers, and ruthlessly evicted miners from company houses during mid-winter in order to accommodate the strikebreakers. The extreme hostility of the men towards Briggs was clearly demonstrated in an anonymous letter sent to him during one of the strikes:

> Mr.Briggs I will tell you what i think by you about this struggle...you shall not live 13 days. Depend on it my nife is sharp but my bulits is shorer than the nife...and if it be at noon wen I see you you shall have the arra if it be in your sharit lik old Abe. Now reade that and pray to God to forgive you your sins to be reddy.[7]

The antagonism led a worker to declare that "All coalmasters is devils, and Briggs is the prince of devils." Another man, named Toft, exclaimed at a union meeting in 1863 that, "if Mr. Briggs only had horn on, he would be the very devil."[8]

For its part, the company had suffered great losses by repeated stoppages. Thus it was that as a last resort, Henry Briggs tried industrial co-partnership. His son, Henry C. Briggs, inspired by Henry Fawcett's 1860 Westminster Review article which had described a system of co-partnership between employer and employee as the most effective antidote for strikes, persuaded his father to take this revolutionary step.[9] In 1865 the firm was transformed into a joint stock company in which the original proprietors retained two thirds of the capital. In allotting the remaining third in L 10 shares to the public, preference was given to the company's employees in order to make them limited partners. In addition to this provision for the employees' shareholding, it was also stipulated that whenever the annual divisible profits exceeded 10 percent, one half of the excess should be divided among the employees, regardless of their holding shares, in proportion to their earnings during the year.

The workers, like Leclaire's employees, at first distrusted the scheme. Antagonism and hostility were clearly too strong to disappear immediately at the initiation of such a plan. One of the men said, "Well, the thing is good, but you know it comes from Briggs, and I have no faith in Briggs."[10] It was a sentiment that reflected the prevailing feelings of the workers. Fortunately, the first year turned out to be a financially good one. There was no strike, although it was unclear if the scheme could claim sole responsibility for that, and the trade enjoyed prosperity At the end of the financial year, the company declared a 10 percent dividend on capital and a bonus of 10 percent on the year's wages to worker shareholders. This was in addition to the dividend on their shares, and a bonus of 5 percent on the earnings of non-shareholder workers was also provided.

This remarkable first year result converted the employees, transforming distrust and hostility into confidence. The same Toft who had called Briggs a devil now asserted that "the scheme had done a vast amount of good and ...has destroyed a vast amount of ill feeling." He even defended Briggs at a miners' meeting when a union lecturer denounced Briggs's scheme as a device for cheating the men. Toft rose to his feet to defend the principle: "it is dear to my life; I have taken it up not for any amount of interest or flattery or benefit I might get from the masters by advocating it, but because I believe it is destined to do a great amount of good." He could not finish his speech, getting a knock on his head.[11]

The Briggses were almost certain that they had won the men's loyalty away from the union, and they were right: within three years, the membership of the union dropped sharply, to about 40 members, from what had been a virtually closed union shop. Although the union membership recovered within another several years, the harmonious relations between the company and the employees remained. Henry C. Briggs could state with some justice that "Our village has been transformed from a hot-bed of strife into a model of peace and good will."[12]

Then a serious conflict took place in 1872. The company's annual meeting and a public demonstration by the miners' union were coincidentally scheduled for the same day, August 19th. The workers requested a day off at the pits but Archibald and Henry C. Briggs, who now took over the business from their father, considered it inconceivable to grant a holiday for the sake of a union meeting on the very day of the shareholders' meeting. The company put the men on notice that any workman who was absent in order to attend the meeting would forfeit his bonus. In spite of this threat, a third of the men attended the meeting and, accordingly, forfeited their bonus. By this time, the miners had returned to their union as, following a business slump, employers were seeking wage reductions. Other issues involving the work process, such as separating coal from smudge, contributed to a worsening of relations. Briggs's employees, while still enjoying cordial relations with their employers, nevertheless sympathized with their fellow miners in a series of conflicts.

Briggs, obviously disappointed in the workers' attitude, nevertheless continued the scheme and on Christmas of the same year, 1872, went so far as readmit those who had forfeited the bonus. In the fall of 1874, the decline in coal prices immediately led to a coalowners' attempt to reduce wages. The men refused to go along and a district strike followed, in which the miners at Whitwood joined. It was the first strike since the adoption of the co-partnership system at Whitwood, but the angry shareholders at their meeting in February 1875 called for the termination of the scheme.

The termination, however, was not complete. The

employees who had bought shares continued holding them, receiving dividends; and the practice of electing a workman director, instituted in 1869, continued as well. While the scheme was in operation, the company had established various welfare programs, such as accident benefits and a pension plan, and these remained in effect after the scheme's abolition. So, for that matter, did the employees' cordial feelings towards their employers. When Henry C. Briggs died suddenly in 1882, the Whitwood miners spontaneously volunteered a subscription among themselves and placed a memorial on his grave.[13]

The Briggs experiment, while in force, attracted attention from various groups in society. Economists such as J. S. Mill and William Thornton, whose description covered only the scheme's initial stage, praised it wholeheartedly, asserting that Leclaire and Briggs were acting upon a principle both intelligent and intelligible. The failure of the Briggs scheme, however, disappointed many enthusiasts. One observer felt that its failure was the chief reason why so few firms ventured to try profit-sharing before 1889.[14]

Both the motivating factors and the actual experience of the Leclaire and Briggs schemes are instructive. The schemes of Maison Leclaire and Henry Briggs and Son opened the eyes of those who had been concerned with the labor question. The initial success of these two pioneer schemes seemed to present a promising solution to the chronic problem of strikes and declining labor productivity. Profit-sharing, which had been devised by a practical employer, soon recruited ardent proponents who provided a theoretical analysis of the system.

II.The Advocacy of Profit-sharing

The proponents of the profit-sharing movement were far from a homogeneous group. Social reformers, such as Christian Socialists, envisaged profit-sharing and co-partnership as a form of industrial reorganization; economists, including William Jevons and Alfred Marshall considered the system ethically right and economically sound; enlightened employers such as William Lever and Seebohm Rowntree, looked at profit-sharing in the context of progressive management; finally, there were those particularly politicians, who viewed it as the best antidote for socialism and the best means of social control.

These various merits of profit-sharing received different degrees of attention as the political and industrial climate underwent changes; yet three basic concepts of profit-sharing can be deduced: first, profit-sharing had a moral purpose; second, profit-sharing was an incentive for greater efficiency; third, profit-sharing was a means whereby to achieve industrial harmony and to persuade the worker of the "identity of interest" between employer and employee.

Profit-sharing as Equity

Profit-sharing derived its initial justification from a sense of equity. Thus, James Bryce, a historian of philosophy, claimed that he was converted to the priciples of co-operation and profit-sharing chiefly by his disgust and discontent with the world as he found it, the world in which power and wealth lay in the hands of a minority.[15] This claim for social justice has remained a constant element in the profit-sharing movement, as shown by the arguments on profit-sharing legislation in West Germany in the 1970s.[16] The principles of profit-sharing were constructed entirely outside the classical political economy, which held that wages should vary with profit and that when the employer was making large gains, his workers ought to enjoy a corresponding prosperity. Shrewd employers such as Charles Carpenter, chairman of the South Metropolitan Gas Company, one of the most famous co-partnership companies, reckoned that workmen would want to possess a share in the prosperity of the country "in the same manner as the middle classes had."[17] It appeared that no plan seemed so feasible and promising as that which, while remunerating all factors in production--capital, management, and labor--at the current market rates, divides the surplus between them in defined proportion and according to mutual agreement.

Radical proponents of profit-sharing repudiated the classical theory, which gave all the credit to capital. "No economic law made it inevitable that all the profits should go to capital," and thus there was "nothing unjust or immoral in labor's claim to share them." The division between capital and labor was viewed simply as a matter for bargaining.[18] J. M. Ludlow, thus, insisted that the profit did not solely belong to the employer because "the worker helps to create it whenever it exists, and has a right to share it."[19] William Jevons, an economist and an ardent supporter of industrial co-partnership, proclaimed that there was no reason whatsoever, except 'long-standing custom, why the capitalists should take all the risk and have all the excess of profits.'[20]

. Indeed Jevons' proclamation was what Christian Socialists and the leaders of the Labour Association (after 1902 the Labour Co-partnership Association) believed. The Labour Association was founded in 1884, as a result of the Derby cooperative congress in the same year. In an attempt to follow the main objectives of the Rochdale pioneers, such Christian Socialists as E. V. Neale, E. O. Greening, J. M. Ludlow, and Thomas Hughes, and G. J. Holyoake promoted the initial organization. A few years later, a younger generation including Henry Vivian, Thomas Blandford, and Aneurin Williams, joined it. The Association sought (1) to aid all forms of cooperative production in the cooperative movement; and (2) to induce employers and employees to adopt profit-sharing in private businesses. In the early days, they concentrated on the first aim, but realizing the limits of the producers' cooperative movement, they turned their interest to private business. Their hope was to build a more homogeneous social structure through profit-sharing. It is interesting to look at the list of the presidents and guest speakers of the Association to see how many public figures were included. Several prime ministers, including Arthur Balfour and Herbert Asquith, were on the list,as were labor leaders as Thomas Burt and David Shackleton, such economists as Alfred Marshall and A. C. Pigou, and such prominent employers as William Lever, George Livesey, and T. A. Brassey. The list might ell create an exaggerated impression of the power of the Labour Co-partnership Association.

Radical proponents, including the leaders of the Labour Co-partnership Association, expected that a wide application of profit-sharing and co-partnership would bring the working class into full membership in the middle class. Under co-partnership, the status of the worker would become equal to that of the owner of capital, and wages would become nominal payments, and possibly disappear altogether, taking with them "wage slavery."[21]

Interestingly, the concept of equity as a basis for profit-sharing received an enthusiastic approval from prominent economists of the time. Indeed, most of the leading economists, including J. S. Mill, Henry Fawcett, William Jevons, William Thornton, Sedley Taylor, and Alfred Marshall, (William Ashley was a notable exception), supported the system. Although, as economists, they tended to look at the issue in economic terms, they supported profit-sharing not so much on economic grounds as on ethical ones.

J. S. Mill and Henry Fawcett were among the first British economists who accepted the principles of profit-sharing. It was Fawcett, in fact, who inspired the idea in Henry C. Briggs, who was to launch the pioneer British profit-sharing plan in 1865. Soon after Briggs launched the unprecedented venture in his Whitwood colliery, Jevons, Thornton, and other economists began to praise the new system wholeheartedly. They saw it not only as a means to improve industrial relations but also as a device whereby to bring about a more equitable redistribution of wealth.

The system dovetailed particularly well with Mill's ideal of modified capitalism: if it was still based upon competition, it yet eliminated the malpractices of capitalism. Mill expected that the relation of the employer and the worker would be gradually superseded by partnership in one of two forms: in some cases, an association of the laborers with the capitalist; in others and perhaps finally in all, an association of laborers among themselves in workmen's co-operation.[22] Profit-sharing was one of these final forms of industrial relations. Mill wrote in Principles:

> Finally I must repeat my conviction that the industrial economy, which divides society absolutely into two portions, the payers of wages and the receivers, the first counted by thousands and the last by millions, is neither fit for, nor capable of, indefinite duration; and the possibility of changing this system or one of combination without dependence, and unity of interest, instead of organized hostility, depends altogether upon the future development of the partnership principles.23

Alfred Marshall was among the most vigorous advocates of profit-sharing and the workmen's co-operative movement. He was a lifelong member of the Labour Co-partnership Association, serving for a time as its vice-president and actively promoting the movement. Although he did not like to elaborate upon any "abstract or metaphysical principles of profit-sharing," he defined the system in ethical terms, lending his support because profit-sharing would give the worker "opportunity and scope or a worthy ambition to act not merely as a hand, but as a thinking and thoughtful human being."[24] Marshall looked at the development of profit-sharing and co-operation with considerable satisfaction and believed that human nature was ready for "considerable advances towards an organization of industry on a plan more generous and under a less rigid cash-nexus than at present."[25] Marshall's conviction was shared by A. C.Pigou, his pupil and the successor to his chair at

Cambridge, who also underscored the theme of profit-sharing on ethical and moral grounds. Although he conceded the relative inefficacy of profit-sharing in stimulating more and better work, Pigou found its greatest merit in its appeal to the non-egoistic side of humanity.[26]

Profit-sharing as a Profitable Business Arrangement

However, the concept of profit-sharing as equity was obviously not a sufficiently powerful force to attract the average employer. Something other than simple philanthropy had to be projected since good feeling alone could not establish a commercial concern. Even G. J. Holyoake, a vigorous promoter of the co-operative movement, recognized that self-interest was also needed, "tempered by good sense." Profit-sharing and co-partnership would be "a plan of a new and enlightened form of self-interest."[27] Indeed, A. Hilton, managing director of a publishing firm in Leceister, noted that there was by 1892 "a distinct change in the way profit-sharing was looked at: some years ago, there had been more or less of a feeling of philanthropy mixed upon it, but now I find employers looking at it from a purely business stand-point."[28]

By this time, indeed, the prevalent opinion maintained that the ethical aspect was an insufficient basis for a viable co-partnership movement. Success would depend almost entirely upon economic efficiency. "However ethically perfect a social scheme may be," it was asserted, "it has no chance of becoming part of the general social organization unless it is also sound economically."[29] The second advocacy, therefore, concerned itself not with the moral improvement of the workers but with the pecuniary effects of profit-sharing, contrary to the first advocacy of "moral concomitants" as important as the material benefits derived from the system.[30]

This was an important point because profit-sharing's cost was vulnerable to severe criticism: its bonus was viewed simply as the sacrifice of employers and shareholders. This was the conclusion of the Royal Commission on Trades Union 1867-69, which investigated the pioneer plan of the Briggs operation:

> It must be remembered that, as regards Messrs. Briggs' system, the principle is to limit the profits of the employer, and to give the workman, over and above his wages, a share in the profits of the concern, without subjecting him to any liability for loss. It is, then, not unreasonable to suppose that many capitalists will prefer the chances of disputes with their workmen, and even run the risk of strikes and temporary loss, rather than voluntarily limit their profits to 10 percent or any other fixed amount.31

Employers in general could hardly be induced to participate in profit-sharing unless the system offered them some tangible benefits in return for altering the established modes of remuneration and power structure. Thus, the proponents had to demonstrate that profit-sharing "pays back." The system was described as "a new form of enlightened commercial shrewdness which pays," and a business arrangement under which all parts concerned--capital, management, and labor--would receive greater remuneration.[32]

Judging by early results, profit-sharing constituted a seemingly sound financial procedure. South Metropolitan and Lever Brothers were remarkable examples of profit-sharing success, and other companies, such as Clarke, Nicholls, and Coombs, a London confectionery firm, and J. T. and J. Taylor, a woollen-worsted manufacturer in Batley, had also reportedly accrued greater profits since implementing the scheme. At Clarke, Nicholls, and Coombs, the dividend on capital rose from 5 percent to 12 percent in twelve years. Many factors, of course, contributed to the success of a business, and profit-sharing was probably not the major reason. Yet proponents spoke up warmly for profit-sharing. William Lever asserted that "the balance remaining to the shareholders has always been greater and not less by consideration of the employees."[33] George Livesey declared "every penny of bonus was earned by co-partners themselves." Other employers who could not establish that there was a positive monetary benefit in the system nevertheless felt that they lost "nothing and probably gained something by the scheme."[34]

Subsequently a basic question arose--if all workers were to have more and the employer and capitalist were to have no less, where was the more to come from? The answer lay in the creation of new profits: profit-sharing would produce such an effect by purchasing the worker's interest as well as his labor. Under profit-sharing, every person engaged in the business would have a direct interest in its prosperity since the effect of any success or downturn would almost immediately produce a corresponding change in weekly salaries or wages. Everyone concerned would have an immediate interest in preventing any waste or mismanagement in any department.[35]

The prevention of waste, then, formed the economic basis of profit-sharing. When a factory owner remarked to Robert Owen, "If my men liked, they could save me L 10,000 a year by better work and the avoidance of waste," Owen replied, "Then why don't you pay them L 5,000 a year to do it?"[36] The existing profit-sharing firms reportedly derived considerable benefits from preventing waste. Workers in those firms were said to pick up even a nail and say "This is so much bonus saving."[37] Furthermore, the cost of supervision would diminish tremendously under profit-sharing as each worker would become a foreman in relation to every other worker, or as George Thomson put it, his or her own manager. Under the profit-sharing system, "everyone has upon him not one," William Thornton wrote, "but hundreds perhaps of pairs of eyes, and every eye the eye of a master." In the Briggs colliery, the expense of overlookers was considerably diminished. Workers in some profit-sharing firms would even report a foreman to the heads of the business for neglect in performing his duties.[38]

The successful schemes seemed to confirm the efficacy of profit-sharing in improving productivity. Hubert Fouley, a gas employer in Stafford, stated that after a co-partnership plan was established in his company, the cost of labor fell from 9.2 d. to 7.2 d. per 1,000 cubic feet of gas sold.[39] George Livesey confirmed that view with the before-and-after-profit-sharing statistics of his own company, the South Metropolitan. Archibald Briggs, made an interesting observation in the same vein. "On comparing the respective profits yielded by each of the thirteen seams of coal we are working," he reported, "it appears that those profits--other things being equal--increase in a tolerably exact proportion to the number of workmen who interest themselves in our co-operative movement."[40]

To ardent advocates of the system, such as George Livesey, it was as obvious as a "problem in Euclid that men who have an actual interest as shareholders and receive an annual bonus depending on successful business must be more profitable servants than those who had no connection with or interest in the business."[41] Workers at profit-sharing firms also testified to such an effect. One of Bushill and Sons' employees expressed this way: "I find it has been the means of making me work more economically, trying to get out the most possible work in the least possible time. It has also been an incentive to save, fostering in me ideas of things which perhaps I never should have had." This assertion was echoed by many of Bushill's employees.[42] Impressed by such results, T. W. Allen, councilor of Cardiff, concluded: "Modern industry is continually asking for a system that will combine the greatest degree of efficiency with economy. Co-partnership is the solution." Alfred Marshall appreciated profit-sharing, believing it would increase goods and services, unlike socialism, which he saw as aiming at a fairer distribution of wealth simply by transferring wealth from one class to another.[43]

Industrial Peace

The third theme in the advocacy of profit-sharing was the guaranteed industrial peace that engendered team spirit and a sense of loyalty: this strong corporate feeling would not only make the worker exert his utmost for the company's prosperity but more importantly relinquish his class spirit. The way in which such corporate feeling was established under profit-sharing was manifold. Since the most frequent cause of worker discontent was wages and working conditions, the first solution to the labor problem was to provide him with more wages than he would receive elsewhere. In this light, profit-sharing took a similar line to Taylorism, which argued for greater wages as the solution to labor unrest. Moreover, the worker, under profit-sharing, would develop a keen interest in avoiding labor disputes as strikes stopped not only his wages but his bonus--through curtailing the divisible profits. Profit-sharing, pure and simple, appealed to the instinct of desire for material betterment.

However, material betterment was not the sole reason for labor unrest. As one businessman noted, "Wages and conditions have improved, but the discontent and the unrest have not disappeared."[44] Thus, the problem was tackled from a non-material point of view, such as the dehumanizing factory system with its ever-increasing size and the loss of control caused by mechanization and the loss of interest in work. Profit-sharing similarly promised to solve this problem by satisfying the "righteous desire of every human being to have some control over the development of his life," as well as by enhancing the worker's self-esteem.[45]

Moreover, under profit-sharing and particularly in co-partnership, the employee was taken into the confidence of the firm. He would be treated as a partner and an attempt would be made to show him that the mutual confidence was the foundation of the system. William Lever, a leading welfarist employer, asserted that the attraction of profit-sharing and co-partnership was not mere monetary considerations. "In my own experience, the money element is perhaps entitled to the least consideration of all. It is the great uplift and inspiration that sharing profits cultivates in the employee that constitutes its greater value..."[46]

To the majority of proponents, industrial peace was the most valuable aspect of profit-sharing. Thomas Bushill contended that the highest value of profit-sharing lay in its influence in "bringing proprietor and employee together, breaking down the wall which separates them. It teaches them that constructive co-operation is better than destructive opposition."[47] Profit-sharing was expected to introduce a remarkable stability and peace into the relations between employer and employee. "The day that co-operation and profit-sharing is entered into by all industries," one enthusiast asserted, "the livelihood of the agitator would cease."[48]

The only possible way by which the warfare between capital and labor could be prevented, it was argued, would be by "identifying the interests of capital and labor, either by distributing a definite share in the profits of the business or better still, by making them the actual owners of the capital concerned." "All in the same boat," "all in one big, happy family," were common phrases used by profit-sharing employers. "The toil of the brain and the toil of the arm working together" was another great appeal made by profit-sharing advocates. Some argued for strictly identical interests between employer and employee but less pompous ones stressed "the fundamental unity of interests at the back of all the differences."[49]

The proponents of profit-sharing dismissed conciliation and arbitration as limited because they retained the separation between employers and employees: the perfect combination of the two sides would be realized only under co-partnership. Co-partnership, in A. C. Pigou's view, was a more thorough and far-reaching solution than conciliation and arbitration because "what is aimed at in co-partnership is not so much the conciliation of difference as the amalgamation of interests."[50] Thomas Bushill, the Baptist employer of a Coventry paper-making firm, was particularly active in promoting this unitary ideology. In 1894 he formed the Industrial Union of Employers and Employed, an attempt to educate public opinion as to the "underlying common interests of both classes."[51] The Union also intended to promote industrial reforms including profit-sharing. Not surprisingly, many employers who practiced profit-sharing supported the Union. George Livesey, George Thomson, Theodore Taylor, A. F. Hills and George Mathieson participated in the Union, but it survived for only two years.[52]

Profit-sharing and co-partnership differed in principle, the latter implying industrial democracy by granting the worker the right to become a shareholder and thus to participate in decision making. In reality, however, the subtle distinction between the two was dismissed and co-partnership was conceived of, in general, as an extension of profit-sharing. However, to some advocates, co-partnership seemed much more effective in ensuring identity of interests between employer and employee. Simple profit-sharing with a cash bonus would not be "a permanent benefit either to the workman or to the employer: the effect of such a bonus would soon pass off and no new bond of union between capital and labor is created." According to these proponents of co-partnership, the mere wage-earning attitude to production should be supplemented by the share-holding attitude. It was the shareholding that "creates and sustains the interest in the business, which increases as the investments increase."[53]

Perhaps the best illustration of why employers prefered co-partnership is the scheme of the South Metropolitan Gas Company, which will be explored in detail in Chapter VII. The company's chairman, George Livesey, who introduced a profit-sharing scheme in order to frustrate the newly formed Gasworkers union in 1889 and fought the union's strike to the bitter end, was to become one of the most wholehearted advocates of worker participation in management. Livesey's South Metropolitan allowed two workmen directors to sit on the board in 1898, thus introducing a practice that continued until the nationalization of the gas industry in 1949. He summarized the advantages of co-partnership as follows:

> To make the worker a shareholder in the works, a partner in the adventure, is to immensely enhance his value as a workman. The success of the works would be to him a matter of profit and of pride. He would desire to faithfully serve the enterprise in which he had an interest deeper and stronger than that of a wage earner. He would be concerned to know that everyone did his duty. The workpeople would become a community of people whose interest it was to see that all did their best. Under such a system...strikes would become rare and wellnigh impossible, for it would be of advantage to every man...to avoid all disputes that might militate against commercial success.[54]

Thus it is not difficult to see, contrary to Livesey's assertion, that co-partnership made the worker more, not less, dependent on the employer. He now relied on his employer not only for his wages but for his dividend as a shareholder. It is anything but wise for the worker to invest his savings in the firm where he works, as Paul Samuelson points out.[55] In case of a business failure, he would lose both his wages and his savings.

The Retaining of the Capitalist System and the Parliamentary Debates on Profit-sharing

As Livesey's statement shows, the primary aim of binding the worker's interest to that of the employer was to establish stability in the workplace and in society. That is why profit-sharing and co-partnership received great public attention during three periods: 1889-92, 1912-14, and 1919-20, times of grave labor unrest. Appropriately, this heightened public interest brought about debates on profit-sharing in the House of Commons in 1890, 1911, 1912, and 1920, respectively. The sense of an impending clash inspired Parliament, presumably a barometer of public opinion, to respond with great animation to a system often touted as the best remedy for industrial conflict.

The first discussion concerning the system was initiated by George Bartley, Conservative member for North Islington, in April 1890. Bartley was deeply concerned with social questions and the future prosperity of the country, which faced keen foreign competition as well as labor unrest. He called for the harmonious cooperation of capital and labor to maintain the country's prosperity: "at present, they appear as enemies." Since arbitration seemed to him an "unsatisfactory and clumsy arrangement leading to dissatisfaction on both sides," he came to consider "the great question of profit-sharing," and moved that a committee be appointed to inquire into the system.[56]

After Charles Bradlaugh, a Radical famous for his secularism and thus three times unseated because of his refusal to take the oath, and Sir J. Colomb, Conservative, joined the discussion favoring Bartley's motion, Sir Michael Hicks Beech, the president of the Board of Trade under the Tory government, expressed his opinion of the system in practical terms: "It is good from a philanthropic point of view," he concluded, "but I fail to see why, if it be attempted to be practiced from a business point of view, the employed should not share the losses, as well as the profits." He felt that since the workers would not and could not share the losses, profit-sharing seemed impracticable.[57] At this point, profit-sharing was still viewed by some simply as a philanthropic gesture and not as a workable system in the mundane world. At the end of the debate, Bartley withdrew the motion to appoint a committee as Hicks Beach promised to collect information on profit-sharing. The result was the first report of the Board of Trade on profit-sharing and co-partnership in 1894.

It was more than a decade before the debate on profit-sharing was revived in the House of Commons. The occasion was again turbulent industrial unrest. In December 1911, Lord Robert Cecil, a Unionist, the third son of Lord Salisbury, and the most ardent proponent of the system in the circle of politicians, asked Prime Minister H. H. Asquith to recommend the appointment of a royal commission on co-partnership. Although Asquith rhetorically supported the principles of co-partnership and was once the president of the Labour Co-partnership Association, he did not believe in the effects of the system in practical terms as strongly as Cecil and therefore dismissed the idea of a royal commisssion. However, he promised to instruct the Board of Trade to prepare a report on profit-sharing and co-partnership. The result was the 1912 report of the Board of Trade.[58]

The next debate proved to be far more interesting. In February 1912, Ramsay Macdonald, a Labour member who was to become the first Labour prime minister in 1924, proposed amendment for minimum wages and nationalization, following the King's address. Macdonald's amendment promptly brought about Sir Basil Peto's co-partnership amendment. Peto, a Unionist who once implemented profit-sharing in his building firm, rose to assert his belief in "a better and much simpler way than nationalization, that is a fair division of profit."[59] To Peto, co-partnership was a panacea. It would ensure "the productive capacity of the country, the consequent cheapening of the cost of commodities, the increase of the country's power of competing," and give wage-earners "a human interest in their life and work, and place them on a moral equality with every other class." That was what he believed "from the bottom of my heart."[60]

Profit-sharing and co-partnership were an attractive program to all political parties, and thus were endorsed by people from a broad political spectrum--Conservatives, free trade Liberals, and Tariff Reformers. Arthur Balfour, the Conservative prime minister from 1902 to 1905, served as the president of the Labour Co-partnership Association in 1908. The Liberals were represented by H. H. Asquith who was the president of the Association in 1911. The Tariff Reformers also came out for co-partnership principles, envisaging them as "the domestic policies which should be linked to imperial preferences and tariff reform."[62]

However, the profit-sharing movement found its staunchest activists in the free traders. The majority of the leaders of the Labour Co-partnership Association such as Henry Vivian and Fred Maddison, believed in free trade; so did Lord Robert Cecil, a leading free trade Unionist. Both Cecil and Theodore Taylor, a Liberal from Batley and the owner of the famous profit-sharing woollen factory, followed Peto's enthusiastic advocacy, the latter even stating that he cared "more about profit-sharing" than he cared for "the great honor of representing his constituents in the House."[63]

However, such enthusiastic declarations failed to persuade members skeptical about the system. Richard Denman, the Liberal member for Carlisle, proclaimed that profit-sharing as a substitute for minimum wages was "wholly fallacious." He felt that a minimum wage was the "real" basis upon which the industrial system must be built, whereas profit-sharing was still a "theory."[64] Denman was a director of Marine and General Mutual Life Assurance Company, and also the private secretary to S. Buxton, the president of the Board of Trade under the

Asquith Government. Such a background led him to look at the subject from a practical point of view. He could not see, for instance, how profit-sharing could be applied to such workers as dockers, who were usually employed only several days a week. Although he was sympathetic to the idea of profit-sharing, he clearly understood that it was not a "panacea."

George Roberts, Labour member for Norwich, pointed out profit-sharing's inefficacy in various respects and particularly in its inability to solve the problem of unemployment, which he viewed as the most serious one of the time.[65] Roberts, originally a printer, entered the coalition government under H. H. Asquith in 1915, and when the Labour Party withdrew its support for coalition in 1918, refused to follow Party policy and therefore severed his relationship with Labour. As of 1912, however, he was still loyal to the Labour Party, and shared the labor leaders' criticism of profit-sharing. Keir Hardie wanted to move the discussion to a wider question, capitalism versus socialism. For him, profit-sharing was no solution whatsoever to industrial unrest, for it only helped to maintain the capitalist system, which was based upon competition and private property.[66]

In any case, when Peto's amendment for co-partnership was put to vote after the hours-long debate, it attracted 97 votes. This debate in the House of Commons was followed by one in the House of Lords. Christopher Furness, now Lord Furness, whose short-lived co-partnership venture in his shipbuilding yard in Hartlepools is discussed in Chapter V, initiated the debate. Furness guaranteed that co-partnership in one form or another would ultimately be found to be a solution satisfactory to all concerned, and recommended the appointment of a royal commission.[67]

Soon afterwards, 287 MPs, led by Lord Wolmer and Lord Robert Cecil, signed a memorial to Prime Minister Asquith, requesting a royal commission on co-partnership. They strongly felt the need to point out "that the interests of employers and employed are identical," and believed that co-partnership formed "the most effective method of breaking down the hard line of division between capital and labor."[68] These 287 MPs included members of all parties, but only two labor MPs--Will Crooks, a former cooper from Poplar, east London, and George Wardle, a onetime railway clerk who became the editor of the Railway Review.

Despite all this enthusiasm, the government responded cautiously. David Lloyd George, then Chancellor of the Exchequer, conceded the importance of profit-sharing, but was shrewd enough to recognize the fact that there had been as many profit-sharing failures as successes. It would be too hasty, therefore, to appoint a royal commission; further, "to set up a co-partnership system in the middle of a strike as a solution is totally impossible."[69]

The enthusiasm ignited by Peto's February amendment nevertheless continued for several months and helped spur an important meeting for promoting the co-partnership movement. This was arranged by a group of MPs, the Labour Co-partnership Association, and a number of profit-sharing employers. Among the participants were Lord Robert Cecil, Theodore Taylor, Basil Peto, William Lever, and Charles Carpenter, as well as Henry Vivian and Aneurin Williams, leaders of the LCA. One of the proposals adopted by the meeting was to consider how far co-partnership could be assisted by government action, either administrative or legislative.[70] This was because some proponents felt that no great advance could take place without parliamentary enactment.

To be sure, in his February amendment, Peto had requested the government's intervention to promote profit-sharing. It could be done, he suggested, by imposing a lighter income tax on firms that adopted profit-sharing as well as by giving public works contracts only to profit-sharing firms. However, the idea of government intervention was quickly dismissed by the Parliamentary Secretary of the Board of Trade, S. Robertson. His objection was based on practical difficulties as well as ideological differences. He not only disagreed with government intervention in promoting profit-sharing but also saw problems in setting up an equitable wage scale in different trades and industries.[72]

However, the movement for legislation continued. In June 1912, James F. Hope, Unionist from sheffield, introduced the Co-partnership Bill in the House of Commons, and it passed the first reading in July. The bill would allow all registered and statutory companies to adopt a scheme of co-partnership without applying for any alteration in company regulation and structure. However, the advocates of such an initiative remained in a minority; the majority of the system's proponents supported only the voluntary adoption of profit-sharing. That, in fact, was the Labour Co-partnership Association's unchangeable position. Many supporters including Sir William Lever felt an absolute hostility towards compulsory legislation. Lever, although he strongly believed that co-partnership was a solution to labor troubles, claimed that act of parliament would destroy the spirit of co-partnership: "Co-partnership cannot be forced."[73] The laissez-faire ideology, still prevalent in the early decades of the twentieth century, would not have tolerated any government interference.

The Labour Co-partnership Association was understandably reluctant to see the profit-sharing and co-partnership movement taken up by a particular political party. The fact that the promoters of the Co-partnership Bill were without exception Conservatives--James Hope, Leopold Amery, Lord Robert Cecil, and Viscount Wolmer--also made the LCA uneasy. Thus they proclaimed that "the principle of co-partnership is too high and noble a thing to be dragged in the dust of party controversy."[74]

Meanwhile, a flood of inquiries poured into the Labour Co-partnership Association office--110 in November and December of 1912 alone--and the assistant secretary reported that "the heads of many large businesses are seriously considering the adoption of co-partnership."[75] At the same time, the proponents of the movement were actively engaging in propaganda. William Lever met several leading manufacturers; Theodore Taylor was also communicating with a number of firms in the textile industry; and Basil Peto was busy trying to persuade the building employers.[76] Although the actual number of schemes started in this period fell short of expectations--very great expectations--the profit-sharing movement received no greater attention at any time than in the years 1912-14. Unfortunately, this progress was halted by the outbreak of war and it was not before mid-1920 that another parliamentary debate took place.

The Whitley committee, appointed in 1916 to consider employer-employee relations after the war, inspired great hope among the advocates of profit-sharing and co-partnership. The whitley committee was composed of the equal number of representatives of both sides of industry, as well as such economists as J. A. Hobson and S. J. Chapman, Oxford professor. However, the final report of the committee on the question of co-partnership was disappointing. It declared: "We...have felt bound to come to the conclusion that it does not justify us in putting forward any general recommendations."[77] The fact was that the members of the committee not only held diverse opinions on profit-sharing and co-partnership but felt that the evidence available was not sufficiently conclusive to justify a recommendation for the general adoption of the system.

To Elie Halevy, the historian critical of British development in the direction of industrial democracy in the post-war years, the Whitley councils were merely an antidote used by the government and the employers to avert the revolutionary movement of the working class. He observed that there was "never anything that even remotely resembles working class participation in the management of the firm."[78] However, the Whitley committee did recommend the setting up of joint councils and conciliation boards on an industry-by-industry basis, and the days of Whitley councils certainly contributed to promotion of profit-sharing and co-partnership.

In this atmosphere, profit-sharing and co-partnership were again in 1920 discussed in the House of Commons. This time, the subject was brought up in connection with the debate on the Ministry of Mines, which was soon to be established. T. A. Lewis, Liberal from Glamorgan, moved an amendment for inserting in the bill words to encourage the establishment of co-partnership and profit-sharing in the mining industry. This initiated another long discussion. It would be one in which Lord Robert Cecil, who was never to give up his lifelong belief in co-partnership, and such speakers as Captain Coote, Liberal, Sir R. Horne, the Minister of Labour, and Inskip, Labour member, would participate. The supporters' argument centered on the system's alleged superiority to nationalization--this in response to the miners, who were demanding both nationalization and miner control of the industry. It was contended that experience showed that nationalization could not and would not bring about increased output, but that co-partnership had and would. "Nowhere on the horizon," Lewis proclaimed, "can I detect any other scheme that could do that."[79]

There was also the familiar rhetoric to the effect that in order to achieve permanent harmony and industrial peace, the workers must become partners, not simply industrial hirelings. This time, the advocacy for partnership was more emphatic than ever because of the mounting call for industrial democracy in the early post-war years. Apart from this initiative in Parliament, one enthusiast in 1920 suggested a national system of compulsory co-partnership.[80] Yet, even in the post-war period, the mood remained resistant; the government and the general public were reluctant to "compel cooperation," for compulsion would not so much help industry as endanger it.[81]

Although profit-sharing and co-partnership were a favorite program with both the Conservative and Liberal parties, it was not until 1949 that a major party committed itself to compulsory profit-sharing and co-partnership. The Liberal Party adopted the idea of compulsion in that year because they felt that co-partnership could win working class votes and because it seemed to them that the choice was "between partnership and socalism: there is no other choice."[82]

Thus, with little of the external assistance required to create a true momentum, the fortunes of profit-sharing shifted between extremes: at times it was touted as the best labor remedy, at other times it was almost neglected. It was only in the late 1970s that profit-sharing received genuine legislative help under the Financial Act; this came, surprisingly enough, under the Labour government. It seems ironical that Labour, which had traditionally shown the least interest in profit-sharing, would pass the requisite legislation. To be sure, it did so under pressure from the Liberals, on whom it had to rely to form a parliamentary majority. Yet, the fact that such legislation was enacted under the Labour government is something fitting: it demonstrates once again how the profit-sharing movement throughout its fascinating history has derived support from unlikely quarters and strage bedfellows.

Notes to Chapter II

1\. The account of Leclaire's scheme is based on the following sources: William Jevons, "On Industrial Partnership," in *Methods of Social Reform* (London: 1883; rpt. New York, August M. Kelly, 1965); John S. Mill, *Principles of Political Economy*, *Collected Works* vol. 3 (Toronto: Univ. of Toronto Press, 1965), pp.770-74; Sedley Taylor, "A Real 'Saviour of Society'," *Nineteenth Century*, 8 (Sep. 1880), pp.370-83; William Thornton, *On Labour* (London: 1869; rpt. Shannon: Irish Univ. Press, 1971), pp.363-69; Aneurin Willams, *Co-partnership and Profit-sharing* (London: William and Norgate, Thornton Butterworth, 1913), pp.28-42.

2\. Thornton, *On Labour*, p.364.

3\. Quoted in Charles Fay, *Co-partnership in Industry* (Cambridge: Cambridge Univ. Press, 1913), p.65.

4\. Williams, *Co-partnership*, p.42.

5\. Williams, *Co-partnership*, p.40.

6\. Archibald Briggs, "Memorandum" in *Profit-sharing between Capital and Labour*, S. Taylor (London: Kegan Paul, Trench, 1884), p.118.

7\. Sedley Taylor, "Remarks on the Memorandum by Messrs. Archibald Briggs and Henry C. Briggs" in *Profit-sharing*, p.136; Andrew Yarmie, "The Captains of Industry in Mid-Victorian Britain" Disser. Univ. of London, 1975, p.239.

8\. Nicholas Gilman, *Profit-sharing between Employer and Employee: A Study in the Evolution of the Wages System* (Boston: Houghton, Mifflin, 1889), p.247; Williams, *Co-partnership*, p.66: Thornton,*On Labour*, p. 369.

9\. Fawcett's article was "Strikes, their Tendencies and Remedies," *Westminster Review*, 74 (July, 1860), pp.1-13.

10. Taylor, "Remarks", p.136; Gilman, Profit-sharing, p.249.

11. Gilman, Profit-sharing, p.257; Taylor, "Remarks," p.138.

12. Thornton, On Labour, p.377.

13. Taylor, "Remarks," p.135.

14. Gilman, Profit-sharing, p.290.

15. Labour Co-partnership, April 1902, p.57.

16. See, for instance, H. Sauerman and R. Richter ed. Profit-sharing: A Symposium (Tubingen: J.C.B.Mohr, 1977).

17. Institute of Gas Engineers, Transactions (1908), p.73. (Hereafter IGE).

18. Labour Co-partnership, Sep. 1913, p.138.

19. Thomas Jones, "Profit-sharing in Relation to Other Methods of Remunerating Labour," Accountants' Magazine, 8 (July 1904).

20. Jevons, "On Partnerships," pp.107,141.

21. E. Walls, Progressive Co-partnership (London: Nisbet, 1921), p.225.

22. Quoted in Frank W. Raffety, Partnership in Industry (London: Jonathan Cape, 1928), p.5.

23. Mill, Principles, p.896.

24. A. Marshall, "Co-operation," Memorials of Alfred Marshall, ed. A. C. Pigou (N.Y.: Kelly and Macmillan,

1956), p.252.

25. Marshall, "Co-operation," pp.252-3.

26. A. C. Pigou, "An Economist's View of Co-partnership," *Labour Co-partnership*, June 1909, p.86.

27. G. J. Holyoake, "Partnerships of Industry" in National Association for the Promotion of Social Science, *Transactions*, (1865), pp.483,486. (Hereafter NAPSS).

28. Thomas Bushill, *Profit-sharing and the Labour Questions* (London: Methuen, 1893), p.102.

29. *Edinburgh Review*, "The Principles and Practices of Labour Co-partnership," 209 (April, 1909), p.312.

30. Thornton, *On Labour*, p.329.

31. Royal Commission on Trades Union, *The 11th and Final Report* Cd. 4123 (1869), p.28. Quoted in Jevons,"On Partnerships," p.128.

32. NAPSS, *Transactions*, (1865), p.486.

33. A. H. Mackmurdo, *Pressing Questions* (London: John Lane, 1913), p.291.

34. Board of Trade, *Report on Profit-sharing and Labour Co-partnership in the U.K.* Cd. 6496 (1912), p.71.

35. Jevons, "On Partnerships," p.135.

36. Williams, *Co-partnership*, p.19.

37. Thornton, *On Labour*, p.393. A French employer told how, soon after he had introduced profit-sharing, his composers proposed that their frames should be put closer together so that they might be able to set up type by the

light of one lamp. Taylor, Profit-sharing, p.64.

38.
Thornton, On Labour, p.392.; David Schloss, Methods of Industrial Remuneration (London: Williams and Norgate, 1898), p.185.

39.
IGE, Transactions, (1908), p.64.

40.
Taylor, "Remarks," p.138.

41.
G. Livesey, "Co-partnership," IGE, Transactions (1908), p.58.

42.
Bushill, Profit-sharing, pp.23-31, 218-224.

43.
Labour Co-partnership, Mar. 1904, p.41.

44.
Carter Goodrich, The Frontier of Control (London: G. Bell, 1920), p.3.

45.
Labour Co-partnership Association, Report of the Industrial Conference, (London, 1899), p.32.

46.
Quoted in M. E. Askith, Profit-sharing: An Aid to Trade Revival (London: Duncan Scott, 1926), p.7. William Lever was created a baronet in 1911 and was raised to the peerage as Baron Leverhulme in 1917. In the present dissertation, he is constantly referred to as Lever.

47.
Bushill, Profit-sharing, p.193.

48.
Labour Co-partnership, June 1912, p.94. In Maison Gioffinon of Paris, a profit-sharing firm in Paris, the workers regularly mounted guard in their employers' premises during the Paris Commune in 1871. See Bushill, Profit-sharing, p.36.

49.
Labour Co-partnership Association, Report of London Co-partnership Congress, 1923, p.10.

50.
A. C. Pigou, "An Economist's View," Labour Co-partnership, July 1909, p.100.

51.
Edward Bristow, "Profit-sharing, Socialism and Labour Unrest," Essays in Anti-Labour History K. Brown ed. (London: Macmillan, 1974), p.274.

52.
The Union of the Employer and the Employed, Report of the Provisional Committee, (London: 1894).

53.
G. Livesey, "Co-partnership," IGE, Transactions, (1908), p.159.

54.
G. Livesey, "Another Step in Promoting the Union of Capital and Labour," IGE, Transactions, (1897), p.145.

55.
Paul Samuelson, "Thoughts on Profit-sharing," in Profit-sharing: A Symposium, ed. H. Sauermann and R. Richter (Tubingen: J. C. B. Mohr, 1977), p.15.

56.
Parliamentary Debates, 3rd series v.343, pp.1137-51, April 22, 1890. (Hereafter P.D.).

57
P.D. 3rd series, v.343, p.1165, April 22.

58.
P.D. 5th series, v.32, p.1574, Dec. 7, 1911; p.2701, Dec. 15, 1911.

59.
P.D. 5th series, v.34, p.102, Feb. 15, 1912.

60.
P.D. 5th series, v.34, p.103, Feb. 15, 1912.

61.
Bristow, "Profit-sharing, Socialism, and Labour Unrest," p.283.

62.
P.D. 5th series, v. 34, p.103, Feb. 15, 1912. (The following debates are on the same day and in the same volume).

63.
p.114.

64.
pp.130-1.

65.
pp.138-9.

66.
p.154.

67.
Times, Feb. 15, 1912, 10b.

68.
Times, March 15, 1912, 4f.

69.
P.D. 5th series, v.35, p.1774, March 19, 1912; v.38, p.532, May 8, 1912.

70.
Times, June 13, 1912, 17c.

71.
P.D. 5th series, v.34, p.106, Feb. 15, 1912.

72.
p.117.

73.
"Leverhulme Correspondence," 1321, April 1, 1915, at Unilever House, London.

74.
Labour Co-partnership, Nov. 1912, p.162.

75.
Bristow, "Profit-sharing, Socialism, and Labour Unrest," p.285.

76.
Cecil of Chelwood Papers, British Museum, Add. Mss. 51160, f. 174.

77.
Ministry of Reconstruction, Committee on Relations between Employers and Employed. Final Report. Cd.9153 (1918), p.4.

78.
Elie Halevy, The Era of Tyrannies (Garden City, NY:

Doubleday, 1965), p.168.

79\.
P.D., 5th series, v.132, p.1705, July 29, 1920.

80\.
H. Jordan, _A National Scheme of Profit-sharing_ (London: Industrial League and Council, 1920).

81\.
P.D., 5th series, v.132, p.1709, July 29, 1920.

82\.
Arnold Rogow, "Labour Relations under the British Labor Government", _American Journal of Economics and Sociology_, 14 (1954/5), p.372.

Chapter III. The Criticism of Profit-sharing

> 'Verily, the son of Man is as of old betrayed with a kiss.'--Annie Besant

> 'Many sops have been thrown to the snarling Demos. The earliest on record were "bread and circuses"; the latest are profit-sharing and old age pensions.'--Tom Mann

The objections to profit-sharing centered on several arguments: the first criticism repudiated capitalism itself and viewed profit-sharing as a device to perpetuate the capitalist system; the second criticism concentrated on the unfairness and contingencies of actual practices of profit-sharing schemes; the final criticism was raised on the system's clash with trade unionism.

Socialist Criticism

The first objection to profit-sharing was to be found in socialist theory. Socialists showed keen interest in the development of profit-sharing and co-partnership, as they were fully aware of the fact that the system was advocated as the antidote to socialism. The scheme of South

Metropolitan Gas Company particularly provoked the Socialists for it was the first employer attempt to eradicate a new union of the unskilled workers which was organized and led by Socialists. When 2,000 gasworkers of South Metropolitan went out on strike against the introduction of a profit-sharing scheme in December 1889, labor and socialist journals, including Justice, the organ of the Social Democratic Federation, William Morris's Commonweal, and Keir Hardie's Labour Leader, all came out to condemn the company and to render moral and financial support to the strikers. They believed that the South Metropolitan scheme was nothing more than the employers' attempt to eradicate the newly-born union of the gasworkers.

Since the South Metropolitan strike, the Socialists looked at the development of the profit-sharing movement with gloomy eyes and constantly exposed its "sinister natures." However, it was the years around 1912 that they launched wholesale attack on profit-sharing and co-partnership. The year 1912 saw the greatest enthusiasm and the most vigorous propaganda for the wider diffusion of the movement, as discussed in the previous chapter. The danger of such a situation seemed so great that Harry Quelch, a leading member of the Social Democratic Federation, the Marxist organization founded by H. M. Hyndman in 1884, declared:

> Seeing the possibility of its application to practically all large industries, the steady extension of this application and the amount of support it is receiving from various quarters, I cannot but regard profit-sharing, especially in the form of co-partnership, as the most serious danger and menace to the working class in its struggle for emancipation from wage slavery.[1]

What was more alarming to the Socialists was the fact that the movement was being supported by many trade union leaders who might have been "expected to have a keener appreciation of the sinister character of such schemes."[2]

This concern was shared by other groups of Socialists,. Thus Quelch, on behalf of the SDF, published a pamphlet, in order to warn the workers against "the co-partnership snare." Shortly after that, Edward Pease wrote on the subject to be published as a Fabian tract. The publication of Pease's paper was, however, considered insufficient as "the subject is much to the fore at present, and the Socialist case against profit-sharing as an alternative to the socialization of the means of production has not recently been stated in a convenient form."[3] The Fabian Research Department meanwhile organized a conference on the control in industry under the chairmanship of Beatrice Webb in the summer of 1913. The subject of profit-sharing and co-partnership was most vigorously discussed at the conference, the summary of which was published in _New Statesman_, the organ of the Fabian

Society, in February 1914.[4]

To be sure, if we look at the diversity of theoretical approaches and practical tactics of these heterogeneous groups loosely called 'Socialists,' we may question the validity of including some in the socialist group at all, as Eric Hobsbawm has done concerning the Fabians.[5] The Social Democratic Federation remained a Marxist organization while the Fabian Society was a group of collectivists and social democrats. There were also significant differences between the Fabians and their younger rebels, the Guild Socialists. The Fabians envisaged collectivist society run by highly centralized and efficient bureaucracy whereas the Guild Socialists longed for worker control in workshops in each industry and trade. The former, as Socialists, also aimed at the elimination of capitalism, but not of the wage system, whereas the latter demanded the absolute abolition of both.[6] But as far as profit-sharing and co-partnership were concerned, theirs was indeed a largely homogeneous voice. Moreover, it will be unnecessary for our purpose to attempt to differentiate their perceptions from their ideological backgrounds. Therefore we will simply consider them as if they were, in fact, a homogeneous group.

The Socialists, including the Marxist Social Democratic Federation, the Fabians, and the Guild Socialists, stressed the absolute repudiation of capitalism and the concept of profits, and criticized the wage system as it existed. Thus G. D. H. Cole declared:

> As a Socialist, I am against capitalism and all its work, and the last thing I should wish to do would be to turn the labourers into an inferior sort of capitalists, or to entangle the workers into acceptance of a superficially amended system of capitalist exploitation...[7]

As Socialists they all claimed that the whole productive process of the capitalist system rested on a false basis: first, capital was simply an instrument of which the laborer made use and should be controlled by those who used it and not by private individuals who claimed to be its owners; second, production for profit was immoral: the commodities vital to the life of society should be produced primarily for use or consumption and not simply because they yielded surplus to the capitalist; third, the wage system of capitalism was vicious, making the worker merely a commodity or a wage slave the capitalist bought in a labor market, which left the worker no power over the product of his own labor.[8]

This, they argued, profit-sharing would not change because it would not change the fundamental structure of capitalism. Under profit-sharing, profits would still be obtained by competition and exploitation and therefore the robbery of labor would continue. Under profit-sharing, there would be no general redistribution of wealth, and the bulk of both capital and control would be left in the hands of the capitalist class. Already in 1858, Marx viewed profit-sharing, a recently devised idea, as a means of "buying up individual overlookers etc. in the interest of the employer against the interests of their class," or as "a special way of cheating the workers and of deducting a part of their wages in the more precarious form of a profit depending on the state of the business..."[9] Quelch went even further, claiming that profit-sharing "increases and intensifies the rate of exploitation and the proportion of surplus-value."[10]

Interestingly, some advocates claimed that profit-sharing was a "modified practical" form of Socialism as it would erode the difference between capital and labor and eventually raise the wage earner to the capitalist. The Socialists scorned such a claim and viewed profit-sharing as diametrically opposed to socialism: socialism desired the abolition of profit altogether, J. Morton of the Independent Labour Party declared, whereas profit-sharing tried to increase it. Profit-sharing would only maintain the cash nexus whereas socialists wanted to replace it with the ideal of communal service. Socialism would not secure a "share of the profits for the working men but secure for the whole society; the workers would be partners with the whole society in the ownership of land and capital and in management."[11]

Ironically, profit-sharing seemed to indicate the contradiction inherent in the capitalist system. If employers were willing to divide all the surplus profits, Cunningham Graham, the Socialist MP, declared in House of Commons in 1890, after 5 or 10 percent had been returned to them, that was surely "tacit confession that the whole wage system...at the present is one to be condemned."[12] To him employers' willingness to give away part of surplus profits reflected their uneasy conscience under the existing system. Socialists proclaimed that capitalism was a passing system of the social order: it would eventually meet its demise. But until then, and as long as the capitalist system continued, the employer and the worker "must be armed for a fight."[13] Thus William Morris wrote:

> In the first place, no amount of so-called co-operation or profit-sharing that is possible will prove to be a solution of the labor question as long as land is owned in severalty and capital is the property of individuals...Secondly...ceaseless contest is a necessary condition...it is only by means of this contest, the perpetual antagonism of the classes, that the peace to come can be brought about.14

The cry for the identity of interest of employer and employee was scornfully rejected by these opponents, and so was the idea of co-partnership. The most popular socialist paper, Clarion, printed a poem deriding co-partnership:

> There was a young lady of Riga
> Went out for a ride on a tiger
> They came back from the ride
> With the lady inside,
> And a smile on the face of the tiger.
> They were Co-partners.[15]

Industrial peace, as it was propagated by the employers, was rejected as only superficial. It did not mean the elimination of the causes of the class war, Quelch asserted, but only 'disarming the workers, disbanding their battalions, and depriving them of all power of fighting.'[16]

Annie Besant, a member of both the Fabian Society and the SDF and the organizer of women workers, stated a representative socialist view on the "co-opting" nature of profit-sharing and co-partnership:

> The bonus swindles the worker, gulls him into a belief that he is a partner with the firm. Profit-sharing introduces a new phase in the conflict between capital and labor. It is no longer against capital brutal, coercive, threatening, but against capital subtle, craftful, and insidious. The capitalist of the old school frankly proclaimed the supreme importance of the dividend, and tried to buy his labor in the cheapest market. The capitalist of the new school poses as a philanthropist, yearning to help the workers, and smiles blandly on them as he gently leads them into skilfully laid toils, which will twist round their limbs and bind them into helplessness. The days are not yet passed in

> which Judas betrayed the Son of Man with a kiss.17

Worker Participation in Management

The next point that opponents, mainly the Socialists, raised concerned worker participation in management especially under co-partnership. Profit-sharing was viewed as simply an insidious attempt to give labor vested interest in the continuance of the capitalist system, and co-partnership as an excuse to avoid nationalization of industry by creating "a small army of working class shareholders." Harry Quelch asserted that profit-sharing and co-partnership without worker's control were a "snare and a delusion." Under profit-sharing, power relations between employer and employee remained that of control on the one hand and subordination on the other.

The rules of profit-sharing schemes in general stipulated that a bonus to employee would be declared "after the ordinary shares received the proper dividend." According to this regulation, employee co-partners could never get as high a dividend as the capital co-partners; furthermore, they could never share the ordinary profits with them, but must wait until the ordinary shareholders received either a 5 percent or a 10 percent dividend. Profit-sharing's critics could hardly fail to notice such inequalities and concluded that the system tended to perpetuate the present capitalist system by "intensifying the essential distinction between capital and labor," and "cheating labor of its birthright for a mess of pottage."[18]

The situation of worker directors under the co-partnership scheme was not drastically different. As the Fabians concluded, "the amount of real authority placed in the hands of the workers is apt to be exceedingly small."[19] G. D. H. Cole was even more critical: he flatly rejected the presence of one or two workmen in the board, regardless of the fact that they were given the same nominal powers as the directors representing the capitalist interest as they were bound to be a helpless minority in the board room. It did not show "any likelihood whatever of shifting the ownership of the means of production or the control of industry."[20] Moreover, Cole felt that the worker should not be represented in the boardroom for he could not serve two masters: if he assumed the position of a director, he must cease to represent the workers.[21]

Apart from their other reservations, however, profit-sharing's critics were not enthusiastic about the worker's ability to manage. Sidney Webb, for instance, although insisting on the necessity of worker participation in management, admitted that the workers were not yet competent to undertake such a role. What he wanted to see set up was a consultative body that would include a works committee and the admission of workers to the board of directors even as a minority with a provision for subsequent management training.[22] G. D. H. Cole echoed the same view when he stated that "before labor can control, it must learn how to control."[23] As late as 1946, Sir Stafford Cripps declared on behalf of the Labour Government:

> There is not as yet a very large number of workers in Britain capable of taking over large enterprises. It has always been extremely difficult to get enough people who are qualified to do that sort of job, and until there has been more experience by the workers of the managerial side of industry, I think it would be almost impossible to have worker-controlled industry in Britain, even if it were on the whole desirable.[24]

Practical Difficulties and Problems

Those opponents who were not necessarily committed to socialism found the basis of their opposition in some of the more concrete problems the innovative new system raised. Many trade unionists raised their doubts about the system in this context. It was pointed out that profit-sharing depended on too many contingencies. The prospect of bonus was left to the big ifs: "if" the worker increased his efforts and served his employer well, he might hope to get a bonus at the end of the year, but only "if" prosperity attended the business. Indeed this seemed to be all that profit-sharing offered. Moreover, these ifs were in turn subject to other contingencies because the success or failure of business depended on many factors, such as management skill and market conditions. In this complex process of making profits, the special deligence of the worker was a trivial element and thus the return he would receive for his extra exertion was determined by factors over which he had no control.[25]

The next criticism was focused on employers' arbitrariness in the actual procedure of the scheme. Although many schemes brought the profit-sharing committee into operation, important decisions were always left to the employer. The questions of expansion, depreciation and reserve funds influenced, to a great extent, the balance to be divided, but these were all managed by the employer. As a rule, the profit-sharing employer controlled the preparation of the balance sheet and decided the proportion of dividends, salaries and wages, and reinvestment etc. to gross earnings. And these decisions remained secret. One employer stated that he "keep the bonus as private as possible as regards...the amounts of bonus and the method of calculation.'[26]

There was also abundant room for arbitrary disposal of the gross revenue, and in a few cases, the amounts placed on reserve were increased in order to reduce the divisible profits. The case of the Briggs colliery was the classic example. Employees were to receive one half of the net profits after a 15 percent dividend was paid to the shareholders. Yet in 1873, the fund availble for distribution was decreased well below that level simply because L 30,000 out of the earnings of the previous year was invested in a mine, the shareholders getting new shares, but the employees losing L 15,000 of their prospective bonus. In addition, a large part of it went to depreciation and reserve funds.[27] This sort of arbitrary action on the part of the employer could only be detrimental to the success of profit-sharing schemes. Considering the fact that the causes of many labor troubles are subjective, the possibility of worker discontent was dangerously high.

A more severe attack on profit-sharing was launched against the way in which the whole arrangement was set up. As we have discussed, it was asserted that the essence of profit-sharing lay in the supposed economy that would result from less waste and from greater efficiency stemming from worker enthusiasm. To be sure, under profit-sharing, the employer would not promise to share his normal profits with the worker. He would share only what he called an additional profit in principle. What he said to the worker was this, as Professor Beesley, the leading Positivist and professor of history at University of College in the University of London, summed up:

> The profit I have been in the habit of taking, I still intend to take. I do not intend to let you have any share of it. But I tell you what I will do: if you like to work harder, and take more care of my tools and my material, and so create an additional profit, then I am willing to allow you, not the whole of the additional profit, but a portion of it.28

Generally, profit-sharing employers reported that their profits increased after the new system was instituted, and this testimony appeared to confirm the opponents' view--that the workman earned the bonus and the employer returned them only a "fraction of what they had produced." It seemed obvious that the capitalist had nothing to lose and everything to gain" under the profit-sharing system, and that the worker was like "the dog fed off his own tail."[29]

This argument logically led to the claim that what was shared was not profits but deferred wages. It was argued that the proportion of the total product taken by labor was not greater but less, indeed that there was an actual reduction in the both aggregate and in the proportion. Therefore, it was asserted, "the present disparity is increased rather than diminished," and trade unions contended that if the employer could afford giving away some part of his profits, he could just as well afford to pay higher wages in time of prosperity. They insisted that the worker would prefer regular wages to what H. G.

Wells, the writer who joined the Fabian Society briefly, called "the periodic tipping of employers to prevent strikes."[30] One young worker in Thomas Bushill's employment remarked that he would not trouble himself about a bonus if he received 1s. a week extra somewhere else.[30]

Many workers regarded profit-sharing as piecework and simply as another form of speed-up. W. J. Strachan of Hull Trades Council, for one, identified profit-sharing with piecework and criticized its effect on older workers. The Amalgamated Society of Engineers, suspecting that the purpose of profit-sharing was speed-up, held that it was antithetical to trade union principles.[32] Any form of speed-up caused resentment not only because of its detrimental effect on workers' physical exertion but because of its pernicious effect on his avarice and selfishness. Critics saw in profit-sharing the tendency of intensified competition and therefore reduced the value of labor. Beatrice Webb therefore condemned profit-sharing as a "legacy from individualist ideas."[33] On this ground alone, unions such as the Amalgamated Society of Carpenters and Joiners rejected profit-sharing:

> Our stand for plain time, and that only, is that any system of piecework, payment by results, co-partnership or premium bonus is detrimental to the interests of our members, tending to make them compete selfishly against each other, and undermining their spirit of solidarity.34

The system might increase worker productivity but this result was not welcomed by the trade unionists. They reasoned that increased productivity would lead to increased unemployment and the physical deterioration of the worker.[35] No matter how vehemently the practice of restricting output was criticized, the belief that there was only a limited amount of work available at a given time persisted, and participants in profit-sharing schemes were blamed for stealing work from their fellow workers. When the workers of Irvine's shipbuilding accepted a co-partnership scheme in 1908, the Amalgamated Society of Engineers promptly attacked them: "Now that they have the prospect of rolling up their sleeves an inch higher than on the old rate, to the end of obviating future trouble and gaining 4 percent on co-partnery shares, while knowing that 26.3 percent of their fellows in the shipbuilding and 12.7 percent in the engineering trades are unemployed."[36]

If profit-sharing was a system of payment by results, it was thought to be inferior to other forms in terms of material compensation: in other systems, the return to the worker largely depended on his own exertion, whereas in profit-sharing, the return was decided by the size of profit. In other systems, output was to a large extent within the worker's own control: he could secure additional results by additional effort. In profit-sharing, this was only true to a limited extent even of output, but it was far less true of profits, for profits relied to a greater extent on the general industrial situation, the state of the market, and the skill of management. Obviously, profits were not the correct basis for calculating a bonus. In reality, the average profit-sharing dividend was substantially less than the increase in income that the trade union commonly obtained when it agreed to replace payment by time with a piece-rate system. The point is that profit-sharing was not a form of payment by results in the strict sense, yet some workers and union leaders so viewed it, and its inferiority in comparison with other forms of payment by results was apparent to them.

Profit-sharing's Dangerous Effect on Trade Unioism

The final criticism on profit-sharing concerned its effect on trade unionism. The relationship between profit-sharing and trade unionism was the most sensitive issue due to the general assumption that profit-sharing was an employer challenge to the trade unions. Replying to this assumption, the system's advocates asserted that there were no real obstacles interposed by the basic principles of trade unionism on the one hand and profit-sharing on the other. What trade unionism had contributed to the welfare of the workers was frankly admitted and even praised by profit-sharing's advocates. At the same time, they pointed out the shortcomings of trade unionism as they saw them, insisting that these shortcomings could be overcome by profit-sharing.

First of all, the primary aim of trade unionism was asserted to be collective bargaining: labor co-partnership went a step further, not being content simply with representation but introducing a higher principle--participation. Another aim of trade unionism was seen as the abolition of the sweat of labor: again, co-partnership embraced a higher principle--it not only abolished sweating but promoted industrial peace and a fairer distribution of profits. Upon these grounds, the advocates called for union sympathy and assistance for the further development and democratization of industry through profit-sharing and co-partnership. Trade unions should look sympathetically on co-partnership, it was bravely insisted, and hold it up before their members as an ideal.[37]

"In what way does co-partnership break the solidarity?" they asked. "Granted that freedom of combination exists and the standards of remuneration...are those of the unions, those who work under a co-partnership system lose nothing they claim as trade unionists and gain much more than mere combination can give them."[38] On the other hand, co-partnership should be grateful to trade unionism for its contribution to the improvement of the working class: it basically curtailed "the abuse of the power of capital and raised the wage earner socially, morally, and economically."[39]

Notwithstanding this enthusiastic attempt to link profit-sharing with trade unionism, the unions viewed profit-sharing simply as a means whereby employers attempted to undermine them. Not only the principles upon which profit-sharing and trade unionism rested were mutually exclusive but the policies they employed were obviously incompatible. William Ashley, the economic historian at Birmingham University who supported social reform and worker organization and one of the few exceptions among the economists in criticizing profit-sharing, found the major ground for his opposition to profit-sharing in the clashing principles of trade unionism and profit-sharing. To quote Ashley:

> Trade unionism rested upon the assumption of solidarity and interest between all the workmen of a trade face to face with all the employers of the trade. The unit on profit-sharing is a particular concern, whereas in trade unionism it is a trade or industry. Trade unionism sought to secure as large a share as possible for labor in the form of the highest obtainable standard rate of wages, irrespective of the good or ill fortunes of a particular concern.40

That was in theory; in practice, the contradiction was just as inescapable. Profit-sharing left the employer to initiate or terminate this scheme at will, while the source of the strength of the trade union lay in the protection of it provided against the caprice of the employer. The trade union sought, as far as possible, to secure that the worker should be paid according to the quality of his service, and not according to the amount of profit-sharing each particular business was able to extract from it.[41]

Whereas the proponents of profit-sharing and co-partnership criticized collective bargaining as perpetuating the difference between capital and labor, the critics of the system unanimously agreed to the necessity of collective bargaining in industry and even its superiority to profit-sharing. Even Ashley, who was vigorously opposed to socialist ideas, saw the undermining of trade unionism as the weakening of the necessary basis for industrial peace because it threatened the collective bargaining system. Ashley believed that industrial disputes could be avoided most effectively by conciliation between employers and workers through effective combination on both sides.[42] Although Ashley wished social reconciliation, not conflict, he rejected as unrealistic all attempts to bring about class harmony which took as their starting point the identity of interest between employer and employee.[43] The Socialist critics such as Cole believed collective bargaining by trade unions and the employers would best serve the workers' interest until socialism arrived.

J. A. Hobson, an isolated figure from the

mainstream political economists of the time, also felt it absurd to claim the identity of interest between capital and labor. Like Ashley, Hobson refused to accept the complete identity of interests between capital and labor, although Hobson and Ashley held extremely different views on capitalism and imperial policies of Britain. Hobson admired John Ruskin and followed him in rejecting the principles of classical political economy and trying to humanize economic science. He gave profit-sharng a credit as long as it made an effort to consider the worker not simply a marketable unit but as a human being with mind and interest of his own. Hobson, however, was sympathetic with socialist ideas, and thus repudiated the economic system based on private property and private profit motivation. Therefore he viewed the profit-sharing and co-partnership as nothing more than "the role of amicable fads." and shared the suspicion of trade unionists that employers adopted profit-sharing to undermine the existing trade union power.[44]

To these opponents, the most pernicious effect of profit-sharing on the trade union movement was the breaking-up of its solidarity. The worker's loyalty to trade unionism would be shattered under the profit-sharing system, which by its nature, bound the worker to the employer and the firm, rather than to the union or the class. It not only pitted on workman against another but also "deluded the worker into thinking that his interst was identical with that of his employer."[45] It split up trades and industries into "coteries of priviliged workers, each group with interests different from, and perhaps antagonistic to, the others." This was viewed particularly lamentable because the critics believed orgnization alone could place the worker on the same plane as the employer. If they wanted better wages, the only way to get them was "organize and make themselves sufficiently strong."[46]

Even a few employers who were sympathetic with trade unionism criticized the practice of some profit-sharing schemes which attempted to frustrate the unions. Edward Cadbury, for one, justified the unions' rejection of profit-sharing on the ground that solidarity of labor would be much more precious to the working class than small increase of earnings obtained through profit-sharing.[47]

The objection of trade unions to profit-sharing requires further examination for the greatest part of the system's failure has been attributed to it. Truly, trade unions in general opposed profit-sharing. However, it is another story whether or not they succeeded in deterring the progress of the movement. More examination is, therefore, made in Chapter V.

Notes to Chapter III

1. Harry Quelch, *The Co-partnership Snare* (London: Twentieth Century Press, 1912), p.15.

2. Quelch, *The Snare*, p.14.

3. *Fabian News*, June 1913, p.53.

4. *New Statesman*, Feb. 14, 1914, supplement; *Fabian News*, Aug. 1913, p.65.

5. Eric Hobsbawm, "The Fabians Reconsidered," in *Labouring Men* (Garden City, N.Y.: Doubleday, 1967).

6. Elie Halevy, *The Era of Tyrannies* (Garden City, NY: Doubleday, 1965), p.161.

7. G. D. H. Cole, *The Case For Industrial Partnership* (London: Macmillan, 1957), p.51.

8. Cole, *The Case for Industrial Partnership*, p.52; Bowie, *Sharing Profits*, p.3.

9. Quoted in A. Ramsay, "Cycles of Control," *Sociology*, 2 (Sep. 1977), p.483.

10. Quelch, *The Snare*, p.5.

11. J. A. Morton, "Co-partnership and Profit-sharing Schemes," *Socialist Rev.*, 62 (April 1913), p.114; Quelch, *The Snare*, p.16.

12. *Parliamentary Debates*, 3rd series, v. 343, p.1156, April 22, 1890.

13. Edward Pease, Profit-sharing and Co-partnership: A Fraud and A Failure, Fabian Tract, 170, (London: 1912), p.15.

14. Qouted in Joseph Melling, "British Employers and the Development of Industrial Welfare, c.1880-1920" Disser. University of Glasgow, 1980, vol. 2, p.138.

15. Clarion, Oct. 16, 1908.

16. Quelch, The Snare, p.9.

17. Justice, Dec. 21, 1889, p.2.

18. Bowie, Sharing Profits, p.142.

19. New Statesman, Feb. 14, 1914, p.584.

20. Cole, The Case, p.53.

21. Cole, The Case, p.53.

22. Sidny Webb, The Root of Labour Unrest: An Address to Employers and Managers, Fabian Tract, 196 (London: 1920).

23. Quoted in E. Walls, Progressive Co-partnership (London: Nisbet, 1921), p.228.

24. Quoted in Arnold Rogow, "The Labour Relations under the British Labor Government" American Journal of Economics and Sociology, 14 (1954/5), p.361.

25. A. O'D. Bartholeyns, "Profit-sharing between Capital and Labour," Westminster Review, 177 (1912), p.500; Pease, A Fraud, p.15.

26. Report, 1912, p.71.

27. T. Jones, "Profit-sharing in Relation," p.427.

28. Industrial Remuneration Conference, The Report of the Proceedngs (London: Cassell, 1885), p.323.

29. Commonweal, Dec. 14, 1889, p.398.

30. Quoted in H. Sanderson Furniss, "Co-partnership and Labour Unrest," Economic Review, 23 (Jan. 1913), p,68.

31. Bushill, Profit-sharing, p.45.

32. Industrial Remuneration Conference, Report of Proceedings (London: Cassell, 1885), p.332.

33. Economic Review, "Co-operative Congress," 3 (1893), p.408.

34. Amalgamated Society of Woodworkers, Our Society's History (Manchester: 1939), p.140. Yet some union leaders who supported profit-sharing, while admitted the element of speed-up under the system, attempted to point out the difference: under co-partnership, the results of the driving the workers would benefit the worker himself, while speeding-up benefited only the employer.

35. The Socialists also repudiated the notion of industrial efficiency called for by the supporters of the system as they viewed it simply as creating "a mass of the commodity labor obedient, industrious, and subservient to the will of the captains of industry." See Clarion, Oct. 23, 1908.

36. Amalgamated Engineers Journal, Dec. 1908, p.5.

37. Labour Co-partnership, Nov. 1899, p.191; Dec. 1903, p.189.

38. Labour Co-partnership, Oct. 1913, p.148.

39. *Labour Co-partnership*, Nov. 1899, p.154; March 1904, p.42.

40. William Ashley, "Profit-sharing," *Quarterly Review*, 219 (Oct. 1913), pp.522-3.

41. Cole, *The Case*, p.52.

42. Ashley, "Profit-sharing," p.524.

43. Bernard Semmel, *Imperialism and Social Reform* (Garden City, NY: Doubleday, 1960), p.214.

44. J. A. Hobson, *The Condition of Industrial Peace* (NY: Macmillan, 1927), p.18.

45. Quelch, *The Co-partnership Snare*, p.4.

46. Pease, *A Failure*, p.15.

47. *Yorkshire Factory Times*, Feb. 28, 1908.

Chapter IV. Employers' Objections to Profit-sharing

Now that the merits and advantages of profit-sharing had been demonstrated by its advocates, it was up to the employers to decide whether or not to give it a chance: the employees having no right to demand it. Given the choice, the employers for the most part said no. The figures of the firms practicing profit-sharing and co-partnership between the 1880s and the 1920s, and even today, clearly show the numerical marginality of the movement. Still, unimpresssive numbers should not be

Table 4.1 Profit-sharing Schemes in Great Britain

	1910	1920	1954
Number of schemes in operation	125	279	310
Approximate number of employees participating	58,000	137,000	345,000
Percentage of participants to the total working population	0.3%	0.7%	1.5%

Source: C.G.Hanson, 'Profit-sharing Schemes in Great Britain' in _Journal of Management Studies_, 2 (Oct. 1965), p.345.

equated with insignificance in the development of modern management and labor relations. After all, profit-sharing was a path never before taken in British industry, a precedent-setting innovation that made society look at the workplace in a new light. And yet, why did this seemingly promising system, often touted as a panacea for industrial ills, not succeed in building a strong hold in British industry?

To Lord Robert Cecil, who devoted himself to the profit-sharing movement as much as he did later to the League of Nations, it seemed strange that employers should be opposed to it at all, yet he noticed that profit-sharing and co-partnership were met by "uncompromising opposition from the great majority of employers."[1] John Hope, chairman of John Knight, soap manufacturing company in London, echoed the same view: it was the employers who had the most serious objection to profit-sharing. One London employer reflected that the one thing he had learned from all the profit-sharing schemes that had been submitted to him was "how not to do it."[2] The Labour Co-partnership Association, established by Christian Socialists in 1884, made every effort to convert employers to the cause of co-partnership and cooperation in industry, yet received little response from practical employers. The Association remained chiefly the organization of social reformers,, working class cooperative societies, and sympathizers among politicians and other public figures.

Why did this seemingly promising system fail to recruit practical employers? At first sight, the conservative British temperament and Britain's supreme position in the world economy seem to have contributed to the slow development. Clearly the British would not have been attracted to a new method unless there should seem to be some very important reasons for changing the very system under which England had developed her trade and commerce so successfully. However, a close examination shows that employer opposition to profit-sharing and co-partnership was based on several factors. First, employers believed strongly in the wage contract in the free labor market as the fairest method of remuneration. Second, employers reacted with hostility to any encroachment on the territory of managerial prerogatives, and they perceived profit-sharing and co-partnership as just such an encroachment. Third, profit-sharing and co-partnership were thought of as having only an indirect and remote effect in promoting worker productivity and in reversing deteriorating labor relations. More direct methods, such as payment by results, were preferred by "practical" employers. Finally, British employers who generally held a conciliatory attitude towards trade unionism refrained from committing themselves to the new system--simply because they were aware of the unions' vigorous objection to it.

Laissez-faire ideology

The most discernable phenomenon in the British experience was a strong influence of individualistic liberalism.[3] To be sure, the declining position of the British economy and commerce began to be felt already in the last quarter of the nineteenth century, and various efforts were attempted to convert the decline in their economic condition. A notable movement to achieve such a goal was the Tariff Reform movement, launched by the staunch imperialist Joseph Chamberlain in the years after 1903. Chamberlain was famous for the radical reform programs he established in Birmingham while he was the mayor of the city, yet his fiscal plans, including imperial preferences, stormed the political scene of the first decade of the twentieth century. The Tariff Reformers condemned the Cobdenite beliefs in free trade and cosmopolitanism, and urged active state intervention in both economic and social action.[4] The Tariff Reform movement obviously reflected the changing attitude of the British public toward laissez-faire ideology and free market system.

However, the majority of the British employers still remained complacent and still thought of economic activity in terms of free market system. Basically, employers understood profits as an absolute right of property and saw no reason to give away what was theirs to their employees. After all, the capitalist system assumed the perfect fairness of a wage contract between employer and employee in a free labor market: wages were decided by the classic process of supply and demand, if left free from artificial intervention. Profit-sharing, by contrast, assumed that the share in the results of an enterprise in the form of wages was not a just and adequate share and that consequently, equity called for a further distribution of money to the workers at the annual balancing. Advocates of profit-sharing, such as G. J. Holyoake, asserted that profit-sharing was a right of labor. He argued that if the worker, whose labor did most to create the profit, had no right to a share in it, "no man has a right to anything."[5]

However, employers viewed the matter from a diametrically opposite perspective. Profits were conceived of as a just remuneration to the capitalist for his investment and risk-taking. Non-Marxist theories of profit have generally agreed on the fundamental point that profit arose out of risk-taking: the capitalist is prepared to take the risks because of the expectation of rewards for doing so, but no return is guaranteed on their own investment, nor is security provided for it.[6] The worker, who had "never saved, contributed and risked capital," had no right to profits.[7]

Moreover, employers saw wages as the first rather than the last charge on the product of industry, and considered the employer rather than the worker as the residual claimant. Under the wage system, the employer was the buffer, it was insisted, that softened the shock of the collision of the industrial train. One employer put this argument bluntly:

> If the capitalist guarantees to the laborer a weekly wage, whether there are profits or losses, and the laborer accepts the term, the arrangement is equitable. Why the laborer, guranteed the full rate of wages, should also be entitled to a share of mamagement in which he has no share, it is not easy to see.[8]

To this objection, it was pointed out that the share of profits given to the working man would be earned by the working man himself through extra diligence and economy. This argument, however, could not persuade those critics skeptical of the economic value of employee good-will. There seemed to be only two ways, as one employer summed it up, "by which you can pay your bonuses; either you underpay your men or you sweat them."[9] Over and over again, employers asked "Where does the money for a bonus come from?" On the whole, they thought that profit-sharing would inevitably diminish the reward of the capitalist.

Cost considerations were indeed a very crucial element in the way of employers' welfare provisions, as R. Hay has pointed out. Many employers abstained from profit-sharing simply because it seemed to cost too much. Employers sometimes found the cost of profit-sharing was not worth spending because it required much complicated extra booking and extra cost for administration.[10]

However, profit-sharing could be a less costly provision than other plans such as non-contributary pensions, for the profit-sharing bonus depended on the annual profits of the undertaking and in case of no profits earned, the employer met no obligation to provide bonuses. Indeed, some employers adopted profit-sharing on the ground that it was a benefit to the workers without too great cost to the employer.[11] Yet the average employers' reluctance to profit-sharing, a form of welfare provisions which was conceived as less costly, indicates a lack of employer enthusiasm for welfarism in general, as recent studies on employer social policy have shown.[12]

To many employers, profit-sharing and co-partnership seemed to serve not to undermine socialism but to precipitate it--by eroding the difference between capitalist and worker. Profit-sharing and co-partnership would give the worker not only larger portion of wealth but greater voice in management. Co-partnership in particular seemed to contend that the employer and the worker "should be all partners in the same work."[13] When George Livesey, a famous profit-sharing employer, tried to convert a group of his fellow employers to the cause, one of his auditors promptly attacked him, calling him "Socialist." Co-partnership was defined as "Socialism of the best kind." If socialism was to be met, it was obvious for them that it must be done through means other than another form of socialism.[14] "These attempts which urged people how they should conduct their business," one enraged employer claimed, "all lead up to socialism, and form no remedy whatever."[15]

Even if it was agreed that profit-sharing schemes brought about increased profits as the advocates proclaimed, problems still remained: there were so many factors that contributed to the success of business, and it was by no means easy to differentiate among them. Profits could increase through general prosperity in trade, through better management, through improved machinery, through effective advertising, or through the workman's increased zeal and productivity. To the employer, labor's part seemed less than all-important in this complex process of profit-making. The average capitalist certainly had no intention of allotting any part of profits not directly owed to the workman. An employer named Thomasson, claimed that no one had so far discovered a means of deciding "mathematically what the shares of the laborer, the superintendent, manager, and the capitalist in the total produce should respectively be," and until that was done, "no one can say that the actual arrangement is inequitable."[16]

Tomasson's argument shows the vacuum in economic

theory on wages after the wage-fund theory passed out of favor. That theory, which had occupied an insurmountable position as a "science" in mid-Victorian England and powerfully dictated employer policy and trade union behavior, held that there was a fixed amount of funds available for wages in society at a given time, and that if one section of labor received a greater share, the allotments to the other sections inevitably diminished. According to the wage-fund doctrine, the working class could never improve its lot much beyond the subsistence level, and the unions were blamed because they were thought to obtain a greater portion of the fixed fund for their members at the sacrifice of non-union workers. But the theory, as mentioned earlier, lost ground in the early 1870s, and no other theory was put forward that would provide a satisfactory principle whereby to assign labor's share of the economic pie.[17]

The strong influence of laissez-faire ideology was revealed even among the employers who practiced profit-sharing. The commonest method in England of distributing the profit-sharing bonus was by payment in cash, which formed 71 percent of the total number of the profit-sharing schemes in operation in 1920. Other countries presented a different tendency. In France, for instance, it was usual to devote the whole or a large part of the bonus to a provident fund from which the workman could only draw after a prescribed and protracted period of service: if he left earlier, he forfeited all claim on the fund. The purpose was obviously to attach employees to the particular concern.[18] However, the British employer was different. An employer in Halifax proclaimed that he did not believe in binding any workman. Employers must trust the workman, he insisted, "pay him a fair day's wage, and not hang over his head a sword in the shape of a threat that if he broke his word, he would be discharged and lose the benefit of the bonus scheme."[19]

Loss-sharing

The conviction of profit arising out of risk-taking logically led to employer repudiation of profit-sharing with employees who took no part in meeting losses. A manufacturer's view that "We can give away profits, but would like to know how we can share losses," was echoed by a number of employers. Sir Benjamin Browne, prominent engineering employer, asked George Livesey: "If you invite all the workpeople to share in the profits, are you going to ask them to share in the losses also?"[20] William Gladstone made a similar comment to the House of Commons in 1891:

> There is, I think, no one of those means more attractive in itself than the operation of what is called profit-sharing. But what

> is to be done when there is no profit at all, but even...a heavy loss? Are you willing and able to share alike in the loss as well as in the profit? Those are questions which it is not likely I should be able to find a solution for.21

To the employers, the dividing up of all surplus profits in the good years and the non-sharing of losses in the bad years seemed both unfair and unreasonable. Thus it was argued that until profit-sharing involved loss-sharing, it could never be regarded as being founded on strict justice. It would continue to be founded on sentiment only--"a generous and noble sentiment, but not one likely to have a very widespread application in this mundane sphere."[22]

In response, however, there were a number of proposals for solving the difficulties. The most feasible of such plans called for the establishment of a reserve fund: a certain percentage of profits was to be set aside in good trade years before the employee bonus was paid; the reserve fund would then be available during a commercial depression or other calamity. Yet this idea had its drawbacks: if the object of the profit-sharing scheme was to give the worker an incentive, the putting aside of profits in the reserve fund would reduce that incentive since the worker could not be certain any of the money would be his. Presumably he would not exert the same degree of diligence and enthusiasm for an uncertain reward as he would for a guaranteed bonus.

The motive involved was a decisive consideration. When the object of profit-sharing was increased efficiency, the issue of loss-sharing was crucial. Employers insisted that unless the workers assumed part of the risk involved, they would never exert themselves to the fullest. When the motive was philanthropy or loyalty, the question of sharing losses was seldom discussed. Theodore Taylor, who could be defined as an autocratic, benevolent employer, said flatly that employers who raised the question of loss-sharing had better leave profit-sharing alone. For the years 1897 and 1898, he pointed out in an address to the Textile Students' Association, his firm had had no profits to divide. All the same, he did not expect "the workers to return any part of their wages."[23] Employers who were chiefly motivated by the desire for control preferred to exclude the notion of losses and restrict their workers' participation only in shared profits. William Lever, for one, was emphatic in his insistence that there should be no loss-sharing and that management was to exert total control of the business and was to be prepared to take all losses: "Just as taxation and representation must go together, so loss-bearing and control must go together."[24]

Most employers, however, continued to think of profit-sharing without loss-sharing as unfair, and steered clear of both. Their cry of unfair, however, presents only half the picture. Obviously labor suffered losses that employers normally did not: unemployment, underemployment, and wage reduction. There was the further consideration that, under profit-sharing, they had presumably been putting extra effort into their work. But if there was no profit or if there was a loss, they received nothing for that extra effort.

The diffusion of ownership among shareholders that was taking place to an increasing degree in the second half of the nineteenth century put still another obstacle in the path of profit-sharing. This seems ironical because in theory, profit-sharing was an attempt to combine the interest of the worker with that of the shareholder by directly relating bonus to the worker to the dividend on capital. That, however, was not how shareholders viewed the matter. On the contrary, they failed to see any reason to sacrifice any portion of their profits for the cause of greater worker harmony and efficency. Perhaps worker satisfaction would in the long run produce greater profits, but they preferred the status quo to any such radical experiment. They treated the idea with undisguised hostility. This seems to have been one reason why profit-sharing was more often to be seen in companies dominated by a single individual: there would thus tend to be a small number holding the majority of ordinary shares, and fewer aggrieved shareholders complaining about the size of their dividends.[25]

Alfred Palmer, director of the Palmer Shipbuilding

Company, believed that profit-sharing could not be carried out except in a few instances where business was controlled or owned by one man. His belief was indeed supported by the statistics of the official report on profit-sharing. About half of the firms which practiced profit-sharing in 1919 were mentioned in the Stock Exchange Official Intelligence. If the gas companies, which were nearly all mentioned and numbered more than one fifth of the total schemes, be excluded, about one-third of the remaining firms with profit-sharing schemes were recorded in the Stock Exchange, while two-thirds were private firms or private limited liability companies. The private limited liability firms represented a typical British compromise. Its object was to obtain limited liability while retaining the original management and maintaining the privacy of the past.[26] In this form of companies, control was left in the hands of the original employer. It would therefore appear that profit-sharing had its greatest extension in private or semi-private businesses such as private limited liability company.

Archibald Briggs, whose scheme at the Whitwood colliery in the 1860s and 1870s represented the first venture in profit-sharing in Britain as examined in Chapter II, recalled the difficulties he had had with his shareholders who asked, "What is the use of giving away 1,800 pounds to the workmen, when they have been amply repaid for their labor?"[27] It was necessary, therefore, to prove that profit-sharing was not simply giving away money and that bonuses would come, not out of normal profits, but out of extraordinary profits resulting from labor's increased productivity. Naturally enough, outside shareholders who had no daily contact with the workers and saw none of the enthusiasm supposedly inspired by the bonus plan, were skeptical. They were more than a little alarmed at the amount of money working men were receiving.

Another objection of shareholders was what they saw as the possible destruction of the traditional power structure under the impetus of profit-sharing and co-partnership. This was especially true in companies where the bonus was given in the form of ordinary shares. Shareholders feared that "a vast voting power would be transferred to the workers of the company."[28] This was conceived as a real danger because of the growing militance of labor and the socialistic tendency of trade unions. The latter was demanding the nationalization of the means of production, distribution, and exchange, as well as the "complete emancipation of labor from the dominion of capitalism and landlordism," as passed at the TUC conference each year since the 1890s. The call for a socialist economy and the demand for nationalization made it abundantly clear that the interests of the worker and the interest of the shareholder were not identical.

Yet the fear of a transfer of a vast voting power

to the employees was groundless. No shareholder could exercise sufficient influence until his investment was substantial, and most workmen would never be in a position to make such an investment through a small sum of profit-sharing bonus. Still, those shareholders, who were at all open to a sharing of surplus profits, preferred that it be in the form of old-age pension and other welfare benefits.[29] They preferred paternalism to a businesslike arrangement which was implied in profit-sharing: paternalism meant a clearer and firmer separation of powers. Besides, it meant they could share if they chose, not share because they were contractually obliged to do so.

The Impediments of Managerial Prerogatives

The second reason for employers' rejection of profit-sharing stemmed from the same fear as shareholders'--the democratic implications of profit-sharing and co-partnership. Employers unanimously objected to any encroachment of managerial prerogatives and they simply did not want the employees to have a voice in the running of the company. In principle, profit-sharing did not necessarily include employee participation in management; employers could simply distribute a cash bonus at the end of the financial year. However, a number of successful profit-sharing schemes, such as that of the South Metropolitan Gas Company, included a profit-sharing committee with employee representation. Since the committee was concerned not only with administering the scheme, but also served as a consultative body in the firm, a seemingly dangerous precedent was being set.

Indeed, the very nature of profit-sharing was problematic, being very different from such gestures of managerial good will as the Christmas bonus. Profit-sharing was defined by the International Congress of Profit-sharing held in Paris in 1889 as "a voluntary agreement, by virtue of which an employee receives a share, fixed beforehand, in the profits of an undertaking."[30] The bonus was to be given on the rate fixed in advance and not on the arbitrary discretion on the part of the employer. Among other things, employers feared that this condition could lead employees to demand the right to inspect company accounts---indeed, that workers might not be content with their bonuses until they had seen the yearly profits as set down in the books with their own eyes. This employers would never allow, for secrecy was considered indispensable to the security and to the prosperity of a business. Secrecy was necessary, it was insisted, whether the firm was enjoying profits or suffering losses: if the firm was doing unusually well and that fact was discovered, capital would immediately flow into that industry and subsequent competition would force down profits. On the other hand, if the firm was losing money, its credit would rapidly disappear.

Thus, many firms that instituted profit-sharing insisted vehemently that employees had no right to see the company's accounts. The rule of the profit-sharing scheme of Clarke, Nicholls, and Coombs, London confectionary firm, stipulated: "It is clearly understood that having this guarantee of good faith the participants shall possess no right whatsoever to intermeddle in any respect with the book-keeping."[31] Again, Thomas Bushill, an ardent exponent of profit-sharing, refused to provide the Royal Commission on Labour with details of his firm's accounts under profit-sharing even though it was a good opportunity to show the profitability of the system. Obviously, this problem of secrecy could have been solved with little trouble--for example, by appointing a disinterested accountant to inspect the company's returns and report to the employees. But only a very few profit-sharing employers relied upon this method, and they did so, presumably only because the dividend had to be published in any case and thus the company's financial condition would be released at least in part.

Theodore Taylor, a non-conformist owner of a successful profit-sharing woollen factory in Batley and Liberal MP, conceded that the question of secrecy had been his greatest objection to profit-sharing. Yet he overcame this difficulty for he did not

> expect to make so much profit as to be made ashamed by the public knowing it, and I contend that no firm ought to trade in such a precarious condition that its credit would be destroyed if it were known to have a bad year.[32]

The issue of opening the company books was so vital one employer stated that "I can say without any exaggeration that the future of profit-sharing depends entirely on the solution of...the problem that the employer, the proprietor of the business, or the manager of the company shall or, as a result of the profit-sharing scheme, be liable to find himself faced with a demand on the part of his employee to interfere in the management of the accounts."[33]

The fear of possible interference with managerial prerogatives under the profit-sharing system did not involve simply the question of opening the company books. One employer exclaimed, "You will have your workpeople wanting to overhaul your books and I do not know what besides!"[34] The deeper issue was the retaining of absolute managerial authority and control. One employer asserted that 'You will have "Jack as good as his master," and no business will stand many masters.' One employer who advocated profit-sharing at the gas engineers' meeting was vigorously attacked on the ground that the workers' participation in the decision making was "the fifth wheel."[35]

Relationship between employer and employee is twofold: it is political as well as economical. Radical historians and students of industrial relations have indeed considered control as the basic issue in the struggle between employer and employee. Even a strike demanding larger wages implied a wider dimension in the strikers' perspective, Richard Price argues, for going out on strike for greater wages implies that workers feel they are strong enough to force concessions from the employer and immediately suggests a changed power relationship.[36] Other studies on the labor process have also shown the crucial role which the issue of control has played in the process of capitalist modes as well as in the development of industrial relations.[37] Employer attitude towards profit-sharing and their concern for management authority ought to be understood in this broader context of struggle for control.

The cry for the retention of managerial prerogatives was accompanied by passionate justifications. In the first place, managerial authority was seen as deriving from property rights: it was unthinkable for men to claim a voice in management without having invested any capital. If working men wanted to manage the capital, it was insisted, "let them save up capital of their own and go in for co-operative undertaking."[38] Jeremiah Head, owner of an ironworks whose profit-sharing scheme was marked by heavy paternalism and anti-unionism, contended that it was a 'forced ad unnatural thing to put working men in the position of capitalists,' and insisted that the employers "ought to retain control because the property is theirs." It seemed to him preposterous that man should have control over property not his own.[39]

A second justification was that absolute control was required if there was to be true efficiency: in order to manage the business with maximum effectiveness, management needed absolute freedom to make decisions and organize production. It was for the cause of efficiency, for instance, that Frederick W. Taylor rejected the co-partnership system: "The world's experience in all directions has demonstrated the utter impracticability of successfully doing executive work under the management of a body of men larger or smaller."[40]

The working class was seen as immature and incapable of managing. Even Benjamin Browne, generally considered one of the more enlightened industrialists, dismissed any potential worker contributions to efficient management on the grounds that management required great talent, experience, and training. "Whereas it takes years of laborious study to make a man a good mechanic, an artist, or an accountant," he estimated, "it takes far greater study, and far more labor, and probably far greater natural gifts, to give a man the experience, the nerve, and the moral qualities...to manage a large business."[41] When the National Association for the Promotion of Social Science discussed the possibility of industrial co-partnership in 1866, the chairman of the meeting, Malcolm Ross, contended that "with uneducated men, so ignorant that they are easily made the dupes of others and irritated into combinations against their masters, 'mild despotism' may be more successful than cooperation," and concluded that only "when the morality and intelligence of the working class are elevated, would cooperation become possible."[42]

The possibilities for employee encroachment on managerial territory were less apparent in profit-sharing than in co-partnership. The two terms were often used interchangeably, but the implications of co-partnership were more democratic of the two as examined in chapter II. Employers understandably embraced the idea of profit-sharing more readily than they did co-partnership. Unlike co-partnership, profit-sharing retained the classic separation of the distinct functions of capital, management, and labor. Whether or not there was an identity of interest between employer and employee, it was argued, there was no identity of function: the function of direction must be kept distinct from the function of doing.

F. D. Marshall, a gas industry employer, asked what the workman would perform in the board of directors. "Will he take in hand the purchase of the coals and the financing of the company?" If that was the case, he concluded, "it will not be long before all the directors will be working in the retort house and all the retort house men will be seated in the board room."[43] Another employer contended that, "If we are ploughmen, we do not want to be plough makers, nor grain distributors, nor yet agricultural managers, as well as ploughmen; co-partnership would lure us into these pursuits."[44] Even in profit-sharing with the rudimentary form of profit-sharing committee, employers saw a potential threat to management authority and therefore vigorously objected to it. It was not until the post-war years that British employers responded to the call for industrial democracy with less hostility.

The Inefficacy of Profit-sharing as an Incentive System

The third objection to profit-sharing mainly came from the employers who pursued efficiency as the prime goal. They rejected the system because they viewed it as less effective than other incentive systems, such as payment by results. The decades after 1880 were the period when labor productivity came to be seriously studied because of Britain's economic difficulties, as discussed in Chapter I. Understandably, they turned to labor, a manageable variable in the process of production, and studied the techniques that seemed to produce the best results.

To reiterate, it was argued that profit-sharing and co-partnership would bring about increased profits: first, through improved worker productivity, and second, through less waste of material and less need for supervision. These effects, it was assumed, would result from the worker's expectation of a bonus. And yet, profit-sharing, being a form of collective remuneration, was not so effective as individual incentive schemes, such as piecework and the premium bonus system. Its flaw was that it made no distinction among the contribution of individual workers. This was Frederick Taylor's criticism of co-partnership: Taylor's own principles, by contrast, rested upon individual incentive system.[45]

At the same time, the reward under the profit-sharing system bore no direct relation to output. If the assumption is accepted that the worker would be motivated to work better if rewards and penalties are tied directly to his performance, as the scientific management methods asserted, profit-sharing had indeed very little incentive value. It was also obvious that the system produced little effect on the large group. A representative opinion was that of Captain Noble, vice chairman and managing director of Sir William Armstrong and Co., giant armaments manufacturers, who dismissed profit-sharing as pointless in his firm, where 15,000 workmen were employed. He insisted that the effect of any individual worker, when its advantage was divided among 15,000 others, would amount to nothing. Instead, he advocated piecework, which he thought to be real profit-sharing.[46]

Piecework was touted by employers who thought day wages a direct temptation to carelessness and dishonesty. It was also thought of as the cure for restricting output. J. S. Mill, for one, resented the worker resistance to piecework as one of "the most discreditable indications of a low moral condition." Dislike to piecework in itself must be dislike to justness and fairness, he wrote: "piecework is the perfection of contract, and contract which in the present state of society and degree of civilization most favorable to the worker."[47] William Denny, a prominent shipbuilder in Dumbarton who was famous for his philanthropic provisions for his employees, thought piecework the direct reverse of the policy of the "degradation" of labor, by which he meant the attempt to make labor scarce, either by reducing the number of skilled workers or by reducing the output.[48]

Therefore, for the most part, employers who concerned themselves with greater industrial efficiency considered profit-sharing and co-partnership remote from tangible objectives and therefore irrelevant. Not to be overlooked among the various forms of incentives that employers used to promote individual efficiency was the device of higher wages, although many employers still failed to accept the high-wage economy. Yet it was pointed out that the workman was concerned with wages and nothing else: "Double or substantially increase his wages and he will be content." Their approach was simply to pay the highest amount of wages they could afford.

However, the more sophisticated employers turned to various systems of payment by results, a technique that was spreading rapidly. The superiority of payment by results to any form of sharing profits or participation in the business seemed almost self-evident: when each man knew that he was paid according to his personal productivity regardless of the output of others or the profit made by the firm, he was getting the strongest inducement to produce his maximum.[49] These direct incentive systems made profit-sharing, by comparison, look not only indirect but far inferior. In short, employers who were chiefly concerned with labor productivity tended to prefer payment by results to other systems in general and profit-sharing in particular in spite of the advocacy that profit-sharing would bring about greater productivity.

The effect of profit-sharing came to be thought of as remote and indirect not only in promoting worker productivity but also in subverting industrial unrest. Lloyd George, then Chancellor of Exchequer in the Liberal government, put this point bluntly when he said to the

House of Commons in 1912: "To set up a co-partnership system in the middle of a strike as a solution is totally impossible."[50] In a larger prospective, employers who wanted to do something about increasingly deteriorating labor relations found profit-sharing wanting in answering the classic difficulty: how to decide that relative proportion of profits should respectively reward capital and labor. It seemed to them that profit-sharing could not bring about any permanent solution to this fundamental question.

Daily wages were more important than a bonus, after all, and wages were still a matter for bargaining under the profit-sharing system. William Denny, thus, predicted the failure of profit-sharing on the ground that the workman who was fighting for higher wages would, under the profit-sharing system, argue for the highest possible bonus.[51] This view was shared by many employers. At least one employer, however, contended that profit-sharing did away with the perpetual negotiating with his employees as to their remuneration. "They know that if business is good, their salaries rise automatically," he testified.[52]

But this was a rare case. The remark of Seebohm Rowntree, a benevolent Quaker owner of Rowntree chocolate manufacturing company, appears to indicate a more accurate picture: "My own feeling is that however high the profits are, the workers believe them to be higher. My experience is that a worker's idea of the profits of his employer is always exaggerated."[53] There is evidence that once a high bonus was announced, the workmen immediately requested a wage increase. Wages, after all, were a regular remuneration whereas the bonus was looked upon as occasional tipping. The workman naturally wanted to share the fruits of business in a fixed form.

Employers' Conciliatory Attitude toward Trade Unions

Finally, British employers hesitated to try profit-sharing because they did not want to provoke the wrath of the trade unions, for they were well aware that the unions felt a strong hostility towards the system. George Livesey observed that the most serious difficulty in the way of the general adoption of profit-sharing was fear of trade union opposition. The special committees, appointed by the Federation of British Industry to explore alternatives to working-class demands for the nationalization of industry in the post-war era, decided not to recommend profit-sharing. Their conclusion: it was not desired by the workers.[54]

The relationship between profit-sharing and trade unionism has been the most sensitive and important question we have so far considered. This is because of the contemporary perception that many such schemes were motivated by a wish to destroy the trade unions, and because this common perception doomed many schemes to failure even before they were given a serious trial. It is also because historians and students of profit-sharing have accepted this view without reservation and interpreted the development of profit-sharing and co-partnership mainly in the context of confrontation between employers and trade unions.

In the next chapter, we will examine the question of whether the failure of profit-sharing can validly be attributed to trade unionism. Here, our interest must be confined to the fact that many employers indeed chose to believe so and therefore refrained from putting profit-sharing in practice. As we have seen, it was alleged by trade unionists that the motive of employers in adopting profit-sharing schemes was primarily to crush the unions or at least to diminish their power. Some publicized cases, such as those of the Briggs' and Fox and Head's, appeared to support this allegation. Even the scheme of the South Metropolitan Gas Company, the most successful and admired of all, clearly had the same objective. George Livesey, chairman of the company, asserted that profit-sharing and co-partnership were incompatible with trade unionism: "The two things are directly opposed. Trade unions are antagonistic to the employer, they are the union versus the employer; whereas profit-sharing is the union of the men with the employer." Trade unions were "organizations of socialists, with evident antagonism with capital," and "as we are capitalists, or represent capitalists, there cannot be any union between us."[55]

Yet the desire to destroy trade unionism, or at least the plausibility of succeeding in an attempt to do so, had mostly disappeared in British industry by the late 1890s. Employers accepted trade unionism as a fait accompli, realizing that trying to ignore it was simply a mistake.[56] This transition by no means followed a unilateral process, and the gasworkers and the railway men still had to fight for union recognition as late as in 1912, yet the recognition and conciliation from the British employers were generally obtained throughout industry by the late 1890s. Thus Clegg and others conclude that most employers were not anti-union: the experience of the first five years of the twentieth century suggests that despite the Taff Vale, "the majority of organized employers preferred to make a serious attempt to work with the unions."[57]

The recognition of craft unions had been extended as early as the 1870s, yet the militant new unions among the unskilled workers that sprang up in 1889-90 were far from acceptable to most employers. It was precisely these new unions that inspired anti-unionism in the years after 1889. However, as time went on, recognition was granted even to these "unpedigreed" unions. Surprisingly, as

Hobsbawm has pointed out, the new unions which had at first alarmed the upper classes with their militant and socialistic approach, would obtain status and stability, winning the support and recognition of employers.

The Royal Commission on Labour, which was appointed in 1891 and reported in 1894, made it clear that many employers were coming to reject the extreme anti-union and laissez-faire point of view. One such employer stated:

> I have no feeling of expectation, or desire, to see unions of workmen made less powerful than they are today. I believe, cordially, not only in the right, but in the desirability of combinations of workmen in order to secure and advance their own power and influence socially...58

The potential usefulness of trade unions was evident to such employers as Benjamin Browne, who asserted that it was "far better that the workmen should act together under trained and experienced leaders than that each man should act separately. The difference between unions and no unions is much the same as the difference between any army and a mob."[59] The path to union recognition was smoothed by the unions themselves, by their greater moderation in policies and organizing efforts. The objectives of the craft unions had always been modest. At the Amalgamated Society of Engineers, for instance, they included so modest a one as assisting members when in distress and when needing burial. Among their higher aspirations was the goal of extending investment in co-operative societies to alter the competitive system and securing for the worker a full share of the fruits of labor.[60]

If the old unions like the ASE seemed modest in their stated goals, neither did the new unions, such as the Gasworkers Union, aim at more radical purposes. Its objects, when it was first formed in 1889, included these: (1) to shorten the hours of labor and to obtain wherever possible an eight-hour working day; (2) to abolish wherever possible overtime and Sunday labor or to obtain payment at higher rate; (3) to raise wages and to obtain for the same work the same wages for women as for men. In 1891, the union altered its rules to include the settlement of "all labor disputes by amicable agreement of arbitration wherever possible," facing a trade depression.[61]

In 1892, Will Thorne, general secretary, insisted that all disputes should be settled in the "most quiet and expedient manner." In 1894, he even declared that it would be better for the union to lose a few members by not supporting strikes that seemed doomed than having them on the strike fund for six months and then at last have to surrender. "A firm stand should be made against men coming out on strike, unless oppressed to such an extent that their position is unbearable."[62] They were thus able to present themselves as a buffer between the employer and the more radical elements of the working class.

The main reason for union recognition, however, was the employers' realization that repression was neither the most workable nor the most desirable policy towards labor. The heightened class solidarity manifested by such events as the formation of the Triple Industrial Alliance of the miners, transport workers and the railaymen in 1913 was sufficient to frustrate the employer's desire to undermine the unions.

In 1890, the year in which the trade union movement gathered increased strength with the emergence of the new unionism, J. S. Nicholson, professor of political economy at Edinburgh University, observed that trade unionism had been so successful that it had now reached "the point of development at which the danger to be feared is the danger of excessive power."[63] After all, the unions were so strong in a great number of industries that it would have been extremely impolitic for a new and weak institution such as profit-sharing to provoke their hostility. Nicholson might have changed his view when the powerful thrust of the new unionism lost momentum several years later. In any case, trade unions had done so much for the improvement of wages and working conditions, they had won the loyalty of the workers. The employers had to concede that hardly perhaps one or two percent of trade unionists would entertain for a moment the thought of abandoning their union membership for the chances of a new and untried system.

To sum up, British employers were generally not enthusiastic for profit-sharing and co-partnership. The first three reasons for their reluctance--the belief in the wage system, the wish to maintain managerial prerogatives, and the desire for more direct methods in improving productivity and in controlling the workforce--are self-explanatory. The final reason, however--the strength of union opposition--leads to a further significant question that must be answered: were trade unions really so strong a force as to obstruct the progress of profit-sharing? We must turn to this crucial question.

Notes to Chapter IV

1. Cecil of Chelwood Papers, British Museum, Add. Mss. 5115, f.61.

2. *Labour Co-partnership*, Mar. 1917, p.26; London Chamber of Commerce, *Journal*, (1898), p.8. D. Marshall, gas employer, declared that profit-sharing was "utopia: We have heard of the new woman; now it appears that we are to have a new man." Institute of Gas Engineers, *Transactions*, (1897), p.156.

3. The virtual non-existence of effective associations among the British employers has been pointed out by historians. See E. H. Phelps Brown, *A Century of Pay* (London: Macmillan, 1968), p.188.

4. Bernard Semmel, *Imperialism and Social Reform* (Garden City, NY: Doubleday,1968).

5. *Labour Co-partnership*, Dec. 1901, p.193.

6. E. G. Hanson, "Profit-sharing Schemes in Great Britain," *Journal of Management Studies*, 2 (Oct. 1965), pp.348-9.

7. *Labour Co-partnership*, June 1902, p.93.

8. *Labour Co-partnership*, Dec. 1901, p.193.

9. Thomas Bushill, *Profit-sharing and the Labour Questions* (London: Methuen, 1893), p.47.

10. Roy Hay, "Employers' Attitude to Social Policy and the Concept of 'Social Control' 1900-1920" in *The Origins of British Social Policy*, ed. Pat Thane (London: Croom Helm, 1978); David Schloss, *Report on Profit-sharing and Labour Co-partnership in the U.K.*, Cd. 7458 (1894), pp.109-10. (Hereafter, *Report*, 1894).

11\.

Board of Trade, Report on Profit-sharing and Labour Co-partnership in the U.K., Cd. 6490 (1912), p.71. (Hereafter Report, 1912).

12\.

Craig Littler, The Development of the Labour Process in Capitalist Societies (London: Heinemann, 1982).

13\.

Institute of Gas Engineers, Transactions (1908), p.74.

14\.

Institute of Gas Engineers, Transactions (1908), p.74.

15\.

George Sole's letter to Lord Robert Cecil (Feb.27, 1912), Cecil Papers, British Museum Add. Mss. 51160, f.80.

16\.

Labour Co-partnership, Dec. 1901, p.193. The same employer, Thomasson, went further and proclaimed that "It would be just as true to say that workman, receiving a day's wage, as a rule conspire to give employers less than a fair day's work."

17\.

The importance of the retraction of the wage-fund doctrine is that it was now admitted that the reward of labor depended on the terms which the worker could succeed in securing for himself even if within certain limits.

18\.

William Ashley, "Profit-sharing," Quarterly Review, 219, (Oct. 1913), pp.514-5.

19\.

Institute of Gas Engineers, Transactions, (1908), p.72.

20\.

Labour Co-partnership, Aug. 1911, p.118.

21\.

Quoted in Labour Co-partnership Association, Report, (1891/2).

22\.

Bushill, Profit-sharing, pp.98-9.

23. Theodore Taylor, "Profit-sharing and Labour Co-partnership in the Woollen Trade," rpt. from the _Journal of the Leeds University Textile Students Association_ (London: 1913), p.17.

24. William Lever, _The Six-hour Day ad Other Industrial Questions_ (London: George Allen and Unwin, 1918), p.69.

25. The separation of ownership and management helped to mold this position. Management which held no right of control of the business through proprietorship had to legitimate itself through the achievement of the highest efficiency, the only stand for judging their ability. However, the degree of such a separation ought not to be exaggerated. What is surprising is, P. L. Payne writes, "the tendency throughout the nineteenth century of forms of business organizations characterized by a marriage of ownership and control almost as complete as that encountered during the Industrial Revolution." _British Entrepreneurship in the Nineteenth Century_ (London: Macmillan, 1974), p.23.

26. Ministry of Labour, _Report on Profit-sharing and Labour Co-partnership in the U.K._ Cd. 544 (1920), p.16. (Hereafter _Report_, 1920); P. L. Payne, "The Emergence of the Large-scale Company," _Economic History Review_, 20 (1967), p.520.

27. National Association for the Promotion of Social Science, _Transactions_ (1866), p.707. (Hereafter NAPSS).

28. Gas Light and Coke Company, _Report of Proceedings_ (Feb. 1909), p.7. (Hereafter GLCC).

29. GLCC, _Report_, (Feb. 1909), pp.6-7.

30. D. Schloss, _Report on Profit-sharing and Industrial Co-partnership in the U.K._, Cd. 7458 (1894), p.2. (Hereafter, _Report_, 1894).

31. Clarke, Nicholls, and Coombs, _Profit-sharing Rules_ (London: 1890).

32. Taylor, "Woollen Trade," p.17.

33.
Albert Trombert, _Profit-sharing: A General Study of the System as in Actual Operation_ (London: P. S. King, 1920), p.77.

34.
Thomas Bushill, _The Relations of Employers and Employed in the Light of the Social Gospel_ (London: Alexander and Shepherd, 1889), p.13.

35.
Bushill, _Profit-sharing_, p.176; Institute of Gas Engineers, _Transactions_, 1882, p.38.

36.
Richard Price, _Masters, Unions and Men_ (Cambridge: Cambridge Univ. Press, 1980), p.60.

37.
Richard Edwards, _Contested Terrain_ (London: Heinemann, 1979); R. Edwards, D. Gordon, and M. Reich, _Segmented Work, Divided Workers_ (Cambridge: Cambridge Univ. Press, 1982); C. Littler, _The Development_.

38.
George Sole's letter to Robert Cecil, Cecil Papers, British Museum Add. Mss. 51160, f.80.

39.
NAPSS, _Transactions_, (1870), p.493.

40.
Quoted in L. Urwick, "Co-partnership and Control," _The Human Factor_, 8 (Nov. 1934), p.393.

41.
Benjamin Browne, _Selected Papers on Social and Economic Questions_ (Cambridge: Cambridge Univ. Press, 1918), pp.237-8.

42.
NAPSS, _Transactions_, (1866)

43.
Institute of Gas Engineers, _Transactions_, (1897), p.156.

44.
A. H. Mackmurdo, _Pressing Questions_ (London: H.John Lane, 1913), p.126.

45.
Edward Walls, Progressive Co-partnership (London: Nisbet, 1921), p. 265.

46.
Royal Commission on Labour, Group C, Minutes of Evidence, Cd. 6894-ix (1893-4). Q. 25814-7.

47.
J. S. Mill, Principles of Political Economy (Toronto: Univ. of Toronto Press, 1965), Collcted Works, vol. 3, p.783n.

48.
William Denny, The Worth of Wages (Dumbarton: Bennett, 1877), p.16.

49.
Keith Burgess, The Origins of British Industrial Relations (London: Croom Helm, 1975), p.28; H. Clegg, A. Fox, and A. F. Thompson, A History of British Trade Unions since 1889, vol.I (Oxford: Oxford Univ. Press, 1964), p.429. The premium bonus system was even more attractive than simple piecework to the employer because the bonus paid under this system was proportionate; that is, the time saved was divided between the worker and the employer in varying proportions. In practice, this made the labor cost of any job fall with every increase of output. Even with the increased wages, the employer's production expenses were so reduced that he had less reason to cut rates than he did under piecework.

50.
Parliamentary Debates, 5th series, v.35, p.1774, March 19, 1912.

51.
Denny, The Worth of Wages, p.vi.

52.
Report, 1912, p.70.

53.
Cecil Papers, British Museum Add. Mss. 51103, Fols. 101-7, p.14.

54.
Labour Co-partnership May 1903, p.68; Times, Aug. 2, 1919, 10a.

55.
G. Livesey, "Another Steps in Promoting the Union of Capital and Labour, Institute of Gas Engneers, Transactions (1897), p.161. Similarly, a writer in the Edinburgh Review

asserted that co-partnership greatly reduced the need for trade unions. Trade unions, he said, existed for the purpose of protecting labor from "the tyranny of capital and they assume an opposition of interest between capital and labor." When this opposition no longer existed, he reasoned, "they can be dispensed with." Edinburgh Review, 209 (1909), p.320.

56.
Simultaneously, the working clas realization that capitalism had come to stay made them learn to live with or within the system. They accepted and pursued resigned attitude and imposed on themselves a separate life style and perception from those of the upper classes, as scholars such as Gareth Stedman Jones and Standish Meacham have exposed. G. Stedman Jones, "Working Class Culture and Working Class Politics in London, 1870-1900" Journal of Social History, 7 (1974); S. Meacham, A Life Apart: The English Working Class, 1890-1914 (Cambridge: Cambridge Univ. Press, 1977).

57.
Clegg, Fox, and Thompson, A History, p.363.

58.
Institute of Gas Engineers, Transactions (1897), p.153.

59.
Benjamin Browne, Selected Papers, p.102.

60.
Charles Carpenter, Are Trades Unionism and Co-partnership Incompatible? (London: Labour Co-partnership Association, 1913).

61.
National Union of Gasworkers and General Labourers of Great Britain and Ireland, Rules, 1890; 1892. (London).

62.
Gasworkers Union, Report, 1894.

63.
J. S. Nicholson, "Profit-sharing," Contemporary Review, 57 (Jan. 1890), p.68.

Chapter V. Trade Union Attitudes toward Profit-sharing: Objection, Acceptance or Acquiescence?

I.The Myth of the Union Opposition

Did trade unions really feel such strong hostility towards profit-sharing as to attempt to deter employers from installing such a system? Given the alleged importance of profit-sharing's impact on trade unionism, it is peculiar that the TUC did not make clear its official opinion until 1923 which condemned the capitalist attempt to introduce forms of co-partnership as "designed to mislead the workers to prevent trade union solidarity."[1] Again in 1925, the TUC passed a resolution put forth by E.Joseph, a delegate of the Tailors and Garment Workers Union, which read:

> The congress warns the workers against all attempts to introduce capitalist schemes of co-partnership which in the past have failed to give the workers any positive rights, but instead have usually served as fetters retarding the forward movements.2

This resolution was much milder in tone than the 1923 resolution, and it was carried by a majority of two to one.

The fact is that the TUC largely neglected the

question of profit-sharing and co-partnership, as Walter Citrine, leader of the Electricians Union and later general secretary of the TUC, admitted in 1927. At the same time, trade unionists were far from being of one mind about it--as the TUC's split vote indicates. There was a great deal of confusion and a diversity of opinion. As late as 1957, the report of the General Council on the subject was repeating the old refrain that "some affiliated unions are either unaware of, or are not interested in schemes which are affecting some of their members."[3]

Why this indifference? In the first place, many unions were not directly involved in the system, probably, in part, because its scope was still limited. Also trade unions represented only a minority of workers in the 1890s and in the early years of the twentieth century, and thus there was a considerable number of firms whose workmen were not yet organized or only partly organized. In either case, trade unions do not seem to have seriously interfered with the introduction of profit-sharing.

John Ward, the leader of the navvies and Labour MP since 1906, testified to the Poor Law Commission that he had never been brought into personal contact with the question of profit-sharing for it was never suggested to the members of his union and therefore he knew nothing about its effects--except theoretically. George Barnes, the former general secretary of the Amalgamated Society of Engineers, also admitted he had considered the subject only "theoretically."[4] When David Schloss completed the first survey of the British profit-sharing schemes for the Board of Trade in 1894, almost half of the profit-sharing firms which returned the answer had no unions among their employees. Even those unions whose members were involved in the system did not consider the queston seriously. The unions of seven firms either replied that they had not so far considered the question or sent no reply. Two of the unions that had members in profit-sharing firms took a neutral position, and unions representing another fifteen companies claimed that the scheme was unsatisfactory, viewing it as an employer attempt to keep wages down, to put pressure on the men, and to impede the operation of trade unions. But significantly, unions at five other firms approved of the system. In twelve cases, union wages or the disrict rate or even higher wages were paid, and in addition, the workers received a bonus. Indeed in one case, the union concerned regarded the company as the best employer in the district. One union even stated that they "would be pleased if the employers adopted the principle."[5]

These diverse union opinions suggest that any attempt to generalize worker perception is extremely dangerous. It is difficult to draw a general picture of labor's perception of profit-sharing and co-partnership because of the many points of view represented by the all-inclusive "labor." Various groups reacted differently, and even the same group's response varied with time and circumstances. Many thought that the working class on the whole was against the profit-sharing system. A writer in the Westminster Review observed that the working man was by no means favorable to the principle of profit-sharing because the worker was "half-educated and in most cases unaccustomed to consider and solve intricate mental problems."[6] A similar judgment came from Sir Benjamin Browne, who observed that "the working classes dislike profit-sharing though nearly every employer would be content to adopt it with very slight encouragement."[7]

It is wrong, however, to generalize worker perception as if it were a homogeneous phenomenon. In contrast to the two men just mentioned, the Yorkshire Factory Times noted worker enthusiasm for profit-sharing and co-partnership, and contrasted it with employer indifference.[8] If employer reaction to the system was mixed and complex, worker response was no less so. Numerous factors influenced worker reaction, among which were the degree of labor organization, the nature of industry, the strength and nature of the union, union leadership, the previous history of industrial relations in individual firms, and perhaps most importantly, the employer motives apparent or real, in introducing the scheme. Allen Gee and Ben Turner, two prominent leaders of the textile workers, participated in George Thomson's co-partnership venture at Woodhouse Mills not because they particularly believed in class collaboration but mainly because Thomson's motives seemed pure and noble. John Burns, who had originally been a Marxist but became a Liberal minister in 1906, by contrast, vehemently attacked George Livesey's profit-sharing scheme not because he had an ideological bias against the system but because Livesey's object was plainly and simply the eradication of trade unionism in his company.

Ideology appears to have played a decisive role. While the socialists, whether they were Marxists or non-Marxists, Fabians or Guild Socialists, unanimously opposed the newly devised system as discussed in chapter III, "respectable" old union leaders and Lib-Labs such as Thomas Burt and George Howell warmly greeted profit-sharing and actively promoted the movement. Although they were originally workers, Burt and Howell were more liberal than the Liberals in their ideology and political beliefs. Again, it was on ideological grounds that socialist leaders of the new unions such as Will Thorne and Ben Tillett vigorously attacked the system.

The resistance to profit-sharing was strongest where a union's socialism was strongest--as in the case of the Gasworkers Union, which had been organized by the socialist leader Will Thorne and aided by Eleanor Marx. However, ideology was not the only consideration; the stability and strength of the union also shaped their attitude. Old, established unions which had little fear of being undermined by the new system, were more willing to give it a chance whereas the new unions, composed of unskilled and semi-skilled workers, saw in profit-sharing a serious threat to their still young and feeble organization.

Understandably, the actual progress of the scheme at a company was heavily influenced by previous relations between employer and employee. In the companies where relations had been good, the introduction of a profit-sharing scheme caused hardly any trouble at the outset and consequently the system tended to prosper. In those firms, on the other hand, which had a tradition of troubled labor relations, the schemes were usually met with suspicion and resistance, and tended to fail.

Supporters of Profit-sharing among the Union Leaders

Contrary to contemporary assumption and the current beliefs of the historians, many influential union leaders wholeheartedly supported the system. Thomas Burt, the leader of the miners and one of the first Lib-Lab MPs, and David Shakleton, leader of the textile workers and also Lib-Lab MP, served as presidents of the Labour Co-partnership Association. The supporters of the movement included George Howell, the first secretary of the parliamentary commiittee of the TUC and Lib-Lab MP, Henry Broadhurst, successor of Howell in the parliamentary committee, W. A. Appleton, general secretary of the General Federation of Trade Unions, and John Wilson, the leader of the Durhahm Miners' Association and Lib-Lab MP, to name a few, although most of them were leaders of the "respectable" old unions. We must then ask on what grounds these leaders justified their support.

As discussed in Chapter III, the principles of trade unions and profit-sharing were in obvious contradiction. Trade unionism assumed an antagonism between employer and employee whereas profit-sharing presupposed an identity of interests between the two. Trade unions aimed at the improvement of the working class as a whole and required class solidarity; profit-sharing attempted to benefit employees of particular concern, and nothing more.

However, the Lib-Lab leaders did not see such contradictions between the two. They all rejected the revolutionary transformation of social and economic structure, and accepted Liberalism as their political and ideological bases. Henry Broadhurst was the secretary of the parliamentary committee of the TUC during the period 1875-1890 which was marked as the "Broadhurst era" in the history of British trade unionism. The chief achievement of the Broadhurst era was the recognition of the craft unions and the consolidation of the harmonious relationship between these craft unions and the employers. They did not believe in the organization among the unskilled labourers and succeeded in protecting their members' interests through tight regulation of the union membership, apprenticeship, and skill training. Not surprisingly, such policies were bitterly criticized by the new generation of the Socialist trade unionists such as John Burns, Tom Mann and Ben Tillett. The young generation attempted to disentangle the working class movement from the Liberal Party, and finally succeeded in ousting Broadhurst from secretaryship of the parliamentary committee of the TUC.

For those who believed in class collaboration, no other excuse was necessary except for "the toil of the brain and the toil of the arm working together," as John Wilson put it.[15] They found not only no conflict between the two but believed profit-shaing to be a facilitating system for achieving certain objects of the trade union movement. These leaders, who never embraced socialism, envisaged profit-sharing as the most promising way to improve the workman's lot. They did not want a revolutionary transformation of capitalist society, and therefore wholeheartedly welcomed any change of the division of profits within the existing system. Charles Fenwick, orignially a collier and the successor of Broadhurst as the parliamentary secretary of the TUC in the years 1890-94 and a Lib-Lab member since 1885, asserted that "voluntary co-operation" was the best form of socialism and denied the possibility of state socialism because the British were "not revolutionary."[16] Even this form of co-operation was viewed as remote. They hoped someday it would be possible to pass beyond the individual business and operate the industry on co-operative lines, but it was a problem "for another rather than for our own generation."[17] Since they rejected the assertion that capital and labor were basically antagonistic, it was not a difficult step to accept the idea of bringing the two more closely together.

Another powerful justification of their position was the obvious decline of the British economy and the anxiety to reverse the trend. The eradication of industrial inefficiency, and particularly strikes, was viewed as an absolute prerequisite for retaining Britain's supremacy in world trade. Besides, strikes were a painful weapon, in spite of the employers' frequent allegation that union leaders--"agitators" in employer language--were thriving on strikes. Ben Turner thus insisted that co-partnership must be established in the first place for the sake of efficiency and preventing waste. Another trade union official, James Whitburn, stated that it was the enormous waste caused by industrial disputes that made him come to the conclusion that co-parnership was the soundest way to avoid it.[18] When Sir Christopher Furness offered a co-partnership scheme for just this purpose, Charles Fenwick declared that the offer made by Furness showed that "shrewd, farseeing captains of industry are realizing that our commercial position depends more and more on our industrial efficiency."[19]

More positively, profit-sharing and co-partnership were seen as one of the most practical ways, possibly the most practical of all, to transform the existing capitalist system along non-revolutionary lines. Thomas Burt, in his letter to a profit-sharing employer Thomas Bushill, wrote that profit-sharing was "good in itself, and it is one of the best ways out of the present wage system."[20] At a conference of delegates from some 50 trade unions and kindred bodies held under the auspices of the Labour Co-partnership Association in London, March 1898, the following resolution was adopted:

> This conference...convinced that it affords a <u>practical means</u> of emancipation of the workers from the evils of the wage system, giving them a real share of the profits, responsibilities and control of their labor; and it earnestly calls upon all London trade unionists to promote co-operative production in every possible way.21 (My underline).

After all, if the working class did not intend to seize capital and power by revolutionary means, the alternative would be a gradual accumulation of capital and gradual assumption of power. The view of Hugh Boyle, president of the Northumberland Miners' Association, represented this sort of reasoning. If the workmen could not be in a position to finance and manage the concern, he stated, "the next best thing is to accept partnership with those who possess the capital and accept the management of those who were able to manage."[22] Moreover, profit-sharing brought about material benefits for the workers. "Half a loaf is better than none" was a powerful excuse. If profit-sharing did not give the worker his full dues, it nevertheless gave him a "larger share of the pie than he would have without its help."[23]

And all progress was interpreted as more enlightenment and more development in the direction of altering the position of labor. Profit-sharing indeed meant for those who worked under it better pay; some knowledge of actual business, including facts about profits and losses; and sometimes even a voice in management--even if to a very limited extent. Although profit-sharing would not change the power structure, it gave the wage earner a different status within the firm because it recognized his claim to share in what hitherto had accrued to capital alone. This understandably was regarded as a major advance. Thus a writer in <u>Justice</u>, a Marxist newspaper and the organ of the Social Democratic Federation, declared that "Nevertheless I welcome the inauguration of profit-sharing because whatever may be the ulterior motives, it is an admission of the rights of labor to share the surplus profit."[24]

J. Clynes, when he dropped his old opposition to profit-sharing, declared that there was no sense in refusing to take something which "in itself would give benefit to the trade union movement beause it does not give us the new heaven we desire, and because it does not complete the whole sum total of social and industrial change that many of us would like to see."[25] Clynes started working in a textile mill at the age of ten and then worked as an organizer for Will Thorne's National Union of Gasworkers and General Labourers, which manifested the most vigorous opposition to profit-sharing. Clynes understandably objected to the system and yet changed his view over the time. In response to John Burns, at this time still a Marxist, who declared that "Profit-sharing is merely a golden link to bind the men to their employer," profit-sharing advocates maintained that "It is still better to be bound by a golden link than by an iron or copper link."[26] Yet one must wonder if the men were to be bound at all, if it really mattered by what they were bound. Obviously, some preferred to be bound by a golden link than to try to break the link itself.

This logic conceived of trade unionism not as the goal itself but as a means to the goal, material betterment of the working class, and it would eventually lead to evaluating everything in terms of its utility as a means to achieve that goal. Some union leaders were indeed broadminded enough to admit that trade unionism ought to face the test of utility, the claim that was put forward by anti-unionist employers and ani-unionist working men's organizations such as the Free Labour Association. Appleton put this position with surprising frankness: "Trade unionism has achieved many things, but it may not have achieved permanence, and it is possible that, in the changes that are inevitable, it will be affected, or even superseded." This view echoed the declaration of the Free Labour Association that "If trade unions get smashed in the process, it will be because there is no further use for them."[27]

Even workng-class solidarity was to be judged according to its utility. Solidarity was "but the instrument to achieve the very thing for which co-partnerhisp stands--the equitable distribution of the rewards of industry." If that goal could be achieved without working-class solidarity, so be it. The supporters of the profit-sharing movement, in conclusion, urged their fellow unionists to consider it the broadest possible aspect and to seek to "control rather than to destroy it."[28]

Union Leaders Opposing Profit-sharing

The union leaders who were committed to socialism,

by contrast, were unanimously hostile to profit-sharing and co-partnership. Keir Hardie, one of the first two Labor MPs elected in 1892, for one, had been a vigorous opponent of the system from the early days, proclaiming that this new invention of the capitalist was doing 'positive harms' to the working class not only by making the working man accept conditions of employment which he would refuse if he were not a shareholder in the concern, but by breaking down the sense of his own consciousness.[29]

The staunchest oppponents were, however, found among leaders of the new unions that burst into existence around 1889. Will Thorne and his Gasworkers Union were to fight a most prominent profit-sharing employer, George Livesey, immediately after the formation of the union. John Burns, when he was still a faithful member of the Social Democratic Federation, was busy disclosing the "viciousness" of the profit-sharing system. He told the Industrial Remuneration Conference of 1885 that he regarded profit-sharing as "nothing less than a delusive bait on the part of capitalists to goad the working on the greater intensity of toil."

In fact Burns contributed to frustrating at least one profit-sharing scheme. Basil Peto, a building contractor in London and later a Unionist Member of Parliament, proposed to distribute a quarter of the net profit among the workers when his firm assumed a contract for L 80,000 in 1889, on the condition that the workers did not strike while the work was proceeding. Two days after Peto's proposal as printed in the *Times*, Burns rushed into Peto's private office and said, "You had better drop it or we will ruin you." In spite of Burns' influence, the workers accepted the offer. Unfortunately the contract resulted in no profit to divide in the three years it was in force. Peto years later recalled the event and blamed Burns and other malicious influence for the failure of the scheme.[30]

These leaders all shared the view that profit-sharing was a system to ensure a larger output of labor for a given wage, to bring about the docility and subservience of the workers, and, by getting workers to believe that their interest lay in the side of employer and not with their own class, to destroy working class unity and solidarity. Their conviction stemmed from their ideology. Yet another crucial factor contributed to their opposition to profit-sharing: their unions had only recently been formed, were made of unskilled or semi-skilled workers, and thus were vulnerable to employer counterattack. Indeed, the profit-sharing scheme of the South Metropolitan Gas Company was one of the first attempt by an employer to counteract the new unionism.

The Transition from Hostility to Acceptance

However, as the circumstances under which the unions operated changed, so did the unions' reaction towards profit-sharing and co-partnership. Bitter suspicion and distrust were replaced by tolerance and a more positive willingness to participate. Such a change appears to have been a gradual process and it became clearly visible by the first decade of the twentieth century. George Livesey, Basil Peto, and A. F. Hills, to name a few, all met with vigorous opposition in the period of the 1880s and 1890s. However, when William Lever introduced the system in 1909, it received the blessing of trade union officials. About the same time, Christopher Furness announced a co-partnership scheme in his shipyards in Hartlepools, and prominent union leaders either welcomed it or acquiesced in it. Even Will Thorne, who suffered a disastrous defeat in the struggle against profit-sharing, did not urge the members of his union to refuse Furness's proposal. Thus, in 1913, Charles Carpenter, the successor of George Livesey at South Metropolitan, remarked on the diminishing degree of union opposition.[31]

George Barnes, former Socialist general secretary of the Amalgamated Society of Engineers, reflects these changes in the union leaders' attitude. When the Furness scheme at the Hartlepool shipyards was abandoned after a one-year experiment in 1910, Barnes, then the chairman of the Labour Party, was delighted. In 1921, however, he declared that there was no reason "why trade unionism and co-partnership should not run hand in hand," and criticized labor leaders who "still speak in terms of the condition of the last century and still in terms of revolution."[32]

The same change is discovered in J. Clynes of the General Municipal Workers Union, formerly Gasworkers Union. Once an organizer of the gasworkers and general labourers, Clynes had the common mistrust of profit-sharing schemes. Criticizing the Liverpool United Gas Light Company bill in 1914, which included a compulsory co-partnership scheme, he was convinced that the intention of the company was simply to destroy trade unionism. Yet in 1919 we hear him declare himself to be a supporter of co-partnership: "I see no reason why trade unionism should any longer assume an attitude either of hostility or suspicion towards co-partnership or profit-sharing."[33]

The most interesting conversion was that of Ben Tillett, the leader of the great strike of the dockers in the summer of 1889 and the member of the SDF and the ILP. Tillett challenged William Lever at the very outset of the famous Port Sunlight scheme, denouncing it as "a soft-soap bubble." He stigmatized the scheme as "the worst taste of class-swank and patronage, capitalist's carrot, clever juggling cointrack, and empty and heartless bribe, a hoax on the willing slaves of our industrial system," and branded Lever as "Caesar, judge, and the lord-high-executioner in one."[34] However, these flamboyant denunciations had given way to genuine compliments by 1929. Tillett, speaking at a luncheon of the Industrial Co-partnership Association, formerly the Labour Co-partnership Association, praised co-partnership as a good human basis for the employer-employee relationship and even traced the origin of co-partnership in the Sermon on the Mount. He also suggested establishing a research department and inquiring into national and international co-partnership.[35]

The Amalgamated Society of Engineers even paid tribute to George Livesey on his death in 1908: "The busy life he had led in the scientific world, and his renowned endeavours to act a fair part as the chairman of the company, prompts the expression of a measured admiration rather than the cherishing of old bitterness now that at a ripe old age he has passed away."[36] As late as 1927, the Labour Party condemned profit-sharing and criticized labor leaders who had declared in favor of it.[37] Even this customary hostility, however, had disappeared by 1951, when Hugh Gaitskell, who had been just elected the leader of the Labour Party, suggested:

> We should not exclude altogether from our considerations as one possible contribution to for example, the distribution of bonus shares reflecting the rise in undistributed profits. I throw it out as an idea which you can chew

over.38

The Increased Stability of the Trade Unions

What brought about this change? The change in attitude on the part of union leaders certainly derived in large part from changes in personal beliefs and experiences. But if we look for more general causes, the first appears to be the change in the status of the unions.The fear that trade unionism would be eradicated or undermined through the profit-sharing system had now disappeared. When profit-sharing was first introduced in British industry in the 1860s, trade unionism was by no means generally recongnized. Collective bargaining was still in its infancy in many industries.

Under these circumstances, the eradication of trade unionism seemed possible and certain employers such as Briggs and J.Fox were clearly motivated by such a desire. Fox adopted profit-sharing simply because he refused to accept collective bargaining and because he believed that profit-sharing would be constructed on the ruins of the unions. The same concern was felt over the South Metropolitan plan. If the plan were accepted, it was asserted:

> not only would the present union (the Gasworkers and General Labourers Union) be broken up--for what use would a union be if the workers were bound over to keep the peace by the beautiful scheme?--but it would be impossible to form another one, and the men would sink back into the old state of degrading slavery.[39]

But the hostility of the unions gradually disappeared because of the confidence that came as their strength increased and as they won recognition by employers, and because employers ceased to use profit-sharing as a weapon against trade unionism. It was mostly the unions of unskilled or semi-skilled that felt threatened by the new system. No employer would have attemped to destroy a union like the Amalgamated Society of Engineers by profit-sharing. Even if the employer succeeded in detaching the men from unions as in the case of the South Metropolitan, the main victims were the militant, socialistic unions of the unskilled such as the Gasworkers and the Coal Porters Unions. Livesey allowed what he thought reasonable unions to remain, but not the Gasworkers Union, which he believed to be a group of Socialists.

Interestingly, when the Suburban Gas Company of London, of which Livesey was also chairman, introduced a similar profit-sharing plan several years later, no clause was included in the agreement banning members of Gasworkers Union from participation.[40] This was partly because the union did not hold power in the company any more, but also because Livesey's anger with the union had calmed down a bit by this time. Measured against the full span of his life, therefore, Livesey's notorious anti-unionism, which was the ground of considerable distrust of his plan as well as of the entire profit-sharing system, seems to have been exaggerated.

The Rank and File Perception of Profit-sharing

The second reason for the change in the union leaders' attitude concerns a controversial question about the democracy of the trade union structure, and before we reach an answer, we ought to detour and first consider the rank and file perception of the profit-sharing system. How did the average worker perceive profit-sharing and co-partnership? As we have mentioned, it is extremely dangerous to attempt to generalize the worker's response. The rank and file opinion of organized labor is difficult enough to identify; the voice of the unorganized, almost impossible. Even among organized labor, the opinions were diverse, as we have seen. To make things more uncomfortable we can only judge from segmentary evidence available here and there.

It was mostly the national leaders who set themselves against profit-sharing. However, national executives were prevented from directly engaging in such schemes in two counts: first, the structure of the British trade union movement was such that they were not involved in plant level negotiation; profit-sharing, on the other hand, took a firm or a works as its unit by its very nature, and thus local branches were usually left to deal with cases as opportunities presented themselves. At the same time, a firm or a works was not a one-union affair: workers usually belonged to only one of a wide variety of unions. Lever Brothers, a soap manufacturer, for instance, employed workers belonging to more than thirty unions. These factors prevented national union executives from assuming responsibility for accepting or rejecting the scheme.

If the national leaders lacked personal experience of such schemes and tended to envisage them in a more abstract and ideological context, local officials found themselves personally involved and understood them in more concrete terms. One thing was obvious to them: the system in most cases benefited the men materially. Lever's famous scheme in Port Sunlight and Theodore Taylor's in Batley were both brilliant examples of what the profit-sharing system could do for the worker's well-being. Thus whereas national leaders pronounced disapproval of the system, William Glennie, the Tyneside district secretary of the Amalgamated Society of Engineers, testified: "I have spoken to and consulted with many of my fellow-workmen on the subject. I may say that cooperation and profit-sharing are very popular in the district I come from."[41]

There is plentiful evidence for the enthusiasm of a number of union workers for profit-sharing an co-partnership. A member of the Amalgamated Society of Railway Servants proclaimed that "there is only one method which would provide all the elements of industrial stability--co-partnership of the kind inaugurated by Sir George Livesey."[42] George Livingstone, a Newcastle gas stoker, had been a strong belever in the scheme of the South Metropolitan ever since it was inaugurated and asserted that if such a scheme was laid before the workmen at the Newcastle company they would accept it.[43]

There were few contemporary studies on worker opinion on the subject, especially during the period we are concerned with. Fortunately, one survey of employees of a profit-sharing firm is available. In 1892, Thomas Bushill conducted a general inquiry concerning his employees' attitude to profit-sharing. The business was printing and papermaking, employing about 140 workers, both men and women. The scheme had been in operation since 1886 therefore the employees had had six years' experience. The profit-sharing committee conducted survey by ballot under absolute secrecy. Here are some extracts of employee replies:

> First employee: I am sure it is by all means the best thing that ever has been brought forward for the benefit of employees, not only for its good sources, but for the way in which it causes that great motto to be preached, "Help one another." I feel that we, the employees, generally have done our very best endeavours to help our masters to this great success; it is a sure system that it is to our advantages we do our utmost to please our masters.
>
> Second employee: The principle is very good, as it helps to bring employers and their employees in harmony with each other, and causes us to know our employers are thinking of our welfare as well as their own, and I should think causes every employee to give more thought to his work, both in pleasing his employer and for his own benefit. I can only add that other employers of labor would do well to adopt the same.
>
> Third employee: I cordially approve of the principle of profit-sharing. The results have been good not only financially but also for operating a feeling of brotherhood and mutual helpfulness throughout the whole staff, and for adding a new and pleasant zest to all our duties.
>
> Fourth employee: The principle is very good, and undoubtedly more beneficial to the workman than to the employer. I look upon it as a free gift, for I should have had to work had nothing of the kind ever been started. I wish it had been started years before.44

These replies must be taken only as indicative. However, all the replies, which numbered 66, displayed an affirmative opinion on the system; none expressed a negative view. We may take this as an obvious evidence of worker satisfaction with the profit-sharing system.

And yet not all the workers were eager for profit-sharing benefits. In fact, one of the major reasons the employers cited for abandoning the schemes was "apathy of employees." Sometimes it was even more than apathy. Employee opposition had the effect of terminating some schemes. And that opposition could be fierce. A certain Watson, a member of the Amalgamated Society of Engineers, asserted his beliefs powerfully:

> The employers own and control the whole of the means of producing and distributing wealth. Their and our interests are diametrically opposed...The only permanent way to settle industrial disputes is for the workers to recognize the antagonism of interest between the employer and worker and organize themselves so that ultimately they will once and for all shift this idle, parasite, employing class from off their backs.45

A boilermaker, identified only as Macleod, vigorously ridiculed the claim of the identity of interest between employer and employee: "No workman is credulous enough to swallow such bunkum. The worker's interest is to secure as much wages as he can in exchange for his labor...while the employer's is to get the maximum of labor or the minimum of wages. Socialism is our only hope and salvation." Above all, they resented the fact that employers employed them only as "profit-making machines."[46]

However, the relative calmness of the employees in firms that practiced profit-sharing indicates that such a system could retain employee loyalty and peace even in the stormy days of prewar industrial unrest. In 1912, the general manager of the Commercial Gas Company reported that "largely due to the influence of profit-sharing, the company's employees loyally observed their duties in spite of outside attempt to undermine their loyalty."[47] The South Metropolitan never experienced any strike after the introduction of profit-sharing except for a minor incident during the General Strike in 1926. During the General Strike, the gas industry, where profit-sharing and co-partnership were most extensively applied, was one of the few industries that experienced only a minor impact. The Gas Journal proudly reported that "Unlike the employees of electrical supply undertakings, gas works in general were left undisturbed in their employment."[48]

Even if the Workman's Times blamed the South Metropolitan employees for having sold "their birth-right for a mess of pottage," they did not mind giving up the "sacred right of strike."[49] H. T. Manley, a worker on the Old Kent Road station, summed it up this way: "The co-partnership scheme has given us peace.(Hear, hear). We never have strikes--we never think of it."[50] They were shareholders of the company, and they took great pride in it. A workman of Theodore Taylor's woollen factory confirmed the effect of profit-sharing in creating a sense of identity and superiority: "I don't think it was entirely the money point of view then--you took a pride in working there and trying to make his scheme a success."[51] Joseph Newbold, an South Metropolitan worker, urged his fellow workers not to be influenced by the "agitators":

> Seeing that we have such a heritage left to us--a heritage that has lifted us from mere wage earners to shareholders--let us see to it that we are not made the tools of agitators, who would like to capture us because they see that if co-partnership should become more general, then their occupation as professional agitators would be gone. Let us not sell our great heritage for a mess of pottage...but each realize our individual responsibility and duty.52

Concepts such as "birth-right," "great heritage," and "a mess of pottage" obviously implied different meanings to the workers of the South Metropolitan and those who felt otherwise. The lack of class solidarity and sympathy was revealed vividly when the South Metropolitan workers protested against the miners' eight-hour bill in 1908 beause it would threat their bonus and dividend. One of the effects of the bill would have been to increase the price of coal and thus the price of gas and thus damage the earnings of the company and themselves![53] They seem to have lived in a world of their own, caring little for the world outside their own industry. Therefore, one observer lamented that for him at least, the spectacle of the workers "split up into little groups, each struggling for profits without any class consciousness or high ideals is not a pleasing one."[54]

To the painful disappointment of those with socialist aspirations, British workers did not accept what the Marxist Harry Quelch called "the elementary economic fact that all profit is due to the robbery of labor and that labor will continue to be robbed until profit-taking is superseded by socialism."[55] When William Lever said to his employees "You and I make profits together; you are not the only force to make profits," they applauded him and shouted "Hear, hear."[56] The eagerness with which the workmen were ready to embrace the very antithesis of socialism by becoming shareholders and accumulating savings was the clearest proof that English labor was not as a rule imbued with socialistic ideas. Thus shrewd employers concluded that the best way to fight socialism was not by arguing but by giving the men the opportunity of becoming capitalists.[57]

The conservatism of working men who accumulated some savings was well known. Before the Labour Commission, it was somewhat extravagantly stated that worker shareholders in certain cotton mills were ten times greedier than the big capitalist. One trade unionist sadly pointed out the "menace" to the trade union movement to be the "100 pound millionaire."[58] An engineering driver at the

Taff Vale Railway refused to come out at the 1890 strike, remarking that "I cannot strike against myself." He was holding 5 pounds of the company's stock. It was in fact this story of the engine driver that inspired George Livesey the idea of making workmen shareholders of the company.[59] The co-partner workers had a double disincentive for going out on strike, because they would thus be going against themselves twice: against their regular wages and against their dividends.

The foremost concerns of the working man were present consumption and future security. The survey on the earnings and livings of the English working class conducted by the U.S.Labor Department in 1891 underscored these considerations. The survey discovered that virtually all the workers thought it necessary to buy life insurance and to join "sick clubs." The same survey also discovered that at least 75 percent of the families in each of the industries in skill levels surveyed bought some form of insurance. In addition, most of the rest probably purchased it indirectly through the friendly societies to which many belonged.[60] If such security was provided more easily by profit-sharing, there would be no reason not to subscribe to it. Thus a workman named C. Carter insisted that if trade unions examined these schemes with an "unbiased mind," they would see that the advantage and safeguards "more than counterbalanced the voluntary limitation of the right of strike," which was usually imposed by the scheme.[61]

Profit-sharing seemed to guarantee a greater share in the fruits of capitalism than mere wage bargaining, and thus it was insisted that if profit-sharing brought the worker more than the unions were reasonably demanding, there should be no further antagonism.[62] Some workers indeed thought that if there was regular employment and the provision of a pension, or if there was a good and generous employer, it would be no longer necessary to join a trade union. One non-union worker at the Gas Light and Coke Company asserted his conviction about not being a union member as follows:

> Because I did not see there was any necessity to form a union in place like this, because any petition that was placed in the hands of directors and engineers was conceded. We do not want the keys of the cash-box...or anything else. We want to do what is just and fair, and honorable, but you could not have anything more fair according to my idea.[63]

Although socialist newspapers such as the Clarion constantly suggested to the working men that they were chained to the system and that profit-sharing and co-partnership would make this chain permanent, such warnings were disregarded. "If you wanted, you could cast off those chains and upset the system," the Clarion insisted.[64] However, it is quite clear that the English working class did not want to cast off its "chains," particularly when the arrangement seemed profitable.

The workers seldom refused an employer's offer to establish a profit-sharing plan. There were very few cases in which they did reject such an offer, and when the unions tried to prohibit them from participating, the workers often defied union orders. As we have seen, when Basil Peto offered a scheme to the workers employed for a building contract, the unions concerned vehemently repudiated it. This was understandable, for it was about the same time as the gas stokers of the South Metropolitan were on strike against a profit-sharing proposal. There were other elements that provoked the unions. Peto not only imposed the non-strike condition but delegated great power to his foremen. Consequently the unions, represented by the London United Building Trades Committe, comprising the Amalgamated Society of Carpenters and Joiners, General Union of Carpenters and Joiners, Operative Bricklayers' Society, and National Association of Plasters etc. urged the men not to accept the offer. Yet the men did accept it.[65]

When the Liverpool Gas Company proposed a compulsory co-partnership scheme in 1914, Will Thorne and J. Clynes, two MPs from the gas industry, with the support of other labor members, tried to obstruct the introduction of the scheme. The company's workers, however, passed unanimous resolution approving the scheme and declared that they did not desire the intervention of trade union officials.[66] When the national executive of the Amalgamated Society of Carpenters and Joiners forbade its members to participate in co-partnership schemes, the Pudsey branch of the union protested against the decision and urged the reconsideration of the case on the ground that "the object of trade unions is to obtain a just and equitable share of the profits earned to be paid to the workers."[67] The co-partner carpenters and joiners of Lever Brothers eventually sued the union in order to continue to receive their co-partnership bonus. The workers at Taylor's woollen factory in Batley agreed to join the union only it was conceded that if there was a strike, they would not come out because they did not want to lose their profit-sharing bonus: if it was not conceded, they told the union officials, "Right then, we're not coming in." The union accepted the situation and conceded to the men's demand.[68]

The Relationship between Union Leadership and the Rank and File

Here arises the sensitive question of the relationship between union leadership and the rank and file. Historians and sociologists have habitually formulated the schema of moderate leadership versus militant rank and file.[69] However, this view must be seriously questioned. If the rank and file found the leadership opposed to their aspirations more often than not, why did they tolerate it? What forced them to accept leaders whose policy they conceived of as incompatible with their own? Richard Price argues that they may have done so on the realization that they had no other organizational alternative to turn to.[70] This view, however, is inadequate to explain the retaining of the leader-member relationship and worker loyalty to the union. To be sure, there were cases when the members of a union rebelled against their leaders. The Durham miners struck against the new hours, which enforced nightwork, negotiatd by the executive in 1900. In the same year, the engineers forcibly ejected the autocratic full-time executive from their union offices.[71] But these were rare incidents. In most unions, the leader-member relationship was free of such discord.

What seems more likely is that labor leaders in fact tried to meet rank and file aspirations even if it meant changes in policy and it went against the leaders' personal beliefs. When the carpenters and joiners of Lever Brothers defied their union's order to refrain from co-partnership or be expelled, the union executive secretly decided not to pursue the issue any further. The case eventually developed into a lawsuit, and Lever's employees and the union, the Amalgamated Society of Carpenters and Joiners, engaged in prolonged litigation, but the union's initial policy was acquiescence. When the officials of the

Gasworkers Union were among the first to sign the agreement of the co-partnership scheme of the Commercial Gas Company, in spite of the executive decision to reject it, the executive council could do nothing to the defiant members.[72]

Although much of British syndicalism can be accounted for on the ground of rank and file discontent with union leaders, it also seems true that the leaders nevertheless tried to suit their policy to their members' aspirations. The raison d'etre of the trade union, after all, was to look after the welfare of the members. When the members made it clear that they appreciated many of the advantages of profit-sharing and were willing to receive benefits from it, the union had to accept it--if only out of deference to the feelings of their members. At least one contemporary observer pointed to this and asserted that the attitude of trade union leaders was not in fact hostile, but when not favorable, was at the worst only expedient. "Looking sincerely to the welfare of the laboring man as their one aim," he observed, "they realize that there might be surer means of obtaining their welfare than trade unions, and are willing to give profit-sharing a fair trial."[73]

Therefore, we conclude that trade unions were not sufficiently powerful as to obstruct the progress of the profit-sharing movement. In the first place, many influential leaders, including almost all the old union leaders, supported the system. In the second, even those who had originally opposed it changed their attitude as trade unionism gained more confidence and strength, a development that had become quite clear by the post-war years. Third, it was mainly national leaders who set themselves against the system, and by the nature of the profit-sharing arrangement and the trade union structure, national executives could neither enforce nor reverse the decisions made by local branches and members. Fourth, lower union officials and the rank and file were enthusiastic for profit-sharing and co-partnership mainly because of the accompanying material benefits. When the unions tried to prohibit their participation in such schemes, the rank and file defied union orders and willingly accepted the employer's offer. Finally, the union leadership eventually had to accept the system because the relationship between leader and member could not have persisted on a basis of constant contradictions. It seems accurate to say that the union leadership tried to accommodate itself to the rank and file unless it was a question of life and death. Profit-sharing, although it was originally conceived of as just such a threat, ceased to be that, and thus made smaller the gap betwen union policy and rank and file aspirations.

Now we turn to the close examination of a

particular scheme, that of the Irvine Shipbuilding Company, to evaluate the influence of trade unionism on the failure or retardation of profit-sharing. This particular scheme perfectly serves our purpose because its abandonment after a year's trial was generally attributed to trade union opposition. Through close examination, we will find out whether this particular allegation is valid and furthermore, we will obtain an insight into our general question: were trade unions so powerful an opposing force as to obstruct the progress of profit-sharing and co-partnership?

II. The Co-partnership Scheme of Irvine's Shipyards

Sir Christopher Furness, probably the largest individual shipowner and shipbuilder on earth, offered a co-partnership scheme to his employees at Hartlepool shipyards in 1908 for the simple reason that he was tired of labor disputes. His sole object was to eliminate the industrial waste which he thought was causing the nation's industry to lose out to foreign competitors. Shipbuilding occupies a peculiar position in the history of industrial relations, for it was an industry that had well-organized unions and employers' associations at an early date. Yet, despite a conciliation system that had existed from the relatively early days, labor relations were as bitter as in any other industries. The closely organized skilled trade unions could threaten to inflict cripping damage on the employers during periods of full employment. In slack times, employers could easily dispense with the tradesmen and wages fell quickly.[74] The tense state of labor relations is clearly revealed in the following statistics. Between 1890 and 1906, there were 130 industrial stoppages on Northeast shipbuilding--75 of which were on the Tyne--compared with only 24 stoppages in engineering in the same area over the same period.[75]

By 1908, the industry was in the middle of the worst depression it had known owing to overproduction in previous years. The Tees and Hartlepool branch of the Boilermakers' Society reported that "the year 1908 will be long remembered as having been one of the worst experienced in the history of the shipbuilding trade. The shipbuilding industry at Hartlepool was practically at a standstill."[76] To make things worse, the serious strikes took place on the Northeast coast in the engineering and shipbuilding trades in 1908. Not surprisingly, they affected the same employers--as so many of the shipbuilders were also marine engine builders. Owing to the serious depression, the employers had decided on a reduction of wage. In both cases, the majority of the men had agreed but in the shipyards, the carpenters and joiners refusd and in the engineering works, the three engineers' unions also refused.

After the strikes began, the local employers appealed to the national body of the shipbuilding employers, and that of engineering employers. The shipbuilders carried out a general lock-out but in the engineering trade, the employers' mere threat of a lock-out was sufficient to get the men back to work at reduced wages. As a result, four steamers, built by the Furness company during the period around 1908, were late by the respective totals of 152, 173, 173, and 304 days. Since the shipbuilding companies were liable to the risk of heavy pecuniary penalties for delays beyond the stipulated time of delivery, the company lost over L 17,000 on the work done during 1907-8. Furness considered closing the yard, but was afraid that his doing so would lead to strikes in other yards throughout the district.

The position of a giant employer in shipbuilding, an industry heavily dependent on export and the business cycle, caused Furness deep concern about the industrial crisis England was facing. He made a trip to America in 1902 and was shocked at what he called 'the American invasion."[77] He at once seriously began pondering the question of how Britain could retain her preeminent position in world trade. He found a most serious obstacle in trade unionism, and while he conceded the benefits that the unions had brought to the working class, he was quick to point out the other side of the coin. He was especially critical of the unions' opposition to the introduction of labor-saving machinery, for he saw this impediment to management as hampering trade, increasing the cost of production, and causing the loss of much work to other countries. In Furness' own words, "To put an end to waste, and institute in its place thorough efficiency...is not a local question. If England is to remain the workshop of the world in the future, as in the past, it must become a national question."[78]

To help achieve this "national goal," Furness decided to employ a new method: not confrontation but instead, collaboration and incorporation. The result was a proposal which he presented to 135 delegates from 19 trade unions in October of the same year. Furness had no reputation as a benevolent employer. He was "not popular in his own neighbourhood, or among business competitors, and his business methods were severely criticized."[79] He had even dismissed some workers for being members of trade unions, although he himself was originally the son of the laborer.[80] There is no evidence that his company had established any welfare services before he proposed the co-partnership scheme. His co-partnership was not a gesture of philanthropy: the sole cause of his decision was a desire to avoid the serious threat of strikes. It is not even clear whether Furness had acknowleged the legitimacy of trade unionism before 1908. Unionism was a powerful, though divided, force in the shipbuilding industry and seemed the primary cause of the severe labor disputes.

His first proposal to the labor delegation that October was that trade unions would take over his business and run it since they were sufficiently wealthy and powerful to buy and manage the firm. "We hear much that the day of the capitalist is over," he said in his address to the delegates, "that the hour has arrived for substantial experiments in labor co-partnership in its extremest form." The trade unions being capable, organized, powerful bodies, "why should they not go into the business on their own account?"[81]

No one took Furness' first proposal seriously. The employers, the unionists, and even the press understood it as a good joke. Furness, however, appears to have seriously meant it because he had made a similar proposal eight months earlier: "If, as Socialists so freely and persistently state, they regard every employer as the working man's enemy," he stated, "if they believe shipbuilding to be so profitable as one gathers from their expressions of opinion, let them invest some part of such funds as they have been able to acquire to invest control in the establishing of a shipyard, and work it in their own account and in their own way."[82]

His second proposal was to make the workers limited co-partners of the company. The employees were invited to buy at least ten special employee shares priced at 1 pound each, paying for the shares from their wages: 5 percent was to be deducted until the total amount of shares were covered. In turn, for his shares, the employee partner was guaranteed 4 percent per annum as fixed interest. In addition to this, after the ordinary shareholders received a 5 percent dividend and depreciation and other expenses were met, the remaining profits, if any, would be divided in proportion to the holdings beween the ordinary shares and the employee shares.

As usual, the Furness scheme included an offer to set up a works council for the purpose of conciliation. The formation of a court of arbitration was also suggested, a court composed of three members each from the employers and the men and a referee for appeals if the works council failed to settle a dispute. In fact, the Furness scheme was a combination of profit-sharing, conciliation, and arbitration. However, all control was left to "co-partners governing the administration of the business." Control of the company's affairs was to be vested in the board of directors; "No one but the management will possess authority to discharge and engage workmen."[83]

The novel elements of the Furness scheme were three: it called for the absolute eradication of strikes, it recognized and even encouraged trade unions among the workers, and it required the employee to buy special shares out of his regular wages, there being no gift from the employer. The most peculiar of these was unquestionably the guarantee to recognize trade unionism. The proposal stipulated that "Every employee to whom the scheme applies must be a trade unionist." It represented, as Furness himself put it, "the full recognition and frank concession to the authority and influence of the trades unions."[84] Aware of the power of the unions in the shipbuilding industry, Furness had simply decided to make a deal with them. But the imperative condition of the agreement he sought was that "under no circumstancs whatever shall the employee co-partners go on strike against the directions and decisions of their co-partners governing the administration of the business."[85] In exchange for the no-strike condition, Furness proposed to relinquish the corresponding weapon, the lock-out.

The whole purpose of the scheme appeared to be the increase of efficiency through the prevention of dispute. However, Furness was obviously motivated by other considerations as well. Among other things, it seems that he was aware of the advertising effect of his proposal--for the proposal would serve both his commercial and political interests. He had entered Parliament in 1891 as a Liberal and Home Ruler, defeating the Unionist candidate from Hartlepools, but had been defeated in 1895 and again in 1898. Although he was returned in the 1900 and 1906 elections, he was eager to increase his popularity with the electorate, the majority of whom were the area's working men. Co-partnership promised to enhance his political prospects, for the mere fact of his offering such a seemingly generous plan, whether or not it was accepted by the workmen, suggested an enlightened and sympathetic employer.

Furness' proposal galvanized the nation, and all sections of society responded with either praise or criticism. Never before had such a captain of industry adopted so revolutionary a principle and applied it so dramatically to his business. But for all those who praised it as a remarkably brave action on the part of an employer, there were those who dismissed it simply as an advertisement: "He cannot get orders, and he wants to sell out."[86]

Trade unionists, in general, were flattered by Furness' recognition of union power. Predictably, all the labor leaders who had favored profit-sharing and co-partnership expressed hearty approval. Thomas Burt and Charles Fenwick, to name only two, urged the workers 'not to be foolish' and accept it. Havelock Wilson, having already forgotten the bitter strike against the South Metropolitan Gas Company in which his union rendered support to the beaten gas stokers, only wished that Furness would extend his offer to sailors and firemen of the Furness shipping companies.[87]

Furness received hundreds of letters from people of

all walks of life, ranging from cabinet ministers to working men. Hundreds of letters from the latter asserted in effect that 'it is just the thing that is wanted.' The letter from Henry Broadhurst, former general secretary of the TUC, stated that "it is a national blessing and a lasting honour and benefit to both the parties concerned. Surely it would help in attracting more and more of the world's shipbuilding to our country."[88] However, the other shipbuilding magnates neither welcomed nor praised Furness' action. Walter Runciman, for one, one of the leading shipbuilders in the Tyne district, doubted that the system would prove workable.[89] Later, Furness would recall that some members of the Shipbuilders Federation had manifested so much hostility that he would not have been surprised had they voted to oust him from the organization.[90] Meanwhile, presumably as a result of all this national attention, Furness was appointed to sit at the Arbitration Court formed by the Board of Trade in late October of the same year, even though he had never been an authority on arbitration.[91]

The unions had been delighted at Furness' first proposal of selling them the shipyard. It seemed a sign of increased union status, although no one thought its intention was truly serious. Neither did they consider the investment of union funds desirable, finding it risky at a time when the industry was suffering through a period of insecurity. Thus, Ramsay Macdonald called the proposal "absurd."[92] The second proposal was more tempting and the union delegates held secret meetings to discuss it. Furness had requested their final reply in five weeks time. After several meetings, union representatives, by a ten-to-one majority, recommended the acceptance of the proposal.

It is important to consider the reasons for the union leaders' decision. Above all, it seems that they greatly appreciated both Furness' conciliatory attitude and his uncompromising recognition of trade unionism. The Furness scheme was a combination of profit-sharing, conciliation, and arbitration, and nobody could have denied the need for conciliation in the shipbuilding industry after month-long strikes and lock-outs. Union officials were exhausted not only by all the bitter confrontation but also by the tremendous cost, and thus were ready to accept any reasonable offer of industrial peace. Their intention was "to support any plan that would bring about the total abolition of strikes and lock-outs."[93]

Union leaders were also encouraged by a frank concession from such a giant figure in industry: an offer made directly to organized labor. No employer at the same level as Furness had so frankly recognized the strength of the unions and invited their cooperation--at least in shipbuilding. Furthermore, union officials would be admitted to the works council as aldermen, a further difference from other experiments, where only company emplyees were allowed to represent the men. With such recognition and guarantees, it seemed that trade unionism might establish a firmer foothold under the system.

All that Furness requested in exchange was an increased efficiency through the elimination of confrontation. Whether trade unionism, deprived of the strike weapon, could fulfill its function as well as it had previously was the risk the unions had to take. Significantly, they were indeed to take it, enticed as they were, by the guarantee of full recognition. Even Will Thorne, who had every reason to detest such a system, appears to have been tempted because of the requirement of compulsory trade union membership. The same attitude is found in Ramsay Macdonald, who previously attacked profit-sharing and co-partnership but now proclaimed that there was "nothing antagonistic to trade unionism and co-partnersip, provided it is safeguarded."[94]

The scheme was launched on the first of April, 1909, after some necessary preliminaries. The scheme seems to have gone well for the first year, and the company kept its promise of full union recognition. The commercial aspect of the scheme was also successful because as soon as the scheme was accepted by the workmen, the company received new orders for ships and for abundant repair work. In February 1909, the two shipyards in which co-partnership was to start were fully occupied and prospets were bright, although the depression was by no means over. In 1909, the

Irvine shipyards more than doubled their output over the previous year. It was particularly remarkable in comparison with other yards in the same district. On the whole, output increased by 26 percent in 1909; in Irvine's shipyards by 140 percent.[95]

	1908	1909
William Gray and Co............	25,071 tons	30,517 tons
Irvine shipyards...............	12,549	30,126
Total in Britain...............	96,061	122,733

All the steamers built and repaired had been delivered on time, and in one case work was even completed six days earlier than stipulated. The Irvine's shipyards were ranked fifth in tonnage for 1909. Speed-up was said to be practiced in the yards, but it was not attributed to the firm. The people responsible were zealous workers trying to get the best results out of the scheme.[96] While the scheme lasted, there was peace. It was in fact the only shipyards in the country that suffered no stoppage during that period.[97] Peace and friendship appeared to have replaced antagonism and strife.

The works council consisted of twenty members, ten representing the company and the remaining ten, the employees. The company members included the managing director,the secretary, and eight managers and foremen; the other half were elected from groups of artisans and laborers at the meetings held in the yards. In addition, there were 'aldermen' nominated from outside, who were actually the chief executive officials of the unions in the area. The aldermen were to be summoned in case of the failure of the works council's conciliation.

In December 1909, the company announced a dividend at the rate of 5 percent over and above the guaranteed rate, 4 percent, thus making the total rate 9 percent. The ordinary shareholders received 10 percent--5 percent on ordinary shares plus a contingent additional rate of 5 percent. The 10 percent dividend on ordinary shares was higher than in previous years, and the result seemed satisfactory. However, although 9 percent sounded impressive, the actual money the worker received was negligible. The total amount was L 3,375; there were over 2,000 employee shareholders, and thus the checks each of them received amuonted to L 1 12s. although they depended on the amount of shares held. Since the average skilled worker's wages approached L 100 a year, the shareholder supplement seemed ludicrously small. Nevertheless, the guaranteed interest of 4 percent in deposit was higher than the current interest rate at the post office savings bank--and thus, had the workers been able to buy a greater number of shares, they would have done very well, particularly with the additional 5 percent bonus. The return was for nine months: the scheme had started on April 1st; the board chose to make the financial year end on December 31st. This made the return smaller.

Perhaps too optimistic, Furness, at the end of the first year, decided to leave the question of the continuation of the scheme not to the works council, which represented the employee co-partners and the company, but to the branches of trade unions whose members were employed in his shipyards. He asked, with obvious confidence: "Where, indeed, are artisans and laborers doing so well--indeed, approximating to you--today?"[98] In retrospect, it seems an obvious misjudgment. The works council would have voted unanimously for continuation, but things went differently in the hands of the unions. Five unions took a full-membership vote, not confining the voting to those employed by the company. The remaining ten unions, by contrast, decided to confine the vote to the members working in the shipyards.

Everyone was confident of the result; the press and even the local union branches, not to mention the employee co-partners, predicted an affirmative outcome. At the meeting of the employee shareholders, Thomas Liddle, a local official of the Amalgamated Society of Carpenters and Joiners, expressed the earnest hope that the men would continue the scheme, and similar sentiment were heard everywhere. Yet there was obvious hostiilty on the part of workers in other shipyards against the Furness scheme and Furness' employee co-partners. They were seen as enjoying privileges not given to other workers. Worse yet, the no-strike stipulation created a deep confict between Furness' employees and other workers. In case of a strike, the workers in the Irvine's shipyards would not come out to support their mates and indeed they did not.

Surprisingly, however, the voting result upset every positive expectation whatsoever. The result was as follows: in the case in which the entire local membership voted: 564 against, 85 for; in the case of the ten unions that confined the vote to co-partner members: 354 against, 302 for. This mixed voting was held to be unsatisfactory, so a further vote was taken, this time among the co-partners only. The result was dismayingly similar: 598 against, 492 for. Some 300 or 400 abstained from voting.[99] The shipwrights and the members of the Gasworkers and General Labourers Union were the two most prominent unions in opposition.[100] The negative result of the votes of the entire union membership was understandable, but to many observers, the rejection of the scheme by the employee co-partners did not make sense.

Why did the co-partnership scheme of Irvine's shipyards come to an end after only a year? Perhaps the most important reason was the lack of generosity on the part of the employer. The Furness scheme differed in that respect from others, more generous ones such as those of the South Metropolitan and Lever Brothers, which we shall examine thoroughly in other sections. Briefly, though, in the South Metropolitan scheme, a nest egg was provided at the initiation of the system; at Lever Brothers, at the outset of the scheme, employees received co-partnership certificates nominally worth approximately ten years of salaries and wages on which they received interest. Therefore, both schemes started with a sizable free gift from the employer. The Furness scheme was different: the workers had to purchase his employee shares out of his ordinary wages. Furness, as we have seen, did not add anything to it, simply providing for the purchase of special shares. Not surprisingly, this ungenerous arrangement led to worker discontent, particularly among the lower-paid.

Many of the unskilled workers in the shipyards earned so little, frequently not more than 18s. a week, that they simply could not afford to buy shares. This was finally recognized and the rule was changed so that for those who earned less than 24s. per week, the deduction from wages was reduced from 5 percent to 2.5 percent. Nevertheless, any deduction from regular wages whatsoever was a great burden to most of semi-skilled or unskilled men. Not surprisingly, they were largely responsible for the defeat of the scheme. At times even the skilled workers needed every penny available, for even at the Irvine shipyards work was often irregular, and even a deducted shilling could be greatly resented.

This suggests a further reason for the scheme's failure: unemployment and adverse economic conditions. The main reason the men accepted Furness' initial offer was the expectation that co-partnerhsip would bring about full employment. This was, as it turned out, a groundless expectation, for no co-partnership scheme whatsoever could have produced full employment. But the workers appear to have entertained such a quixotic hope, and when it was not fulfilled they were deeply disappointed. Like 1908, the year 1909 was one of widespread unemployment, and in 1909, the Shipconstruction and Shipwrights' Association, for one, paid the highest sums ever for unemployment benefits. About 5,000 men, constituting more than 25 percent of the total membership, received unemployment grants and other special grants during the year.[101] Although the co-partner shipyards had more work and kept fairly busy in comparison with other yards, the work was by no means continuous.

Maintaining constant employment was the worker's greatest concern. When employee-shareholders held a huge meeting to discuss the continuation of the scheme at the end of the year 1909, the questioning was concentrated on the prospects for trade and work in the coming year.[102] When co-partnership could not guarantee a remedy for this, the workers lost interest. As we have seen, the actual amount of co-partnership money which the workmen received was insignificant. The fact that the return was made not for the normal twelve months but for nine was of only minimal consolation. The workers' holding was pathetically small and the 9 percent dividend, though generous in theory, was negligible in cash value.

To the workers with their exaggerated expectation of a king-size bonus, it seemed little more than a joke. After a year's hard work, the fulfilling of a no-strike agreement, and major expectation, the result was disappointing. Even the aggregate of the workers' holdings was too small to be of any real value, and the employee shares carried no voting power. As a result, the employee "co-partners" were left without any decision making power. The works council served only as a conciliatory and consultative body, nothing more.

Finally, Furness' workers, when they were temporarily unemployed, were unable to get work in other shipyards because of the hostility of the workmen at those yards. If they did not accept the need for class solidarity, they must have felt grieved and uneasy about others' hostility and the impact of the co-partnership scheme in practical terms. If permanent employment was not guaranteed in the Furness shipyards, they had to find work in other places, which was tremendously difficult due to the jealousy and hostility of other workers.

Furness was greatly disappointed and blamed the union for the result. He believed that if the men had been left free to act without interference from the other members of the various unions, they would have wanted the continuation of the scheme.[103] But by contrast, G.Barnes, secretary of the Amalgamated Society of Engineers and the chairman of the Labour Party, was pleased to hear the men's decision. The scheme had come to the end he had hoped although he had thought it would last longer. Keir Hardie declared, "In these modern days of keen competition and growing solidarity of the working class movement, all such schemes were foredoomed to failure."[104]

In any case, Furness remained a faithful supporter of co-partnership until the end of his life. We find him speaking to the House of Lords--he was raised to the peerage as Baron Furness of Grantley in 1910--in 1912, asking for the appointment of a Royal Commission on profit-sharing and co-partnershp.[105] He still belived that his scheme would have continued and would have prospered except for the influence of the trade unions, and he insisted that co-partnership in one form or another would ultimately be a satisfactory solution to all concerned.

Were the unions really responsible for the abandonment of the scheme? As we have seen, the main reason the men rejected the scheme was disappointment: first, disappointment in the small size of the actual money returned to their hands; and second, disappointment that co-partnership was unable to bring about full employment. The material benefit was simply too small. If Furness had granted some kind of initial gift, like the nest egg in the South Metropolitan scheme, thus making the deduction from wages less burdensome, the workers would undoubtedly have found the year's result more satisfactory. But more importantly, their disappointment that co-partnership had failed to bring them full employment was the overriding reason. The men seem to have thought of co-partnership as a kind of millennium.

Therefore, we may conclude that the economic uncertainty of the workplace, with its noncontinuous employment, was most responsible for the abandonment of the co-partnership system at the Irvine shipyards. Trade union influence was minimal. Surely, the jealousy and hostility of workers who were not working at the Furness shipyards played a part, but the unions themselves did not try to influence the men's decision either implicitly or explicitly. Indeed, the trade unions had little to complain about. The company kept its promise to maintain a closed-union shop, and when a non-union worker happened to be hired, and became an object of union complaint, the company fired him. Councillor Liddle of Hartlepool, a former plumber, testified that trade unionism was not suffering "in the slightest degree, but has obtained a firmer foothold than ever before in Irvine's Shipbuilding Company."[106]

Even so, the unions were blamed for the abandonment of the scheme. "Certain external and unfriendly, not to mention malign, influences" were said to be the cause of the men's rejection.[107] But it was the economic conditions of that particular period in that particular industry that defeated co-partnership, as we have discussed. If the scheme had been introduced at a time when the industry itself was in better shape, it would presumably have survived much longer, and would have formed a more significant part of the history of the profit-sharing and co-partnership movement. Unfortunately, Furness died fairly soon after the experiment had ended, and the workers of the giant Furness combines were not offered such a system again.

Notes to Chapter V

1. Trades Union Congress, Annual Reports, 1923, p.388. (Hereafter TUC).

2. TUC, Annual Reports, 1925, p.437.

3. TUC, Annual Reports, 1957, p.288.

4. Royal Commission on Poor Laws, Minutes of Evidence, Cd. 5060 (1910), Q. 83649.

5. David Schloss, Report on Profit-sharing and Labour Co-partnership in the U.K. Cd. 7458 (1894), App. F. (Hereafter Report, 1894).

6. A. O'D. Bartholeyns, "Profit-sharing between Capital and Labour," Westminster Review, 177 (1912), p.499.

7. Benjamin Browne, "The Ownership of Capital," Economic Review, 23 (1913), p.382.

8. Yorkshire Factory Times, Feb. 28, 1908.

9. Labour Co-partnership, Nov. 1899, p.191; Dec. 1903, p.189.

10. Labour Co-partnership, Oct. 1913, p.148.

11. Labour Co-partnership, Nov. 1899, p.191; Mar. 1904, p.42.

12. Charles Carpenter, Are Trades Unionism and Co-partnership Incompatible? (London: Labour Co-partnership Association, 1913).

13. National Union of Gasworkers and General Labourers

of Great Britain and Ireland, Rules 1890; 1892, London. (Hereafter the Gasworkers Union).

14. Gasworkers Union, Report, 1894.

15. Labour Co-partnership Association, Report of the Industrial Conference held in Newcastle, 1899, pp.26-7. (Hereafter LCA).

16. Labour Co-partnership, Sep. 1902, p.141.

17. Democrat, June 25, 1920, p.11.

18. LCA, Industrial Conference, p.39.

19. Labour Co-partnership, Sep. 1910, p.112.

20. Thomas Bushill. Profit-sharing and the Labour Questions (London: Methuen, 1893), p.105.

21. Quoted in Henry Lloyd, Labour Co-partnership: Notes of a Visit to Co-operative Workshop (London: 1898), p.342.

22. LCA, Industrial Conference at Newcastle, (1899) p.24; Times, Oct. 10, 1899.

23. People's Press, Jan. 10, 1891.

24. Justice, Jan. 11, 1890.

25. Times, Nov. 23, 1919, 7e.

26. Labour Co-partnership, Oct. 1894, p.27.

27. Democrat, June 25, 1920, p.11; Free Labour, Sep. 15, 1898.

28. Labour Co-partnership, Oct. 1913, p.148; Democrat,

June 25, 1920.

29. *Times*, April 5, 1909, 6c.

30. *Times*, Dec. 6, 1910, 12a.

31. LCA, *Report*, 1913.

32. *Labour Co-partnership*, Oct. 1921, p.123.

33. *Times*, May 23, 1919, 7e.

34. *Justice*, March 13, 1909.

35. *Times*, Oct. 4, 1929, 7e.

36. *Amalgamated Engineers Journal*, Dec. 1908.

37. Labour Party, Minutes of the National Joint Council, April 5, 1927.

38. Quoted in Arnold Rogow, "Labour Relations under the British Labor Goverment," *American Journal of Economics and Sociology*, 14 (1954/5), p.373.

39. *Commonweal*, Dec. 14, 1889, p.398.

40. For further discussion, see Chapter VII of this dissertation.

41. Royal Commission on Labour, *Minutes of Evidence*, Cd. 6894-VII (1893-4), Q. 23124. (Hereafter RC on Labour).

42. *Daily Mail*, Aug. 16, 1916. Reprinted on South Metropolitan Gas Company, *Co-partnership*, 8 (1911), p.212. (Hereafter SMGC).

43. LCA, *Industrial Conference*, p.25.

44. RC on Labour, Cd. 7063-I (1893), App. CI; Bushill, *Profit-sharing*, pp.30-2, 218-28.

45. *Amalgamated Engineers Journal*, Sep. 1912.

46. United Society of Boilermakers and Iron and Steelship Builders, *Monthly Report*, Jan. 1910.

47. Board of Trade, *Report on Profit-sharing and Labour Co-partnership in the U.K.*, Cd. 6490 (1912), p.12. (Hereafter *Report*, 1912).

48. *Journal of Gas Lighting*, June 30, 1926, p.743.

49. *The Workman's Times*, Feb. 4, 1891.

50. SMGC, *Co-partnership*, 1 (1904), p.167.

51. S. Pollard and R. Turner, "Profit-sharing and Autocracy: the Case of J. T. and J. Taylor of Batley," *Business History*, 18 (Jan. 1976), p.18.

52. SMGC, *Co-partnership*, 1 (1904), p.53.

53. *Journal of Gas Lighting*, March 24, 31, 1908.

54. H. Sanderson Furniss, "Co-partnership and Labour Unrest," *Economic Review*, 23 (Jan. 1913), pp.68-9.

55. Quelch, *The Snare*, p.15.

56. *Progress: the Magazine of Lever Brothers*, Aug. 1913.

57. Institution of Gas Engineers, *Transactions*, 1894, p.60.

58. TUC, *Annual Reports*, 1925, p.192

59.
Livesey, "Vindication," p.411.

60.
Lynn Lees, "Getting and Spending: The Family Budgets of English Industrial Workers in 1890" in _Consciousness and CLass Experience in 19th century Europe_ ed. J. Merriman (New York: Holmes and Meier, 1979), p.181.

61.
C. J. Carter, "An Employee Co-partner on Co-partnership," _Nineteenth Century_, 85 (Feb. 1919), p.229. The annual distribution of bonuses was accompanied by a ceremony. In Clarke, Nicholls, and Coombs, each profit-sharer had a seat alloted to him or her, and at intervals was placed a wooden support to hold the trays containing the money to be handed around. The various amounts had been placed in little metal cups identified by the number of the recipient; the money was brought to the ceremonial place from the works in an ambulance van, drawn by a pair of horses. _Labour Co-partnership_, Aug. 1912, p.109.

62.
M. E. Askwith, _Profit-sharing: An Aid to Trade Revival_ (London: Duncan Scott, 1926), p.101.

63.
RC on Labour, Cd. 6894-X (1893-4), Q. 38346.

64.
Clarion, Oct. 23, 1908.

65.
The London United Building Trades Committee, "Messrs. Peto Brothers' Profit-sharing Scheme" in RC on Labour, _4th Report_, Cd. 7063 (1893), App. civ.

66.
Times, July 10, 1914, 13c.

67.
Amalgamated Society of Carpenters and Joiners, _Journal_, Jan. 1920, p.20.

68.
Pollard and Turner, p.16.

69.
For instance see Richard Price, _Masters, Unions and Men_ (Cambridge: Cambridge Univ. Press, 1980), p.250. There have been efforts to revise this fixed image of moderate leadership versus militant rank and file. See Jonathan

Zeitlin, "Trade Unionism and Job Control: A Critique of 'Rank and Filism.'" Bulletin of Society for the Study of Labour History, 46 (spring 1983).

70. Price, Masters, Unions and Men, p.250.

71. Paul Thomson, The Edwardians (London: Granada, 1979), p.218.

72. Times, Dec. 30, 1919, 5c.

73. Nicholas Gilman, Profit-sharing between Employer and Employee (Boston: Houghton, Mifflin, 1889), p.276.

74. Sidney Pollard, "The Economic History of British Shipbuilding, 1870-1914" Diss. University of London, 1951, p.187.

75. David Dougan, The History of North East Shipbuilding (London: George Allen, 1968), p.124.

76. United Society of Boilermakers and Iron and Steelshipbuilders, Monthly Report, Jan. 1909.

77. Christopher Furness, The American Invasion (London: Simpkin, Marshall, Hamilton, Kent, 1902).

78. Furness, The American Invasion, p.37; Times, Oct. 24, 1908, 10f.

79. H. W. C. D., "Furness," Dictionary of National Biography, 1912-1921, p.206.

80. Northern Daily Mail, Oct. 8, 1908.

81. Furness, Industrial Peace and Industrial Efficiency (West Hartlepool: 1908), pp.20-1.

82. Times, Feb. 3, 1908, 6f.

83. Furness, *Industrial Peace*, pp.24, 36.

84. *Northern Daily Mail*, Dec. 30, 1909.

85. Furness, *Industrial Peace*, p.36.

86. *Yorkshire Factory Times*, Oct. 17, 1908.

87. *Northern Daily Mail*, Oct. 12, 1908.

88. *Northern Daily Mail*, Oct. 13,1908.

89. *Northern Daily Mail*, Oct. 9, 1908.

90. *Northern Daily Mail*, Dec. 30, 1909.

91. *Northern Daily Mail*, Oct. 19, 1908.

92. *Northern Daily Mail*, Oct. 9, 1908.

93. United Society of Bolermakers, *Monthly Report*, Jan. 1909.

94. *Northern Daily Mail*, Oct. 9, 1908.

95. United Soiety of Boilermakers, *Monthly Report*, Jan. 1910.

96. *Northern Echo*, April 4, 1910.

97. *Yorkshire Factory Times*, Dec. 23, 1909; *Northern Daily Mail*, Dec. 24, 1909.

98. *Northern Daily Mail*, Dec. 30, 1909.

99. *Northern Echo*, April 4, 1910.

100.
Northern Echo, April 4, 1910.

101.
Shipconstructive and Shipwrights Association, Report, 1910.

102.
Northern Daily Mail, Dec. 30, 1909.

103.
Northern Echo, April 4, 1910.

104.
Times, April 4, 1910, 7e.

105.
Times, Feb. 15, 1912, 10b.

106.
Northern Daily Mail, Dec. 30, 1909.

107.
Furness, Whithy and Co., Report, Quoted in Times, July 25, 1910, 16d.

Chapter VI. Motivations of Profit-sharing Employers

We have seen (in Chapter IV) the employers' objections to profit-sharing and co-partnership. Despite these objctions, however, some employers showed themselves willing to accept the system, at least on a trial basis. Who were they and what made them rally to the cause?

Three Types of Profit-sharing Employers

Profit-sharing employers can be classified in three categories. The first group may be identified as authoritarian employers, those who saw in profit-sharing an opportunity to retain control over their employees by containing the unions. This group was particularly prominent during the early days of the profit-sharing movement. The second group consisted of those who viewed profit-sharing as a tool they could utilize as part of a broader management strategy. Increasing industrial efficiency was more often than not the greatest concern for such employers. Finally, there were the benevolent employers, those who genuinely seemed to believe that it was the right thing to do. They were motivated in some cases by Christian beliefs; in others, by Christian socialism or Ruskinian ideas.

To be sure, these motives often overlapped. Thus the authoritarian employer aimed at promoting labor productivity as well as at undermining trade unionism, and many schemes supposedly motivated by pure benevolence also revealed a calculated effort to induce the employees to work with greater efficiency. To be sure, the benevolent employers, although they appreciated greater efficiency, were primarily attracted to profit-sharing mainly because it appealed to their sense of fairness. Indeed, one employer confessed that many capitalists who received large surplus profits felt that they had not earned them and that in equity they should have been more widely distributed. They took it for granted that business had to be conducted not only for greater output, but also for the social and material benefit of the employees. "It is a duty and a pleasure," said Walter Hazell, owner of a printing and bookbinding firm that introduced profit-sharing in 1886, "to make the well-being of their employees their aim and not merely to work for their own profit."[1]

The task of assessing motivations becomes more difficult when, as was often the case, control and efficiency were intricately interwoven. Control and efficiency were indeed two sides of a coin for it was generally assumed that the greatest efficiency could be realized under absolute control while others viewed efficiency as a more urgent need. The difference can be seen in (a) the way in which these two groups of employers perceived labor issues, and (b) in their approach to industrial relations.

In essence, authoritarian employers viewed control as deriving from property ownership: to them, labor was a commodity which they bought in the labor market and which was to be owned by the buyer after the contract was concluded. Here indeed arose the basic conflict in industrial relations: the employer, as a property owner, was merely required to pay the agreed price of labor, whereas the employee, being propertyless, had to surrender control over a major part of his life to his employer.[2] Despite this apparent inequality, the wage contract thus made between the employer and the worker was conceived of as equitable, and the employer's control over his labor was vigorously defended by these employers.

Paternalism also served to legitimate the employer's control. Workers were viewed, as George Livesey so bluntly put it, as "a bulk of lamb...accustomed to act under orders for many generations"; therefore they needed leaders and their "natural leaders are employers."[3]

The proponents of efficiency also viewed control as an absolute necessity, arguing that management based on expertise would be in the most effective position to define what the industrial situation required.[4] However, these employers believed control was not right but something to be sought, and that the ability of management should be measured by its skill to secure this control through voluntary cooperation.

For the authoritarian employers, loyalty remained the most significant measure of a worker's behavior: for the others, the primary measure was efficiency. Obviously, increased loyalty could mean increased efficiency and vice versa; the emphasis on one or the other depended upon the employer's paricular philosophy. Thus, authoritarian employers viewed the profit-sharing bonus as a free gift to the workers, a gift stemming from the employer's goodness of heart and depending for its continuance upon the good behavior of the workers. For the efficiency-oriented employers, a profit-sharing bonus represented an incentive as well as a supplementary remuneration for extra effort: its continuance depended on the profitability of the system.

The attitude towards trade unions also differed in these two groups. The authoritarian employers were determined to maintain worker loyalty against the unions and were ready to confront them on this issue. The efficency-oriented employers, by contrast, tended to acknowledge the existence of trade unions and were prepared to bargain with them. Less concerned over the existence of trade unions, they attempted to eliminate what they viewed as short-sighted union practices, notably the restriction of output. So-called ca'canny and restricted output were, among others, vigorously attacked by these employers, who believed that the tightening of trade union control had resulted in a definite lowering of British productivity.

These two types of motivation, along with the motivation of benevolence, co-existed from the 1880s to the 1920s. Yet the general trend showed a predominence of authoritarian motives in the early stage of the movement, and the ascendancy of efficiency-oriented motivation in the subsequent development. The dividing line cannot be drawn decisively; yet by the first decade of the twentieth century, the second group had emerged as a majority.

When the second thrust toward profit-sharing came in 1912, anti-union sentiment had retreated and efforts to compromise with and integrate trade unionism were more in evidence. At the same time, industrial efficiency rather than control had become the primary goal. To reach it, employers were obliged to substitute a more sophisticated policy of incorporation for the usual approach of authority and repression. Profit-sharing during this period, therefore, reflects the changes in managerial practice and industrial policy.

The Early Phase: Authoritarian and Anti-union Schemes

The early representative schemes were clearly intended to undermine trade unionism and indeed set forth profit-sharing as an alternative to it. The pioneer plan in Britain, that of Henry Briggs and Son, was entirely motivated by anti-union sentiment. The scheme, as we saw in Chapter II, was explicitly intended to alienate the miners from their union. G. J. Holyoake, who assisted Briggs in putting forth the system, recalled that Briggs had "manifestly inherited a distrust of workmen," and thought "too much of disparaging and destroying trade unions."[5] In 1872, the company forced the workers to choose between the profit-sharing plan and the union by issuing a notice to the effect that men who stayed away from work to attend a union demonstration would forfeit all claim to a future bonus. The company's notice read: "We cannot but feel that the trade union is hostile to our industrial partnership and that our workmen must choose between union with us and union against us."[6] The Briggs were strikingly successful in detaching the men from their union within several years of the profit-sharing practice: union membership was reduced to 40 after only three years of the profit-sharing experiment whereas it had been previously an almost closed-union shop with more than a thousand members.

Two out of three profit-sharing schemes started in 1866 also flatly aimed at frustrating the unions. One of the two, the scheme of Fox, Head, was another typical example of anti-unionism. The circumstances in which the scheme was started in fact were similar to the circumstances at the Briggs operation. This ironwork in

Middlesborough, employing some 600 workmen, launched the plan after long and frequent strikes and labor disputes. The employers' sole object was to detach the men from their unions. "Now what we must do is to establish a firm union between you and us," the employers insisted, "you must therefore first cease to have a firm union with anybody else."[7] Jeremiah Head even refused to take part in collective bargaining on a regional basis, for he viewed such bargaining as a superstructure upon which trade unions could build. He saw it as machinery framed merely "to enable employers' and workmen's organizations to battle with less loss than before." He adopted profit-sharing simply because profit-sharing was "not built upon unions; but is based on their ruin."[8]

The Fox, Head scheme laid down that employees should not belong to any trade union; as they saw it, a man could not serve two masters. "If he places himelf under the authority of the officials of the trade union, it is impossible for him to throw his undivided soul into the work, and assist in carrying them on profitably."[9] Another authoritarian element in Fox, Head's plan was its absolute prohibition of employee participation in decision making. The company was determined to retain unhampered control and thus made it a rule that the men should not be made shareholders.

Anti-unionism was also the primary element in many

of the 83 schemes that were introduced between 1889 and 1892. The most publicized of these, as well as the most successful from the employers' point of view, was that of the South Metropolitan, which will be explored in the next chapter. Briefly it should be noted that the company's sole aim in establishing the system was to eradicate trade unionism among its employees. It represented a direct counterattack against a new union, the Gasworkers Union, which had adopted ostensibly socialist policies. Saving money and achieving greater productivity were all very well, but the employers cared far more about defeating the union. More than anything else, the South Metropolitan scheme was probably responsible for the general perception of profit-sharing as an employer tactic to repress trade unionism. This was because of the great publicity it received.

The South Metropolitan approach typified the general attitude. Employers in this period frequently referred to "an agitator coming into the neighbourhood" and reported that "thanks to the profit-sharing scheme," the agitator had been frustrated.[10] These employers believed that profit-sharing would guarantee unhampered control over the worker and predicted the demise of trade unions once profit-sharing became generally established. Archibald Briggs bluntly stated this very belief:

> If our system of partnership of capital and labor succeed, as I hope and believe it will succeed, every legitimate object of the trade union will be attained; and it must die a natural death or better still, be converted into a benefit or accident club.[11]

This tendency was noted by the Labour Co-partnership Association, the propaganda organization for promoting cooperation and profit-sharing, which observed that employers might be "tempted to regard profit-sharing as an easy means of getting rid of what they regard as the dictation of trade unions." The Association, however, warned such employers on the ground that, although some employees might gladly accept the new conditions, others would see in them "only an insidious attempt to weaken their unions," and would be inclined to cling "more tenaciously to the trade organizations which hitherto have been their chief aid in the struggle of existence."[12]

Although anti-unionism had largely retreated throughout industry by the first decade of the twentieth century, profit-sharing schemes were still being put forth as an alternative to trade unionism as late as 1914. In that year, the Liverpool Gas Company tried to introduce a scheme chiefly to undermine the power of the Gasworkers Union.[13] And at the 1913 meeting of the British Association, an employer named Kirshaw bluntly advocated profit-sharing as an instrument for containing trade unions. When William Ashley, the economic historian, and

Edward Cadbury, the enlightened employer who was concerned with industrial welfare, attempted to defend the unions and justify their existence, Kershaw was quick to attack: "I should like to ask Professor Ashley and Mr.Cadbury whether they have ever seen Mr. Tom Mann and Mr. Ben Tillett in the flesh (laughter), or studied their speeches, or whether they were in Liverpool in the stormy strike days of 1911, for I have done all these things."[14]

It should be noted, however, that even schemes motivated by anti-union sentiment were often preventive rather than an angry reaction to a labor dispute. The schemes of the Briggs and the South Metropolitan were unquestionably devised as a solution to prolonged and deteriorating labor relations. The majority of the schemes, however, were not the direct result of concrete industrial conflict even during the turbulent years of 1889-92. Evidence shows that many schemes were established in firms where labor relations had been good and that only a minority of schemes were introduced in firms that had experienced serious disputes with trade unions.[15] Out of 34 schemes in which employer motives can be assessed, only six cases can clearly be traced to previous industrial disputes and a consequent determination to prevent the men from being influenced by trade unions or "outside agitators." The majority of the firms had experienced no strikes or disputes immediately before the initiation of such plans.

It is true, however, that employers who had suffered no labor disturbances undoubtedly had heard of labor disputes or read about them in the newspaper and wanted to prevent them. In this context, profit-sharing was defensive and paliative in nature.

The Second Phase: the Thrust for Efficiency

As economic and industrial circumstances altered, the anti-union aspect in profit-sharing ventures was modified and the system was looked at from new angles. This different perception of profit-sharing resulted from distinctive developments in industry, developments that were taking place in the last days of the nineteenth century and the early years of the twentieth. The abandonment of employer efforts to contain trade unions through direct confrontation and repression was a reflection of this new departure. It also signaled a movement in the direction of systematic management and the concept of industrial welfare, as has been referred to in Chapter I.

Employers came to recognize trade unionism as an enduring element in industry and to admit its place within the industrial structure. Accepting it as an irreversible process, employers moved away from the idea of eliminating and alienating trade unions to the notion of accommodating and integrating them. At the same time, industrial efficiency was conceived of as the prime goal.

Profit-sharing schemes, that recognized unionism and sought an accommodation with it had emerged by the first decade of the twentieth century. They would become prominent in the profit-sharing movement. The schemes of Lever Brothers and Christopher Furness's shipyards were representative of this trend. In Furness's co-partnership scheme, not only were the union leaders invited for consultation before the inauguration of the system, but the scheme guaranteed a closed-union shop. Significantly, whether or not all profit-sharing employers recognized trade unionism, anti-unionism was no longer openly avowed by the early twentieth century. Professor D. H. Macgregor, Oxford professor and an editor of Economic Journal, observed that the greatest difference in the two reports of the Board of Trade on profit-sharing and co-partnership, published in 1894 and 1912 respectively, was "the disappearance of the argument about collision with the trade unions."[16]

However, if trade unions were recognized, strikes were invariably to be penalized in all profit-sharing schemes. In William Wallace's survey on profit-sharing, only three or four out of 329 cases did not impose such a penalty. In some cases, there was a specific condition that a strike would forfeit the employee's share of profits. In the majority, no such condition was imposed but it was stipulated that a share of profits would be given only to those who were continuously employed.[17]

There were several instances in which the interest of trade unions was especially safeguarded in the scheme and where trade union membership was actively encouraged by the employer. In George Thomson's co-partnership scheme, every worker was expected to join a trade union. The same condition was imposed at Rowntree, a confectionary manufacturer, and Bryant and May, match manufacturers. And in its profit-sharing scheme, William Gray, a well-known shipbuilding and marine engine building concern in Newcastle, showed a most conciliatory attitude toward the unions. While the scheme prohibited any employee who lost more than 12 days' time during any year without good and sufficient reason from receiving a bonus, certain types of strikes were not considered lost time as such. The rule read:

> Time lost by reason of a lock-out, general or district strike, whether authorized by trade unions or not, shall not be considered as time wilfully lost, and shall not debar participation in the divisible profits. Time lost by reason of a strike on a scale smaller than a district strike, shall be considered as wilful loss of time...18

The company was "most anxious not only to continue to work

on the friendliest relationship with the trade unions, but if possible, to improve that relationship." It is indisputable, then, as R. Hay points out, that by the early twentieth century, employers rather endeavored to accommodate and integrate the unions in the face of the internal and external challenges facing the British economy and society.[19]

This change in attitude toward trade unionism represented a distinct departure from traditional British practices. As discussed in Chapter III, British employers were slow to adapt to changing economic conditions. However, by the end of the nineteenth century progressive employers had begun to implement more effective and systematic management methods. As J. A. Hobson observed, employers were realizing that "Business has been conducted too much in the spirit of an art, too little in that of applied science."[20]

Far more considered and deliberate attention was devoted by employers to new methods of organization and control and to more efficient utilization of labor and materials than had previously prevailed.[21] The departure towards greater efficiency in workshop organization and labor coordination went in two directions: scientific management, which was usually identified with Taylorism, and welfare work, as discussed in chapter I.

Profit-sharing as an Incentive and as a Welfare Program

Significantly, profit-sharing fit into both these distinctive developments. In retrospect, we should note that while profit-sharing has been labeled a welfare program by historians, it did not start merely as welfare: a considerable number of employers adopted it as a system of payment by results and as an incentive. Its function was, first, to make the worker's wage greater than it would have been otherwise, and second, to introduce into industry the personal touch and humanitarian consideration. The worker's benefit aside, both tended to increase efficiency, and profit-sharing's ultimate purpose was precisely that.

Both groups stressed the importance of material rewards and viewed efficiency as essential to remove material causes for worker dissatisfaction. They both believed that the happy and fulfilled worker was the most productive. However, the similarity stopped there. Taylorism treated the worker as a unit in the production process and studied him "scientifically" to discover the state in which the worker was most productive. Taylorism was also based on the belief that the greatest productivity would be obtained through incentive wages and scientific coordination of production process. To the employers who were inspired by Taylorism, therefore, profit-sharing was viewed primarily as an incentive.

Welfare employers, by contrast, found one distinct advantages of profit-sharing to be the way it lent itself to the human touch. George Livesey once asked Benjamin Browne, who had questioned the cost under profit-sharing: 'Sir Benjamin, what is the difference in value between cheerfully contended, willing workers, all anxious to make the industry in which they are employed successful, and indifferent, cheerless and discontented workers? Is it 5 percent?' 'Twenty prcent,' Browne replied.[22] An employer named Charles Wickstead asserted that 'Good will and the consideration of the men for the employers and vice versa is worth to the employer something like 20 or 25 percent in expenditure on wages.'[23] Notwithstanding their differences, both groups were convinced that profit-sharing would guarantee higher productivity. Sir Christopher Furness declared that "it may not be too strong a thing to say that the future of British industry hangs on the development of labor co-partnership."[24]

The avoidance of waste was an important objective of profit-sharing. T. W. Allen, councilor of Cardiff, stated that "Modern industry is continually asking for a system that will combine the greatest degree of efficiency with economy. Co-partnership is the solution."[25] The motto of the famous Port Sunlight co-partnership scheme was 'Waste not, Want not.' In many schemes, the employee had to sign an agreement before being admitted to the scheme, promising to be

> regular and punctual in attendance, to be constant and industrious at work, to be economical in the use of materials, and generally to avoid all broken time and slackness, or waste of time, material, or money belonging to the company.[26]

One company stipulated in its scheme, 'no waste of time by courting and love-making.'[27]

When profit-sharing was used as an incentive system, it was often a substitute for piecework or other forms of payment by results. Workers employed on a premium bonus basis or piecework were excluded from participating in several schemes, such as those introduced by Butt, Vosper and Knight, a woollen manufacturer, and Bray, Markham and Reuss, an electrical engineering manufacturer. Firms in which some forms of payment by results were already practiced were less inclined to rely on profit-sharing. In a particular factory, wrote one contemporary student of profit-sharing, "where the wage system has already been supplemented by the introduction of piecework, and prize for economy of material and for increase of production," the need for profit-sharing was less urgent.[28]

Some profit-sharing schemes even introduced crude methods of job measurement. The Lever Brothers scheme was representative. In this scheme, as opposed to the more typical profit-sharing plan, the wages earned were not the unit on which bonus distribution was based, but were used only as a rough index and for fixing a maximum. The reward depended on the subjective estimates of the merits and deserves of each participant. At John Knight, another soap manufacturer in London, the directors reserved "the right to decide in each individual instance, as to whether the bonus has been earned or not."[29]

Unquestionably, profit-sharing was a doubtful incentive as discussed in Chapter IV. All profit-sharing schemes appear to have experienced the same pattern. At first, everybody performed with extra zeal. A year or two later, only the foremen and some others of "the more intelligent workers kept up with the increased zest."[30] After the novelty had worn off, the bonus seemed too remote and was usually not sufficiently substantial to influence the employee's attitude permanently. McVitie and Price, bisquit manufacturers, observed that a positive result could be discerned only for a short time following the payment of the bonus, and that a month after it was paid, the workers lapsed into "the usual condition of 'factory hands' neither worse nor better."[31]

One of the common criticism of profit-sharing was that, if paid regularly, the employee only too frequently would come to regard the bonus as wages, which defeated the whole purpose of the system. Osborne and Young, corn and forage merchants, for one, started profit-sharing in 1890 but found that any extra zeal evoked during the first several years soon died out. Many employees had come to regard the bonus as deferred pay. The firm thus abandoned it and increased the wages of the "old and worthy hands."[32]

Firms like the Allock Manufacturing Company at Birkenhead discovered a different solution: distributing an annual bonus quarterly. In this company, one half of the first three payments was paid in cash and one half was put to the credit of the employee. At the end of the financial year, when the books were made up, the actual amount of profits available for distribution was ascertained and the employee drew as a lump sum his credits plus any further amount due him. This system seemed to succeed in awakening the employee's interest, yet neither this nor any other arrangement seemed able to retain his interest and inspire a greater productivity permanently.[33]

When William Wallace conducted a comprehensive survey on profit-sharing in 1920 at the request of Seebohm Rowntree, he discovered that the failure of profit-sharing as a form of payment by results ranked first as a cause of scheme abandonment. After the category of "information too inadequate," the next largest cause of failure referred to by employers was the failure of the system of payment by results.[34] As this survey shows, a lot of employers genuinely believed in the effect of profit-sharing as a stimulus for greater labor productivity.

When profit-sharing failed to produce the expected

greater efficiency, employers abandoned the system and converted to more direct systems, such as piecework or the premium bonus system. In nearly half of the abandoned cases in William Wallace's survey, profit-sharing was replaced by payment by results in one form or another. Other employers turned to a simple raise in wages.[35]

Even when the shortcomings of profit-sharing as a direct incentive system were fully acknowledged, there was no denying its peculiar value in certain types of industry. There were industries where alternative incentive systems were not practicable, and therefore profit-sharing seemed the most effective way to increase productivity.[36] Coal-mining, an industry in which supervision was highly difficult and where piecework had therefore been adopted in the very early days, was the focus of one of the earliest profit-sharing experiments, that of the Briggs colliery. In the soap work, payment by results was not possible because different shifts were employed on the same work and vats were kept boiling for a number of days--thus rendering it impossible to measure comparative efficiency. William Lever, the famous soap manufacturer, was fully aware of this problem when he initiated a co-partnership scheme in his Port Sunlight factory.

Again, where a great variety of different grades of workers were employed on different, unmeasurable services, as in the gas and electricity industries, it was impossible to distinguish the contributions of the various classes of workers, who ranged from stokers to meter readers. In such areas, profit-sharing was particularly applicable as the nearest approach possible to a system of payment by results. Not surprisingly, the gas industry was the single largest industry where profit-sharing was generally practiced.

Traveling salesmen, another group difficult to supervise, were also likely candidates for profit-sharing arrangements. Still another such group was the managers, whose service was by its very nature incapable of definite measurement. Indeed, profit-sharing made its strongest claim as an instrument for increasing the efficiency of the managerial class. When it was so employed, to some extent, it represented an attempt to devise a payment-by-results method for those whose output could not be objectively measured but who were in a position to influence very considerably the profitability of the undertaking.[37]

One way in which profit-sharing contributed to improved efficiency was by reducing turnover. Workforce stability was an important concern for management as high turnover always implied a loss. The loss of not only skilled workers but even unskilled ones meant the high cost of training. In fact, one study discovered that the retraining of semi-skilled workers was particularly costly.[38] This awareness caused many employers to turn to profit-sharing as an inducement to longer service. Even a scheme largely humanitarian, that of Clarke, Nicholls, and Coombs, set forth as one of its objectives "causing workpeople to remain longer in the employement."[39]

Some schemes made use of special innovations to achieve this goal. Indemnity Mutual Assurance, for example, paid its bonus in two parts, one part in accordance with length of service, the other in accordance with efficiency. The 'Long Service' fund was not given to employees who had worked less than five years. The other half, which was called the 'Efficiency' fund, was distributed among qualified members of the staff as the board of directors determined. Another firm, E.S.& A.Robinson, a paper bag and box manufacturer, paid its bonus in proportion to wages actually earned with an addition of L 1 for each year of service. For example, if a man's actual earnings were L 100, but he had been with the firm for 15 years, his share would be calculated on the basis of L 115.[40]

Profit-sharing unquestionably resulted in greater length of service, for a majority of firms so reported. It was rare, for instance, for a worker at Lever Brothers to leave on his own. Some workers at Bushill and Son rejected offers of higher wages from other firms to remain in a firm with a profit-sharing scheme. Moreover, profit-sharing was likely to draw better workers. One employer believed the system brought all the best workmen to him. J. T. and J. Taylor obtained "the creme of the workpeople in the district," and Lever Brothers' employees boasted that they were the best workers in the world.[41] An observer of a later found that absenteeism and turnover were less marked, or even absent, when bonus earnings formed a large and stable elements of the payment system.[42]

As the limits of profit-sharing as an incentive system became evident and many productivity-conscious schemes were abandoned, the other main aspect of profit-sharing--employer concern for worker well-being--came to be increasingly emphasized. Meanwhile, profit-sharing continued to be the most discussed and the most publicized of all the welfare plans which had emerged by the turn of the century, including model towns, insurance plans, and pensions.

These employers recognized the limitations of the crude and harsh 'engineering' approach which was associated with scientific management.[43] "By treating the men as if they were mere producing machines," Robert Fish told the meeting of the gas engineers, "we mismanage them and our efforts to realize from labor its maximum results are fruitless and nugatory."[44]

The profit-sharing system was perceived in part as an instrument to help restore the personal relationship between employer and employee, the disappearance of which was said to be "the greatest loss to modern industry." A recent study of welfare work in the U.S. has concluded that the most prevalent feeling among businessmen who embarked on welfare programs was "a vague sense that they had lost contact with their employees."[45] Employers such as William Lever emphatically expressed the hope that profit-sharing would bring about closer relations with employees. He addressed:

> Let us recognize the family brotherhood of labor and introduce closer bonds between capital, management, and labor than a mere bald contract for wages. Let us socialize and Christianize business relations, and get back again in the office, factory, and workshop to that close family brotherhood that existed in the good old days of hand labor.46

Profit-sharing was hoped to enhance such a personal contact and modify the psychological ignorance and the social ineptitude embodied in the commodity theory of labor.[47]

The call for worker control in the decade after 1910 fortified the welfare argument for worker participation, and profit-sharing with its aspect of participation received correspondingly greater attention. During this period, the perception of labor unrest was changing: it had been viewed as the desire for material betterment or the result of the "agitators' malice." Now the real cause of labor unrest was thought to be the discontent with conditions over which the worker had no control. "The present industrial unrest is not a mere demand for higher wages and shorter hours," Edward Cadbury wrote in 1913, "but an increasing knowledge of his lack of control of the conditions of his own life."[48]

If industrial unrest was more a "question of status and control," then extra remuneration in whatever form would not be a cure for the trouble. Profit-sharing and co-partnership seemed especially promising on this point, as they recognized the desire of the workers, however latent, to be identified with the ownership and control of the undertakings, as well as to participate in the division of their surplus.[49] Indeed, institutions for worker participation, even to the degree of taking part in a kind of lower level management, were set up in connection with profit-sharing plans. This worker participation took place under various names, such as joint committee, the consultative committee, the wages board, and the committee of the board.

Third Phase: Industrial Democracy

Worker participation under profit-sharing and co-partnership received a further impetus in the post-war years as industrial democracy became a fad. Thanks to this move, 49 profit-sharing schemes were started in 1919 and another 43 in 1920; the highest previous total had been 32 in 1890. In order to understand this exploding enthusiasm for industrial democracy, we should look at the particular historical conditions of the time. First of all, there were memories of pre-war unrest, when labor had called for worker control and received so strong a response from the rank and file.

Then, there was the aggravated antagonism that accompanied the war. During the war, pressure at work intensified, as old work customs and restrictions were discarded and as dilution was set forth. The prohibition of the right to strike forced the workers to the side of militant shop stewards and of unofficial strikes. The issue of profiteering also became keen as "the suspicion" arose that "a portion of the community is exploiting the national crisis for profit," as the report of the 1917 Commission of Enquiry into Industrial Unrest concluded. The workers came to believe that there had been inequality of sacrifice.[50] This sense of exploitation and inequality materialized in labor unrest in the immediate post-war years. The year 1919 witnessed a total of 1,413 trade disputes involving 2.5 million working people and the loss of 34.5 million working days. In 1920, there were 1,715 disputes, involving 2 million workers and the loss of 27 million workin days.[51]

Finally there were the revolutions and social upheavals in Russia and other countries. Severe anxiety and profound uncertainty dominated the mood of the time. It was evident, as the Whitley Committee noted, that "permanent improvement in relations must be founded upon something other than a cash basis."[52] Not only radicals and social reformers, but also industrial and political elites now endeavoured to bring about conciliation and consensus.

The Whitley Committee, which was set up in 1916 in order to consider reconstruction policy after the war, had prophetically pointed to the need for such a consensus. The most famous of a series of the Committee's reports proposed the establishment in each industry of permanent joint bodies of representative employers and union officials. This report helped inspire a true enthusiasm for industrial democracy. Along similar lines, the Sankey Commission, appointed after the miners' threat of a general strike, recommended, on a limited basis, that there be partially worker-controlled nationalization of the mines.[53] The general mood of the time seemed to call for just such radical undertakings. As Seebohm Rowntree observed, "We have finished a war claimed to be fought to establish democracy. It is up to us now to seek to establish the same principle of democracy, so far practical, in our own industry."[54]

Responding to this mood, profit-sharing schemes of the period tended to emphasize not so much the aspect of economic gain but rather worker participation. Companies such as British Cyanides, which started a profit-sharing plan in 1917, emphatically insisted on the role of the consultative committee as by far the most important feature connected with the scheme.[55]

The popularity of profit-sharing and co-partnership, however, is not necessarily evidence of an increasig democratization in British industry. Shrewd employers, such as Brunner Mond, a giant chemical undertaking which set up the eight-hour day, paid holidays, and pensions, as well as co-partnership, took the position that it was a much better policy to give it than to have to give it. It had foreseen the growth of worker power and the further call for worker control.

Industrial democracy was, however, too revolutionary an idea for the average employer. Most employers were horrified by the very idea of co-partnership, as we saw in Chapter IV, and even those employers who adopted profit-sharing felt that co-partnership was too radical. George Livesey, for example, had a tough fight with his fellow directors over the issue of workman directors. There was comparatively little opposition to profit-sharing, but workman directors were too much.

Employers looked upon progressive co-partnership venture with both prejudice and skepticism. George Thomson, a woollen manufacturer in Huddersfield, was so moved by the teaching of John Ruskin that he converted his private business into a cooperative undertaking in 1886, although he quite naturally reserved the position of managing director for himself. To be sure, his was by far the most radical experiment in co-partnership even in the post-war years of "industrial democracy." The firm's committee consisted of three employee representatives, two co-operative representatives, and two representatives from related trade union. Allen Gee and Ben Turner, two leaders of the Textile Workers Union, served on the committee for many years.

Even the profit-sharing employers, however, declined to embrace so radical a plan, and Thomson received favorable responses from very few employers. Thomas Bushill, a devoted supporter of profit-sharing, regarded Thomson's venture as premature because of what he perceived as the "present inadequate condition of working class ability and intelligence." While Bushill was sufficiently progressive as to favor municipal ownership of water and gas, he was flatly opposed to taking on a workman as a partner.

As James Bonar, political economist who experimented a printers'co-operative society, so colorfully expressed it in the presidential address of the Labour Co-partnership Association, too many British employers asked the "jealous question, 'Who is master here, you or I?'"[56] Not only that, but some shrewd employers discerned an apparent relationship between the democratizing process and industrial disturbances. There had been more strikes and labor disputes, they observed, since labor had acquired its parliamentary vote than there had been before. Therefore, they reasoned, "there would be more labor troubles after we have given labor an industrial vote than we have now."[57]

As a result of this employer reluctance to share power, the number of co-partnership schemes remained pitifully limited even in the post war years. The number of schemes that provided employees with shareholding opportunities was mere 49. If the gas company schemes were excluded, the number became 13. Not only the avenues for investing capital in the business were limited, but the opportunity for control through the worker director remained pitifully restricted. Only 15 out of 182 schemes in force in 1919 allowed workers to sit on the board of directors. If the gas companies were again excluded from these 15 cases, (industrial co-partnership was common in this industry not only because of the industry's peculiar economic conditions but because of George Livesey's ceaseless propaganda), only 8 such plans remained. Even in the gas industry where co-partnership received the most favorable response, only seven companies allowed the workers to sit on the board. In only four of the eight schemes outside gas were employees represented on the board of directors in 1919. In one instance, half of the directors were company employees. In the three remaining schemes, the number of employee directors were, two, one, and one respectively.[58]

The term 'co-partnership' was, therefore, misleading. In many so-called 'co-partnership' schemes, the workers were in one sense alone co-partners--for they shared both the company's profits and its shares. But they were not 'co-partners' in terms of control. At J. T. and J. Taylor, for instance, the employees acquired more than half the company's stock through the co-partnership bonus, yet these shares carried no voting power. The amount of the employees' shareholding in this particular company was considerable; in 1919, it stood at L 145,758. Even so, the holders of a majority of shares were absolutely excluded from decision making. Taylor interpreted this in his own way, telling a Rotary Club audience in 1920: "Labor has nothing to do with the management in my firm, and there is no sign that labor is discontented in consequence."[59]

Even in cases where workers were represented on the board, it was one thing to accept their presence, and another to assign them a role. The role of the worker who was also a board member was, if anything, extremely limited and marginal. And because the majority of directors represented the management's interests, the workman directors had no real voice in determining the policy of the firm. Obviously the worker lacked both corporate knowledge and managerial experience. He could do no more than voice the interests of the workers.

In the South Metropolitan Gas Company, the most

frequently analyzed co-partnership experiment, only two of the ten directors were workers. To qualify for election as a director, a workman had to have 14 years' service as well as shareholdings of 120 pounds, a prohibitive sum for the average worker. And even for the few who qualified, the role of the workman director was so limited that Charles Carpenter, the successor to George Livesey and a vocal supporter of the co-partnership system, remarked in a private occasion: "I think the workman's ability to influence the prosperity of the undertaking is greater by their work on the co-partnership committee than by work in the board room."[60]

There were interesting exceptions, however, such as William Thomson and Son, George Thomson's firm, and the Tollesbury and Mersea Native Oyster Fishery. In the latter case, some one hundred employees held more than half of the ordinary shares under the co-partnership system, and subsequently secured a majority on the board. They were then able to press their views in major decision-making areas, including the amount of wages workers were to receive.[61] However, these were extreme exceptions and there is no evidence that others followed these models.

Worker participation in lower level decision-making and consultation through profit-sharing committee or co-partnership committee was a much less revolutionary idea than worker directors, and such committees were more in evidence than worker directors. However, the functions of such committees was also clearly limited. Their primary function was to administer the plan: other duties included supervision of pension schemes, provident clubs, and the like. Sometimes a committee was expected to suggest improvements in welfare work or in minor points of factory management.

All these functions were purely consultative and without executive power. The committee usually dealt only with "the comfort, safety, health, and well-being of all employees." Or, in a critic's words, "any subject but the really important ones such as wages, hours, and conditions of work."[62] The real "right to manage" was never conceded. Thus, co-partnership did not mean worker control of a business but worker participation in it.

The cry for industrial democracy would fade after a brief time--the time it takes for a fad to run its course. The consensus, which had been encouraged by the government, fell apart in the 1920s. The National Industrial Conference, which was set up in 1919 with the blessing of Prime Minister Lloyd George, fell apart as well.[63] Once the post war industrial crisis had passed its peak, enthusiasm for industrial democracy declined. Already in 1920, the Employers' Year Book reported that "the period of 'Co-partnership' is over."[64] And the number of profit-sharing and co-partnership schemes initiated in 1921 dropped to seven. Employers had reasserted their right to manage.

In the view of such critical scholars as A. Ramsay, worker participation did not evolve out of the humanization of capitalism but has appeared cyclically. These cycles are traceable over more than a century, Ramsay writes, and "are shown to correspond to periods when management authority is felt to be facing challenge." Participation was thus understood as "a means of attempting to secure labor's compliance."[65] A similar judgment is made by R. Hay on welfarism as a whole. John Child has argued that even before 1920, it was becoming obvious that "some employers had only dealt with the idea of shared control as a device to buy time."[66]

However, the limitation of worker participation was not necessarily the result of the employers' stubborn determination to retain their authority. The restriction of the worker-director's management may have been necessary for the sake of achieving the greatest possible efficiency. As Daniel Nelson points out, the workers' background, training, and perspective were so limited that joint decision making would have required far too much time and effort for the normal conduct of business.[67]

It was also a result of the workers' indifference. The British working class probably never believed in worker control and neither did they demand it. One shrewd employer was to point out precisely that. The Labour Co-partnership Association initiated a special congress on co-partnership in London in 1920 and 1923, attempting to create a propaganda victory amid the enthusiasm for industrial democracy. All those in attendance--politicians, leading employers, and social reformers--paid enthusiastic lip service to the value of joint decision-making. Then Theodore Taylor rose to his feet and urged the audience to talk less of worker control and more of what was immediately practicable. "The actual workers care far less for control than for income," he contended. "That is the fact and I say it as the result of a long experience and an intimate knowledge of workers." "What they want is dividend--and they are sensible enough to believe that the directors in the business can get dividend better than they can get it for themselves."[68]

At the same time, it should be noted that the failure of worker integration in the board room may not have been as significant as it was once thought. In a complex business, the function of the board of directors is by no means almighty, for decision-making is to a large degree decentralized and dispersed. Thus the influence of the board of directors tends to be limited, as Tomlinson argues.[69]

Moreover, the limitation in worker participation under profit-sharing and co-partnership does not necessarily lead to the conclusion that it reflected an authoritarian labor policy. A recent study of American company unions argues that firms with such unions tended to adopt more enlightened and progressive policies towards labor than firms without them.[70] The same arguement can be applied to profit-sharing committees. If their function was limited, they were nevertheless an open avenue from employees to upper level management and a means for ventilating grievances. This avenue was by no means so accessible in non-profit-sharing firms. In this context, then, profit-sharing firms with even very elementary worker participation still reflected a more progressive labor policy than that to be found at firms without any worker participation whatever.

Indeed, profit-sharing committees did help redress grievances and give the worker a sense of at least partial control. A foreman at Hans Renold, an engineering firm in Manchester which introduced the first systematic Taylorism in the 1880s and then adopted profit-sharing after the war, stated at a meeting of the profit-sharing committee that "the great point of profit-sharing is that it gives us some control of our destiny." The employers professed not to understand him, and we can see why: the committee as we have observed, was not in any sense executive or managerial, but simply consultative. Neverthelsss, as the foreman expressed it, the committee provided a wider view: "We know what is likely to happen, how the business is going, and something about the prospects."[71]

It is true that the connotations of welfare capitalism imply buying employee loyalty at a cheap price.

It is also true that the employers' wish to obtain their employees' loyalty was one of the principal motivations in profit-sharing. Loyalty and harmonious relations, however, were pursued not so much for the sake of control itself as for greater efficiency. At first, profit-sharing and co-partnership were employed as an antidote to trade unionism. But in time that purpose gave way to more progressive motivations--a more systematic management and a more effective industrial relations policy. At the same time, it represented a more sophisticated labor policy. Those profit-sharing employers were shrewd enough to adopt a preventive measure to avert a more serious labor conflict. In their most advanced form, therefore, profit-sharing and co-partnership represented the outgrowth of enlightened management. Now we turn to the third motivating factor in employer's decision to adopt profit-sharing, benevolence, and also to its usual companion, radical ideology.

Benevolence and Radical Ideology

As we have noted, control and efficency were not the only two forces that motivated employers. A trend toward benevolence and visions of a new social order had a major impact on the profit-sharing movement. In the early 1890s, David Schloss observed that it was the custom among a "very considerable number of British employers" to devote a large amount of monies out of the company's profits to various purposes for the benefit of their employees.[72] The same benevolence was found in many profit-sharing schemes. It was often precipitated either by religious beliefs or by ideological convictions: sometimes it was Christianity, at other times it might be Ruskinite principles. In fact, benevolence seemed so conspicuous that James Bowie, an economist, concluded:

> The co-partnership movement was an outgrowth of the increasing sense of social responsibility for the lives of the underdogs. It could be established and developed only on a foundation of genuine good-will.[73]

Yet, Bowie's view appears to have been partisan for not many schemes were derived from pure social responsibility, if such a phenomenon was rather strong in Britain. Interestingly, the U.S. Labor Bureau investigated all the profit-sharing plans operating in America in 1916 and found a notable shortage of the benevolence motive. Of all the employers interviewed, only three stated that their primary purpose was to divide profits equitably as a matter of justice irrespective of the hope of increased efficiency.[74]

Religion seems almost to have been the natural soil for profit-sharing and co-partnership. In fact, the very idea of profit-sharing may be said to have arisen from the teachings of Christianity, inasmuch as the Frenchman Leclaire, the father of the profit-sharing movement, based his thinking on Christian beliefs. The words he wrote immediately before his death summed up the central inspiration behind his life-long venture:

> I believe in the God who has written in our hearts the law of duty, the law of progress, the law of the sacrifice of oneself for others. I submit myself to his will; I bow before the mysteries of him who has told us to do to others what we would have others do to us, and to love our neighbour as ourselves.75

It is well known that Quaker employers had a particular fondness for industrial welfarism in Britain, and as a result, attempts have been made to associate any exceptionally benevolent practice in British industry with the non-conformist tradition. Profit-sharing, however, does not seem to have drawn its zealous disciples exclusively from this source. Those of the Anglican communion were also an influential force in the development of profit-sharing. While Thomas Bushill was a Baptist and William Lever and Theodore Taylor were also from the non-conformist family, George livesey remained in the established church. No matter what their denomination, these employers shared the view of Taylor, who remarked:

> The Christian employer must desire to treat his employees as well as he can. He will wish to pay them not the lowest wages he can get them to take, but the highest wages he can afford to give...The principle of profit-sharing attracted me, in the first instance, as the best method of paying the highest possible wages, consistent with the continued existence of the business.[76]

Ruskin's Influence

Sometimes Christian beliefs were combined with other ideological conviction. Bushill, the owner of a papermaking and printing firm in Coventry, was converted to the cause of profit-sharing as much through his encounter with John Ruskin's teaching as through the teaching of the gospels. Ruskin became interested in political economy in the early 1860s after mainly working on art. He found the most destructive maladies of modern industrial society in the mechanization of work and life and in the competitive system of capitalism. The competitive system particularly appeared as doubly degrading the character of workers: since profit, not excellence of work, was the admitted motive, the individual producer was "purely self-engrossed."[77] Ruskin tried to humanize political economy and put forth his conviction that "honest production, just distribution and wise consumption should replace the mechanical injust and wasteful bodies of the existing system."[78] The final outcome and consummation of all wealth was, Ruskin claimed, "in the producing, as many as possible, full-hearted, brighted-eyed, and happy-hearted human beings."[79] Ruskin thus put forward and demonstrated his contention in his writings on economics, including Unto This Last, that there was nothing more disgraceful to the human intellect than the principle of the political economy, "Buy in the cheapest market and sell in the dearest."

> Charcoal may be cheap among your roof timbers after a fire, and bricks may be cheap in your streets after an earthquake; but fire and earthquake may not therefore be motive beliefs.[80]

Ruskin's influence on the British labor movement was clearly revealed in the fact that Unto This Last was chosen by the newly elected Labour and Lib-Lab MPs in 1906 as the single book that had influenced most in shaping their beliefs.

Yet Ruskin also left his mark on the thinking of British employers. The teaching of his that particularly moved Thomas Bushill was the following passage in Unto this Last:

> The affections only become a true motive power when they ignore every other motive and conditions of political economy. Treat the servant kindly, with the idea of turning his gratitude to account, and you will get, as you desire, no gratitude, nor any value for your kindness; but treat him kindly without economical purpose, and all economic purposes will be answered...81

In the 1870s, Ruskin had tried to put his vision of an organic community into practice in a series of experiments, most prominently in the St. George's Guild near Sheffield. But all of them failed.

Ruskin made at least one other important contribution to the profit-sharing movement, his influence on George Thomson. Thomson adopted the most radical possible form of co-partnership in his woollen factory in Huddersfield by converting his private enterprise into a co-operative undertaking and distributing shares to his employees. Ruskin's idea that competition was corrupt, unjust, ad dishonest left a permanent impression on Thomson's business philosophy, and led him to conclude that "the acceptance of the spirit of Ruskin's teachings is our only chance to escape from the industrial anarchy into which we are drifting."[82]

Thomson longed for the opportunity of putting into practice the principles he had imbibed, believing "the only practical way of applying them was a system of industrial partnership."[83] His company, William Thomson and sons, was registered as a limited company under the 1876 Industrial and Provident Societies Act, and its profit-sharing scheme made it possible for the entire firm to be run by an elected committee of directors composed of employees as well as trade union representatives. Thomson remained manager of the firm with a salary of L 500 per annum. His connection with Ruskin was given a visible form when, in 1910, he became Master of St.George' Guild, the organization founded by Ruskin in 1872.

Christian Socialism

While Thomson's profit-sharing scheme was deeply influenced by Ruskin's teachings, it could also be called a child of the Christian Socialist movement. Christian Socialism was indeed another important force behind the development of profit-sharing as discussed in chapter II. If no profit-sharing employer could be identified as a Christian Socialist, nevertheless its influence was felt through the Labour Co-partnership Association, the propaganda organization of profit-sharing and co-partnership. The LCA was founded in 1884 by a group of Christian Socialists, including E. V. Neale, Thomas Hughes, and Edward Greening. Although the list of their subscribers shows the names of social reformers, politicians, and other public figures rather than employers, it played an important role in promoting the movement.

Christian Socialists first concentrated on constructing co-operative societies of producers, but, recognizing the limitation of the working-class cooperative movement on its own, set up the goal of cooperation between capitalists and workers. As a result, the Labour Co-partnership Association, while still encouraging independent working class cooperative societies, devoted greater effort to converting employers to the cause of profit-sharing and co-partnership.

As its name indicates, Christian Socialism aimed to christianize socialism and to socialize Christianity. It was an ideology promoting reconciliation of two apparently contradictory principles that society had a corporate responsibility for the welfare of its members and that the individual must nevertheless work out his own salvation. Like Ruskin, the Christian Socialsits were critical of the competitive system and hoped to generate productive worker units based on brotherhood. In many ways, at least in theory, Christian Socialism was a middle path between liberal individualism and state socialism.[84]

However, in reality, the Christian Socialists were not so much anti-capitalism as anti-socialism. The majority of the leaders of the LCA, including Ludlow, Holyoake, Neale, and Vivian were indeed vigorously opposed to

Socialist claims. Holyoake, for one, bitterly attacked the Socialists at the Cooperative Congress, and later in his life joined the extreme individualist organization.[85] Henry Vivian and Fred Maddision, two of the younger leaders of the LCA, were Lib-Labs returned in the 1906 election. Although he was originally a carpenter, Vivian refused to join the Labour Party and was censured by his union, the Amalgamated Society of Carpenters and Joiners, for opposing Socialist candidates in 1907.

Not surprisingly, the Christian Socialists were deeply opposed to violent or revolutionary social change. They indeed believed that "the condition of the permanent elevation of the mass of the population is their conversion into capitalists."[86] Apropos of this attitude, George Thomson described profit-sharing as practical and constructive socialism, a genuine alternative to the cash nexus and the outbreak of revolution.[87]

Regardless of ideology behind profit-sharing ventures, these benevolent employers questioned the existing way by which capital and labor were respectively rewarded. Thomas Bushill noticed "uneasiness at the contrast which presents itself between the employers' lot and that of the mass of their employees."[88] They believed that labor in the past had not received its fair share. One employer confessed that it was not the "rhetoric of the so-called demagogue--it is the laborer's dumb endurance--which arouses my sympathy and sometimes stirs my indignation."[89]

Some of the profit-sharing employers were from humble origins and retained a sympathy with the working class. Alexander Horn and George Mathieson, managing directors of Clarke, Nicholls, and Coombs, foodstuff manufacturers in London, were originally laborers and adopted profit-sharing immediately after they founded the company. Leclaire, the shoemaker's son, remarked: "To know the workman, one must have been a workman himself, and above all, remember it."[90] They indeed remembered it and generously gave away a portion of the profit that otherwise would have been theirs to keep.

For some, it was not mere benevolence, but somthing deeper--radical convictions. Most notably, they declined to accept the notion of profits as the absolute right of capital. W. Filene, for instance, established his profit-sharing scheme not primarily on business grounds but on the belief that capital, like labor, was entitled only to its wage; capital should not be the residual claimant, entitled to all that remained after labor was paid at the market rate.[91] They echoed G. J. Holyoake's claim that profit-sharing was equity and a right of labor because if the workman, whose labor mainly created profits, had no right to a share in it, no one had a right to anything. Alexander Horn felt that so long as the employer received a fair return for his capital, it was his duty to share the surplus above such a fair return with those who had helped him earn it. F. Debenham, a London employer, insisted that profit-shring should supplement wages and should be adopted not because it paid, but because it was fair and right.[92]

These employers understood that profit-sharing would probably diminish the reward of capitalists but thought that was quite acceptable: there should be a spark of genuine generosity and a spirit of self-sacrifice. It was this fair-mindeness, in fact, that caused employers such as Alexander Horn to reject co-partnership--for it required loss-sharing on the part of the workers. Horn and other like-minded employers considered this grossly unfair. Horn's own company reported only a limited increase in zeal and efficiency under profit-sharing, but since zeal and efficiency were not the primary purpose of the scheme, the scheme was continued. In this particular confectionery undertaking, the workers received a higher dividend than the shareholders. For intance, in 1909, while the average dividend on capital was 10 percent, the workers received a bonus on their wages of over 14 percent. As of 1912, the total bonus paid to the workers had been three and a half times the amount of the ordinary capital of the company in the 22 years the scheme had been in operation.[93]

Nor was George Thomson's co-partnership scheme profitable to himself. From a financial point of view, the Woodhouse Mills' system was decidedly more beneficial to the workers than to Thomson. He told the Royal Commission on Labour that he was "the only one who gets less remuneration for my services than I would in a non-profit-sharing scheme, providing trade was good."[94] Money, however, meant less to Thomson than to most employers. In addition to a profit-sharing bonus and various welfare funds, Thomson's employees received far higher wages than workers in other firms. "Of course, we cannot go very much above the average of the district. If we did, I should not only get the employers against me, but the workers outside. Indeed, I have often been asked what right I have to pay the workers here better than they are paid elsewhere."[95]

Not surprisingly, a certain paternalism tended to accompany these benevolent profit-sharing schemes. Many schemes contained elements of paternalism and tended to underestimate the workers' ability to handle their bonuses responsibly. Theodore Taylor, for instance, forbade drinking and smoking among his "co-partner" employees.[96] In the rules of the profit-sharing scheme at Bushill and Son, it was stipulated that "Bad language or intemperance will not be tolerated and the sending out for intoxicating liquor is strictly prohibited."[97] One contemporary observed that the impulse behind co-partnership was, in some cases, not so much the desire to knit up the worker's interests with the business as to stimulate him to save.[98] Thomas Bushill insisted that two-thirds of the workers' bonus be deposited in the pension fund because he could not trust the thrift of the working class.

It ought to be noted, however, that not all benevolent employers were paternalitic. Alexander Horn was particulatly critical of the paternalistic practice of compulsory investment in company stock. He challened George Livsey, who insisted that profit-sharing did not harm than good because the workers tended to waste the extra money. "But many men spend their ordinary wages wastefully," Horn pointed out. "Would Sir George withhold these from them on that account? Employers have no right to ddecide what to do with it."[99]

One obvious weakness of these schemes was that benevolent impulses alone could not sustain the scheme. The case of an employer who installed a profit-sharing plan in 1918 clearly points this up. He did so, he said, because he had found it a great temptation to be a 'good fellow' and share his extra funds with his employees during a time of unusual prosperity. However, he had to abandon the scheme in 1921 when the unusual prosperity vanished. Thus, shrewd employers realized that pure benevolence was not enough. Profits could be divided only if there were profits to divide. Perhaps William Lever was right in asserting that the benevolent, but inefficient employer was the worst possible friend to the workman, for his business would soon be compelled to close.[100]

Not surprisingly, both economic calculation and benevolent sympathy figured in the motivations of some employers. Virtually all of them, after all, hoped that profit-sharing would benefit both the employer and the employee. Leclaire laid it down at the outset that profit-sharing must tend to increas, and not diminish, the employer's profit. The employer, he insisted, should be better off financially than before.[101] Thomas Bushill emphasized the importance of economy for the success of the scheme at every employee meeting, and once even threatened his employees with the adoption of a premium bonus system unless they showed more diligence and enthusiasm. Unless bad practices disappeared, he warned, "we shall have to apply very strictly the premium bonus system and try to bring it home to them in that way."[102]

At Clarke, Nicholls, and Coombs, it was expected that the system would develop "in every brain the highest intelligence, in every arm the greatest vigor, and in every heart the warmest loyalty and zeal." "Identify yourselves more closely than you ever yet have done with the interest of the business," the company urged. "Try by every means to minimize waste and above all waste of time and raw material."[103] In this company, long service was particularly desired because two-thirds of the workforce were girls and women, most of whom worked only until marriage.

Thus it appears that in a substantial number of instances there existed a combination of business and humanitarian motives. However, if the appeal to the pocket book was likely to influence these employers to some degree, it was far from all-powerful. Social conscience and religious duty seem to have been the dominant impulse in the benevolent employer. But the influence of such employers should not be overestimated. After all, employers like Thomas Bushill, Alexander Horn, and Theodore Taylor are exceptional figures in the annals of British industry. When Thomas Bushill died in 1907, the profit-sharing scheme of Bushill and Son immediately came to an end. The scheme of J. T. and J. Taylor's met the same fate after the founder's death. Shortly after George Thomson's death, William Thomson and Son ceased to be directly co-partnership. These remarkable employers could not convert even their immediate successors to the cause of profit-sharing, and benevolent schemes remained a very small fraction of the profit-sharing movement.

Notes to Chapter VI

1. "Discussioin on Scientific Management," Sociological Review, 7 (April 1914), p.121.

2. Keith Burgess, The Origins of British Industrial Relations (London: Croom Helm, 1975), p.304.

3. Times, Dec. 30, 1901, 5c.

4. Frederick W. Taylor insisted that management must maintain its prerogatives for efficiency depended on management ability to determine plant and wage structure. See Alan Fox, "Managerial Ideology and Labour Relations", British Journal of Industrial Relations, 4 (Nov. 1966), p.367.

5. George J. Holyoake, The History of Co-operation (London: T. Fisher Unwin, 1908), p.446.

6. Nicholas Gilman, Profit-sharing between Employer and Employee (Boston: Houghton, Mifflin, 1889), p.271.

7. National Association for the Promotion of Social Science, Transactions, (1870), p.493. (Hereafter NAPSS).

8. NAPSS, Transactions, (1870), p.494.

9. NAPSS, Transactions, (1870), p.493.

10. See Report, Cd. 7458 (1894), p.107.

11. NAPSS, Transactions, (1866), p.708.

12. Industrial Partnership Association, Report, (1889/90).

13. The Liverpool Gas Company sent a company officer to

the South Metropolitan to obtain information on the non-union clause and the co-partnerhsip committee. See S. Harris, The Development of Gas Supply on North Merseyside 1815-1949 (Liverpool: North Western Gas Board, 1956), p.108.

14.
Times, Sep. 12, 1913, 10c.

15.
See Report, Cd. 7458 (1894), PP.78-122.

16.
Labour Co-partnership, April 1914, p.63.

17.
Cecil of Chelwood Papers, British Museum Add. Mss. 51103, ff.145-7, p.21.

18.
Report, Cd. 544 (1920), p.98.

19.
Roy Hay, "Employers' Attitude to Social Policy and the Concept of 'Social Control' 1900-1920," in The Origins of the British Social Policy ed. Pat Thane (London: Croom Helm, 1978), p.115.

20.
Joseph Melling, "British Employers and the Development of Industrial Welfare c. 1880-1920" Disser. University of Glasgow, 1980, vol. 1, p. 54.

21.
For the development of systematic management, see John Child, British Management Thought (London: George Allen and Unwin, 1969); Alan Fox, "Managerial Ideology and Labour Relations", British Journal of Industrial Relations, 4 (Nov. 1966), pp.366-78; Howard Gospel, "The Development of Management Organization in Industrial Relations" in Industrial Relations and Management ed. K. Thurley and S. Wood (Cambridge: Cambridge Univ. Press, 1983); W. R. Garside and H. Gospel, "Employers and Managers" in A History of British Industrial Relations ed. Chris Wrigley (London: Harvester, 1982); Craig Littler, The Development of the Labour Process in Capitalist Societies (London: Heinemann, 1982); L. Urwick and E. F. L. Brech, The Making of Scientific Management (London: Management Publishers Trust, 1949); V. Vroom and E. Deci, Management and Motivation (NY: Penguin, 1981).

22.
Labour Co-partnership, Aug. 1911, p.118.

23.
Times, Sep. 12, 1913, 10d.

24.
Journal of Gas Lighting, April 27, 1909.

25.
Labour Co-partnership, March 1904, p.41.

26.
Report, Cd. 544 (1920), p.36.

27.
Edward Bristow, "Profit-sharing, Socialism, and Labour Unrest", in *Essays in Anti-Labour History* ed. Kenneth Brown (London: Macmillan, 1974), p.392.

28.
Thomas Jones, "Profit-sharing in Relation to other Methods of Remuneration of Labour," *Accountants Magazine*, 8 (1904), p.437.

29.
Report, Cd. 544 (1920), p.119.

30.
Royal Commission on Labour, Sitting as a Whole, *Minutes of Evidence*, Cd. 7093-I (1893), Q.5959.

31.
Report, Cd. 544 (1920), p.119.

32.
Report, Cd. 544 (1920), p.119.

33.
Conservative Research Department, *Co-partnership Today* (London: Conservative Political Centre, 1946), p.35.

34.
William Wallace, *Prescription for Partnership* (London: Sir Isaac Pitman, 1959), p.28.

35.
One disillusioned employer called T. Scott asserted "extra supervision would decidedly pay me better than profit-sharing." *Report* Cd. 7458 (1894), p.81.

36.
Piecework was possible only where quantity of output was the prime consideration, and where inspection for quality was easy to manage. Piecework could not

properly fulfill its function where the number of units of output produced was not under the worker's control, but was determined by the speed of the machine he was tending or the particular process in which he was engaged. See N. C. Hunt, Methods of Wage Payment in British Industry (London: Sir Isaac Pitman, 1959), p.46.

37. Hunt, Methods, p.138; James Bowie, Sharing Profits with Employees (London: Sir Isaac Pitman, 1922), p.149.

38. A Study of turnover by General Electric in 1916 discovered that semi-skilled machine operators were the most expensive employees to replace. M. W. Alexander, "Hiring and Firing: its Economic Waste and How to Avoid it" Annals of the American Academy of Political and Social Science, 65 (1916). Cited in Jonathan Zeitlin, "Social Theory and the History of Work", Social History, 8 (1983), p.368n.

39. Clarke, Nicholls, and Coombs, "Profit-sharing Rules" (London: 1890), p.7.

40. Report, Cd. 544 (1920), pp.99-100, 103-4.

41. Report, Cd. 7458 (1894), p.115; S. Pollard and R. Turner, "Profit-sharing and Autocracy: The Case of J. T. and J. Taylor of Batley", Business History, 18 (1976), P.18.

42. Derek Robinson, "British Industrial Relations Research in the Sixties and Seventies" in Industrial Relations in International Perspective ed. P. Doeringer et al. (London: Macmillan, 1981), p.154.

43. Child, British Management Thought, p.40.

44. Institution of Gas Engineers, Transactions, (1887), p.30. (Hereafter IGE).

45. S. Brandes, "Welfarism in American Industry, 1880-1914" Disser. Univ. of Wisconsin, 1970, p.54. Quoted in Daniel Nelson, Managers and Workers (Madison: Univ. of Wisconsin Press, 1975), p.115.

46.
William Lever, "Prosperity-sharing vs Profit-sharing in Relation to Workshop Management," Economic Review, 2 (1901), p.61. Lever's welfare work is discussed in Chapter VIII of this dissertation.

47.
Lyndal Urwick, "Co-partnership and Control," The Human Factor, 8 (Nov. 1934), p.396. As modern industry became more complex and larger-scale, the establishment of some department was neessary to guard and promote the closer relation of management to the workers.

48.
Edward Cadbury, "Some Principles of Industrial Organization," Sociological Review, 7 (1914), p. 105.

49.
Urwick, "Co-partnership and Control," p.396.

50.
James Cronin, Industrial Conflict in Modern Britain (London: Croom Helm, 1979), pp.110-111.

51.
Bowie, Sharing Profits, p.55.

52.
Arnold Rogow, "Labour Relations under the British Labor Government", American Journal of Economics and Sociology, 14 (1954/5), p.358.

53.
Richard Hyman, "Introduction" to Carter Goodrich, The Frontier of Control (London: G. Bell, 1920), p.xix; A. Ramsay, "Cycles of Control", Sociology, 2 (1977), p.488.

54.
Wallace, Prescription, p.13.

55.
Report, Cd. 544 (1920), p.94.

56.
Labour Co-partnership Association, Report of Industrial Conference, (London: Labour Co-partnership Association, 1898), p.32.

57.
A. H. Mackmurdo, Pressing Questions (London: John Lane, 1913), p.122.

58.
Report, Cd. 544 (1920), p.46.

59.
Labour Co-partnership, Nov. 1920, p.155.

60.
Charles Carpenter, Industrial Co-partnership (London: Co-partnership Publishers, 1921), p.45.

61.
Report, Cd. 544 (1920), p.68.

62.
W. J. Reader, Imperial Chemical Industries: A History vol. 2 (London: Oxford Univ. Press, 1975), p.61.

63,
For National Industrial Conference, see Rodney Lowe, "The Failure of Consensus in Britain: The National Industrial Conference, 1919-1921", Historical Journal, 21 (1978), pp.649-675.

64.
Child, British Management Thought, p.40.

65.
Ramsay, "Cycles," p.481.

66.
Child, British Management Thought, p.48.

67.
Daniel Nelson, "The Company Union Movement," Business History Review, 56 (Autumn, 1982), pp.335-379.

68.
Labour Co-partnership Association, Report of London Co-partnership Congress, 1923, p.12; Labour Co-partnership, Dec. 1950, p.22.

69.
James Tomlinson, The Unequal Struggle (London: Methuen, 1982), p.126.

70.
Nelson, "The Company Union," p.347.

71.
Labour Co-partnership Association, Report of London Congress, 1923, p.8.

72.
Schloss, <u>Methods</u>, p.154.

73.
<u>Industrial Welfare</u>, April 1923, p.109.

74.
Bowie, <u>Sharing Profits</u>, p.12.

75.
Sedley Taylor, "A Real 'Savior of Society'," <u>Nineteenth Century</u>, 8 (Sep. 1880), p.383.

76.
George Greewood, <u>Taylor of Batley</u> (London: Max Parrish, 1957), p.34.

77.
John A. Hobson, <u>Ruskin: Social Reformer</u> (Boston: Dana Estes, 1898), p.330.

78.
Hobson, <u>Ruskin</u>, pp.329-30.

79.
Quoted in Hobson, <u>Ruskin</u>, p.98.

80.
John Ruskin, <u>Unto This Last</u>, (London: George Allen, 1907), p.54.

81.
Ruskin, <u>Unto This Last</u> , p.26.

82.
Robert Perks, "Real Profit-sharing: William Thomson a Sons of Huddersfield, 1886-1925," <u>Business History</u>, 24 (July 1982), p.163.

83.
Jo Melling, "British Employers and the Development of Industrial Welfare, 1880-1920," Disser. University of Glasgow, 1980, vol.2, p.133.

84.
Bristow, "Profit-sharing, Socialism," p.272; Perks, "Real Profit-sharing," p.165.

85.
Holyoake, <u>The History of Co-operation</u>, p. 650.

86.
Bristow, "Profit-sharing, Socialism," p.272.

87. Perks, "Real Profit-sharing," p.165; Melling, "British Employers," vol.2, p.135.

88. Thomas Bushill, *The Relation of Employers and Employed in the Light of the Social Gospel* (Alexander and Shephard, 1889), p.8.

89. Thomas Bushill, *Profit-sharing and the Labour Questions* (London: Methuen, 1893), p.182.

90. Thomas Jones, "Profit-sharing in Relation," p.14.

91. *Labour Co-partnership*, Oct. 1919, p. 79.

92. *Report*, Cd. 7458 (1894), p.96; London Chamber of Commerce, *Journal*, Jan. 1898.

93. *Labour Co-partnership*, May 1921, p.47; Clarke, Nicholls, and Coombs, *The Proof of Pudding*, pp.21-3.

94. Royal Commission on Labour, Group C, *Minutes of Evidence*, Cd. 6708 (1892), Q. 7098.

95. *Yorkshire Factory Times*, March 20, 1908.

96. Perks, "Real Profit-sharing," p.161.

97. Bushill, *Profit-sharing and the Labour Questions*, p.242.

98. Bowie, *Sharing Profits*, p.107.

99. *Labour Co-partnership*, Dec. 1906, p.191.

100. William Lever, *The Six-hour Day and Other Industrial Question* (London: George Allen and Unwin, 1918), p.64.

101. Lever, "Prosperity-sharing vs Profit-sharing," p.54.

102. Bushill, *Profit-sharing and the Labour Questions*, p.87.

103. Clarke, Nicholls, and Coombs, *Profit-sharing Rule*, p.8.

Chapter VII. The South Metropolitan Gas Company and the Gas Industry

The gas industry is of particular importance in the development of profit-sharing and co-partnership and deserves close examination for several reasons. First, it was the industry in which the movement received the greatest response and in which the system was utilized in the majority of undertakings. Second, it produced one of the most famous and successful schemes in Britain, that of the South Metropolitan Gas Company, as well as one of the most vigorous proponents of the system, George Livesey, chairman of the South Metropolitan. Third, the primary motive behind profit-sharing was to contain militant trade unionism, and subsequently that was to cause the most serious tension between profit-sharing and trade unionism.

Finally, the industry itself is interesting for the heavy capitalization already accomplished in the early 19th century as well as for the statutory monopoly given to gas companies. The industry was thus in a special position in the predominantly small-scale, privately owned, and liberal British economic structure. While the peculiar aspects of industry itself are not our concern, they ought to be noted because they contributed much to the success of profit-sharing in this particular industry.

Labor Relations in the Gas Industry prior to 1889

Given that the chief motive for establishing the system was to contain trade unionism, the examination of labor relations in the gas industry is necessary before we look into the operation of the system itself. The most distinctive features of labor relations in the gas industry prior to the initiation of the profit-sharing system had been the absence of trade unionism and the presence of paternalism. The workforce in the gas works was composed of three groups: tradesmen, yardsmen, and retort house workers. Among these, retort house workers constituted the majority--in 1889 two thirds of the South Metropolitan workers belonged to this group.[1]

The major work done in retort house was stoking, which did not require a high degree of skill. However, it did require a somewhat long training period and was physically exhausting work. It was "high skilled" work among unskilled labor. The stokers, therefore, were not easily replaceable, and as training a gasworker involved high cost and extensive time, employers paid them higher wages than they paid other semi-skilled or unskilled workers. The stokers' strategic importance in the industry was well recognized.[2]

We need to understand, then, why this particular

workforce, composed of strong males in a hard-to-replace situation, failed to organize themselves until the thrust of the new unionism in 1889, and why they then did so as they did. The reasons for the non-existence of trade unionism among gas stokers were two, as Hobsbawm has pointed out.[3] The first was that they were in essence casual workers and thus possessed little bargaining power. Their casual status derived from the difficulty of storing gas, which meant that production had to coincide with consumption and that therefore only half as many workers were required in the summer months as in the winter. Although the same workers usually came back in the winter season year after year, and many of those who did not work in the retort house in the summer worked in the yards and thus the seasonal fluctuation was less in reality than it might appear--still, the lack of continuity weakened the stokers' bargaining power.

The second reason for the absence of trade unionism was that the stokers were not skilled workers. Their skill, though it represented a degree of irreplaceability, could be acquired by other workers far more easily than craft work skills could be acquired. Moreover, many of them were not simply "gasworkers." They were employed as bricklayers' laborers and deal carriers to dock workers, or even as yard laborers at the gasworks during slack time. For such a group of workers, frequently changing their employment, a sense of solidarity or an understanding of the imperatives of organization would have been remote.[4] Most of them were illiterate. Charles Carpenter, chief engineer of the South Metropolitan told the Charity Organization Society that "it was a very rare thing for a stoker to be able to write his name in 1885. They almost invariably made their mark."[5]

For these reasons, the gasworkers were not effectively organized until the late 1880s. There were occasional attempts to unionize and inspire strikes, but these attempts were brutally subdued. In 1872, the stokers who had formed the Amalgamated Gasmen's Association staged a strike in protest against the dismissal of one of their members at Beckton, the Gas Light and Coke Company. They were defeated and the union was crushed. There was another attempt also unsuccessful in 1884, but except for these incidents, industrial relations in the gas industry experienced little turbulence.

Along with the absence of trade unions, a conspicuous feature of the industry was paternalism, which existed in spite of the large size and public funding of gas companies. The gas companies were pioneers in the area of welfare, providing services that included a sick fund and paid holidays--and these dated to the early years. The managers treated the workmen much the same as the old-fashioned land owners treated their servants. It was usual, for instance, in the Gas Light and Coke Company, when a man fell sick, for the company to pay him his full wages for a period that might be as long as four weeks. If it was an accident, the wages were paid until his return to work.[6] The South Metropolitan, which was incorporated in 1842, established various welfare plans, and the strong degree of paternalism is shown in a remark by a South Metropolitan engineer: "The company had thought of adopting the eight-hour system but gave it up because the more time some men had, the worse use they made of it."[7]

The absence of unions and a paternalistic benevolence rendered the labor relations situation in the gas industry generally comfortable. But there was another reason for the stability of industrial relations: the industry was not vulnerable to violent fluctuations in production and sales, and consequently to heavy unemployment. Competition from other sources of power, such as oil and electricity, were not felt until the early twentieth century. Job security for the gasworkers was thus greater than that of workers in other industries. Because of satisfactory labor relations and the statutory monopoly, then, the gas companies were largely unconcerned with technological innovation and felt no desire to displace labor simply to save money. As a result, the industry lagged far behind the technology of the time in spite of the substantial investment capital that was always available.

If the above presents the general picture of the gas industry as a whole, the relationship beween the employer and the worker at the South Metropolitan, which is at the heart of our story, was even more comfortable. In fact, almost as soon as the company was incorporated, it was introducing a welfare program. A workman's sick fund was established in 1842, the very year of incorporation. Superannnuation was started in 1855, followed by holidays with pay, reduced Sunday labor, and the Saturday half holiday in the 1850s and 1860s.[8] Interestingly, all these provisions were initiated by Thomas Livesey, chief engineer and the father of George Livesey, the cenral figure of our story.

The Liveseys were a professional managerial family. The gas industry required heavy capitalization from the very beginning and therefore relied upon public funds, which made it the usual thing for professional managers to run the business with the board of directors. Thomas Livesey entered the South Metropolitan as an engineer and manager and served it for forty years until his death in 1871, while George entered the company as an assistant to his father at the age of fourteen and became chairman largely through his own ability. George's brother Frank was also an engineer in the South Metropolitan.

Thanks largely to Thomas Livesey, the company went without a strike for the first forty-seven years of its existence. The South Metropolitan workers even refused to join the great 1872 strike of the stokers which involved most of the London companies. The great respect and affection Thomas Livesey inspired in his workmen was attested by the fact that three hundred workers walked in his funeral procession in 1871. We can see just how great a tribute that was by a glance at the employment rolls. In 1875, the company employed about five hundred men in the maximum-employment winter months, so that the gathering of three hundred in October of 1871 would probably have included almost all South Metropolitan employees.[9]

George was a generous employer, following his father's labor policy. For his part, he was the inventor of the sliding scale system applied to gas companies so as to regulate dividends and gas prices. The sliding scale involved two inversely related proposals: dividends might exceed ten percent if the price of gas was reduced, or, conversely, they could be reduced if the price was increased. The purpose of the scale was to link the price of gas with the dividend paid. From this, we can see Livesey's concern with unifying separate interests within society.

The Formation of the National Union of Gasworkers and General Labourers

In 1889, the National Union of Gasworkers and General Labourers came into existence. It was formed in March 1889 by the socialist Will Thorne, who was at the time employed at the Beckton station of the Gas Light and Coke Company. It is interesting to see why the gasworkers, who had been unorganized for decades, suddenly formed a union in

1889. It is an especially important question for the historians of trade unionism, but we ought to confine ourselves to some evident facts.

In brief, the direct cause of the formation of the union was the intensification of work. New machines had been introduced during the period around 1888 and inevitably caused unemployment. Paradoxically, they also meant harder work. Machines were not fully efficient in those days and often required more time and trouble than manual work. And there were changing economic conditions as well: trade revived rapidly in 1889.[10]

In any case, the intensification of work and increased trade were not in themselves conditions sufficient to bring about the sudden organization of gasworkers and unskilled workers in general in the years around 1889. The most important factor appears to have been socialism, as Clegg, Fox, and Thomson argue. What gave momentum to the new unionism was the socialist thrust of the time and some apparent effects of mature capitalism, such as the rise of monopoly power, that seemed to confirm Marxist expectations.[11] Will Thorne had been a member of the Social Democratic Federation from its early days, yet he was not the only socialist who helped to galvanize the gasworkers. Peter Curran and George Waddle, to name only two, were both active gasworker leaders. Also Eleanor Marx, the youngest daughter of Karl Marx, was a sponsor of Thorne, and had in fact taught him to read and write. Both she and her husband, Eduard Aveling, served in the preliminary committee of the Gasworkers Union.[12]

The way in which the union was launched was instructively abrupt. Will Thorne called for a meeting at the Beckton gasworks on March 31: 800 men gathered and a two-penny subscription was collected in a bucket. In the first six months, the membership rose to 30,000. By July, the union had over 60 branches throughout the country. Just that quickly, the organization of general workers and laborers, which had long been considered impossible, was achieved. Already in 1891, Thorne proudly reported that they were one of the strongest labor unions in England.[13]

The objectives and rules of the union were unmistakably socialistic--at least as the Webbs judged them. The rules stipulated that the union would embrace "every kind of unskilled labor and admit workers, women as well as men."[14] Again, the way in which the organization was pursued reflected socialist influence. Contrary to the tradition of the craft unions, the Gasworkers Union comprised workers of some 70 different trades and industries. Most importantly, the Gasworkers Union was among the most ardent advocates of the eight-hour day, which was then closely associated with the socialist movement. Thorne declared that he did not believe in "having sick pay, out-of-work pay, and a number of other pay. We desire to prevent so much sickness and men being out of work. The way to accomplish this is, firstly, to organize, and then reduce your hours of labor or work. The whole aim and intentions of this union is to reduce the hours of labor and reduce Sunday work."[15]

The union's balance sheet is one indication of just how militant the union was in its early years. In the first year of its formation, no less than L 10,000 went into strike benefit payments, of which more than half went to help out the South Metropolitan employees' strike.[16] Now it is time to look closely at this particular strike, the sole cause of which was a profit-sharing scheme.

It is almost no exaggeration to say that the relationship of the South Metropolitan with the Gasworkers Union had been deteriorating ever since the union's formation in 1889. To be sure, the first demand of the newly born union--the eight-hour day with three shifts--was conceded by the company without much objection. Indeed, it was conceded even though it gave a tremendous boost to the new unionism: John Burns repeatedly said that without the gasworkers' success concerning the eight-hour day, the famous dockers' strike in the summer of 1889 could not have taken place at all.[17]

The union's demands, however, did not stop at the eight-hour day: the union went further and began to interfere with the work process. It had been common for stokers to oil the hinges of the retort lids. Now the union ordered stokers to refuse to do so on the principle of demarcation. Livesey, annoyed by it, warned: "If your union is going to act in this way, it will not last 12 months." Thorne, choosing to interpret this remark in his own way, immediately spread the rumour that Livesey was going to "smash the union."[18] Thorne's conclusion was premature, for Livesey was to experience additional humiliation before finally deciding that that was precisely what he would do.

Shortly after the retort-lid incident, another conflict took place over the union's attempt to impose a closed-union shop. One union recruiter went too far in the eyes of management and was promptly dismissed. The union threatened to strike unless the man was reinstated and the right of recruiting fully guaranteed. Livesey again had to concede for he was not yet prepared to cope with a strike. At this point, however, he began to feel the time was at hand to begin containing this seemingly insatiable union. Finally there came the union's demand for double pay for Sunday work. While Livesey had advocated the abolition of such work as early as 1882 on moral and physical grounds, the nature of the industry made it impossible to end Sunday work completely. Now, upon hearing the union's demand, Livesey offered time and a half pay on Sunday, an offer Will Thorne was willing to accept. But the rank and file members insisted on their own terms. This reaction Livesey viewed as a case of the men having gotten "out of hand completely," and he became determined to fight the union.[19] It seems curious that the gasworkers, docile and relatively content for decades, should suddenly became a fiercely militant group--but indeed they did. It appears that the mood of the men changed entirely once a strong organization was behind them. It was also a matter of expecting to have their way. As one of the men put it, "If we ask for a gold watch, we will get it."[20]

Livesey's first response was to make the sort of arrangements that would facilitate coping with future strikes. He first met with the chief of the Metropolitan Police to gain assurance of support in case of a strike, emphasizing that the stoppage of gas would be a public disaster. The police, after being criticized for showing too much generosity towards the dockers in the summer strike, were now quite willing to guarantee Livesey that everything the police could do within the law would be done.[21] That accomplished, Livesey sent his agents to various towns outside London to sign up would-be blacklegs, at the same time ordering accommodations for them. All these preparations were, of course, made in complete secrecy.

Yet, while preparing for a confrontation, Livesey hoped to avoid one. If at all possible, he wanted conciliation and rapprochement. Consequently he came to terms with the idea of profit-sharing, an idea far from unfamiliar to the South Metropolitan which had practiced it among officers and foremen since 1886. Now Livesey planned to expand it to include the entire workforce.

The Alternative to Trade Unionism: A Profit-sharing Scheme and the Strike

When the profit-sharing proposal was offered, the response from the workers was mixed. The yardmen and mechanics accepted it immediately, but the stokers were more cautious. They liked the sound of it, yet refused to give their assent until they consulted with their union executive. Obviously, they were puzzled as to why the company had put forth such a seemingly generous proposal. After all, was it not true, as Baylay of the Southern Counties Labour League stated, that Livesey had not thought of awarding a bonus when his employees were working 16 hours a day?[22]

The proposed scheme was based on a sliding scale. The employee would receive a bonus of 1 percent on his annual wage or salary for every penny reduction of the gas price below 2s. 8d. per 1,000 cubic feet. Since, for example, the gas price in December 1889 was 2s. 3d., the bonus for the year would have been 5 percent. In addition, an initial credit was given to every man who elected to participate in the scheme: the credit represented a sum equal to what he would have received as a bonus if the scheme had been in operation for the previous three years. This nest egg was equivalent to 9 percent on one year's wages.

The main point of the proposal, however, was

neither the sliding scale nor the nest egg. It was the agreement accompanying the profit-sharing plan. Before being accepted into the plan, the worker was asked to sign an agreement binding himself to work for the company for 12 months. This condition was a double-shield protection against a strike: not only was the agreement of each worker to terminate at a different time, thus making collective action impossible, but also a gasworks employee was liable to both criminal and civilian punishment under the Conspiracy and Protection Act of 1875 if he broke a service contract.[23]

Interestingly, and contrary to the general assumption, the union did not reject the proposal at the outset. The rank and file, though somewhat puzzled at what the company's intentions might be, felt they might nevertheless give it a chance. Employees other than retort house men, numbering 1,000 out of a total of 3,000, meanwhile accepted and signed the agreement, as did three stokers. The union, not totally rejecting the scheme, demanded that the clause that prohibited strikers from receiving a bonus be withdrawn, a point that Livesey, after consideration, conceded.[24] Thus, even though he was preparing for a possible confrontation, Livesey appears to have sincerely wanted to give profit-sharing every chance.

Then it was discovered that three members of the Gasworkers Union had secretely signed the agreement.

Enraged, the union demanded that the three men be dismissed immediately and that the profit-sharing scheme be abolished as well. The union later insisted that their notice to the company had contained a typographical error, and what they had demanded was either the dismisssal of the three men or the abolition of the scheme, not both. Will Thorne, who was in Manchester at the time due to a strike there, was not directly involved in the initial disagreement. He came on the scene when the strike threat was issued. Thorne, obviously reluctant to lead another strike so shortly after the one in Manchester, tried to dissuade the men. But having obtained all the concessions they had sought since the formation of the union, the men now came to believe that they only had to make a claim for it to be conceded. Thorne could do nothing, and the strike began Decembr 5, 1889. With the exception of a dozen or so, virtually all of the nearly 2,000 stokers employed at the South Metropolitan went out on strike.

Livesey's preparation strategy worked splendidly. He immediately telegraphed the blacklegs who had been registered and 6,000 new men replaced 2,000 stokers within several hours after the stokers had left work.[25] Accommodation facilities were then brought into the gasworks to make it possible for the blacklegs to remain inside. Meanwhile the police arrived to protect the blacklegs and thus the stoker' picket line achieved little.

Some major elements in the drama should be mentioned here. While the company claimed that participation in the profit-sharing plan was totally voluntary, it suggested at the same time that those who signed the agreement would be given preference when slacktime came. Since employment in the gas industry was essentially seasonal, this suggestion was a most attractive lure. Recognizing this, the union tried to characterize the bonus scheme as a bribe and a snare to break up the union and to put the men at the mercy of the employers. Having been born only six months before, the union understandably saw the struggle as a matter of life and death. For that matter, Livesey's response represented the first major counterattack against it by an employer.

It almost seemed that the entire future of the new unionism lay in the outcome of the gasworkers' struggle with Livesey. If the South Metropolitan triumphed, it was predicted, then profit-sharing schemes would flood the industry. If the bonus system was established, "the union would be of no use: the men would be back to the old state of degrading slavery."[26] Following the same line of reasoning, _Labour Elector_ declared that the South Metropolitan profit-sharing agreement was "nothing more or less than a pecuniary bribe to the men to desert and betray the union."[27]

For their part, the strikers claimed that their object in striking was not an increase in wages, nor did it result "from any matter of self-interest, but on a simple matter of principle." A letter from the strike committee declared:

> We are of opinion that...the bonus scheme... was formulated purely in order to break the union and to prevent all combined action. We are aware that this does not appear on the face of it, but in our eyes it is nothing but a seductive, though most plausible, bribe to throw dust in the eyes of the men and... morally destroy the trade union...28

One important issue was the question of control over the work process and the foreman's power. Livesey, annoyed by the union's attempt to tighten its control in the workplace, deliberately inserted a clause in the agreement stipulating that the employee "agrees to obey the orders of the foreman in charge." This provoked a storm of criticism from the workers. "What we principally object to in this bonus system," one of the men asserted, "is that on the slightest provocation, our foreman would threaten to stop our bonus, thus we should be entirely in his power."[29]

To their pained surprise, the gasworkers received a cold response not only from the public but from fellow workers throughout the strike, which lasted for six weeks. The gasworkers had witnessed the dockers' strike in the summer of the same year, had observed the great sympathy it had elicited from the public and even from the police, and expected the same for themselves. Instead, they found the public against them and the police acting effectively as a strikebreaking force on the side of the employer.

There were few who seemed to feel like Eleanor Marx, who was positively exhilarated by the gasworkers' fight. She wrote to her sister Laura on December 25: "I am glad the gasworkers are saved from the 'patronage' of the bourgeois...The other night I was up at the strike committee...One and all declared themselves Socialists. Things are moving here at last..."[30] Engels also felt relieved at the absence of bourgeois support: "In the gas strike, the workers once more find themselves entirely deserted by all the petty bourgeois. This is very good."[31]

While from the Marxian point of view, the helplessness may have appeared a promising phenomenon, from the strikers' point of view, the lack of support was both painful and detrimental. Yet the fact is that most workers in the trade union world simply did not regard the gasworkers' strike against profit-sharing as a life and death question. The strike committee, of course, as well as newspapers in the labor circle, including _Justice_, _Labour Elector_, and _Star_, blamed the working class for indifference and for failing to provide noticeable support, moral or financial. Indeed, _Commonweal_ went so far as to urge a general strike in the London area--but all such counsel was ignored.[32] The strikers even failed to obtain support from fellow gasworkers in London. The workers of the Gas Light and Coke Company considered a sympathy strike but dropped the idea on the company's promise that it would not supply the South Metropolitan with any commodity whatsoever.[33]

The strikers maintained their spirit for a month, but with no prospect of success, that spirit proved ever more difficult to maintain. The men who had replaced the striking stokers soon learned the work and gas production reached two thirds of its normal level within several days. To bes sure, the number of stokers now engaged was double the former number. Livesey paid the new men 50 s. per week plus a bonus of L 2 bonus, compared to the 40s. he had paid the old stokers. Still it was not simply another case of business as usual. For one thing, many injuries took place. Even skilled workers sometimes burned themselves in the process of drawing and discharging coal. With no experience, then, the new men were much more likely to burn themselves and many had to leave. Others left as soon as they had earned sufficient money. Livesey later admitted that maintaining the workforce was one of his greatest difficulties during the strike.

In hopes of settling the strike, the union now suggested that if the proposed profit-sharing scheme were modified in terms of their suggestions they would guarantee the company no strike for 12 months and do all they could to help the scheme work. Their suggestion included an understanding that the agreement would end quarterly, and that the men would obey the "reasonable" orders of the foremen, not simply "the orders" of the foremen as stipulated in the agreement.[34] Livesey, however, had no intention of accepting this compromise, for he had sufficient funds to carry on the battle, and his new men, despite frequent injuries were catching up to the old level of gas production.

The strike ended on February 14, having lasted six weeks. It was a triumph for Livesey and a disaster for the Gasworkers Union. The cost to both sides was tremendous: the direct cost of the strike to the company was no less than L 50,000 while the indirect expenses and losses amounted to half that sum; the union's lost at least L 5,000. Livesey admitted that it was a tolerably heavy price but insisted that it was probably "the best work ever done, and the most profitable investment ever made by the company."[35]

Why did the strike fail? The reasons were manifold. The first was the potent combination of the company's strike preparation and its extensive financial resources. It was a graphic illustration of the theory that if an employer was truly determined, he could defeat any strike. With its thorough preparation and its monetary reserves, not to mention its assistance from the police, the company was formidable. Yet perhaps an equally important reason lay in the strikers' overestimation of both their power and talent. The well-trained gasworker may have seemed irreplaceable, but his sort of skill was by no means sophisticated and was eventually acquired by his blackleg. Livesey testified that if a yard laborer or a farm laborer was put into the retort house and trained, he could become a skilled stoker in two or three weeks.[36] Also, the timing of the strike was unfortunate. While it came during a period when both gas demand and gas production were at their peak, it also came during the slack season in most other trades and industries, and thus blacklegs could easily be recruited.

Finally, the indifference of both the general public and other working people deprived the strike of any real chance of success. The public misunderstood the issue: many of them thought it was simply a matter of wages and responded with scant sympathy, being aware that the gasworkers were already receiving fairly high wages.[37] Even those who did understand the issue were less than sympathetic. Profit-sharing seemed to them a well-intended gift from the employer, and what was one to make of a trade union striking against an apparently benevolent employer offering an apparently generous bonus? It was viewed as only "a manifestation of that stupid folly of the unions."[38]

Somewhat more surprisingly, a similar feeling was to be found among the working class. Socialists and the more articulate worker groups were aware of the co-opting nature of profit-sharing, but the average workman failed to see the essence of the conflict. There were also those who criticized the gasworkers for being unprepared for the strike. The Boot and Shoemakers' Union, for instance, reproached the Gasworkers Union for calling the strike without being ready: "In those cases where the men had no real organization to depend upon and practically no funds to feed them, as in the case of the South Metropolitan gas stokers' struggle, the men have not been successful, and we cannot but express our opinion that the men were ill-advised."[39] The strike was thus a failure not only from the standpoint of fighting effectively against the company but also in terms of enlisting the sympathy and solidarity of fellow workers.

Meanwhile, even as the strike had been going on, the profit-sharing scheme had been implemented with the new men as its beneficiaries. It was to become one of the most publicized, successful, and admired schemes of its kind and remained so for over 60 years, or until the nationalization of the gas industry brought about its termination. Some idea of the stellar position the South Metropolitan scheme occupied in the profit-sharing movement can be gained simply by looking at the 1920 report of the Board of Trade on profit-sharing and co-partnership. The Board chose 1889 as a landmark in the history of profit-sharing because that was the year in which the South Metropolitan's scheme was launched.[40] Now we turn to examine the operation of the scheme itself.

The Development of the Profit-sharing Scheme and the Transition into Co-partnership

Unlike the Lever Brothers plan, which we shall

discuss in the next chapter, the South Metropolitan scheme was nondiscriminatory and democratic in terms of those participating and also in terms of the bonus rate. The scheme was open to all employees provided they satisfied the requirement of length of employment--one year for the regular staff--and it paid the same rate of bonus to every participant. Establishing different ratios among various classifications of employees was highly complicated and impractical because, even in the gasworks, there were always too many different groups--stokers, fitters, laborers, clerks, lamplighters, etc. A uniform rate made the administration of the scheme much simpler. More importantly, Livesey realized that sharing at the same rate with every employee would help in bringing about a feeling of solidarity between himself and his employees and in creating the picture of a big, happy family, everyone in the same boat.

As fair and egalitarian as it appeared, however, it discriminated in several ways. First, it was subject to discrimination by the very nature of the scheme under which the bonus was awarded on salaries and wages, for the larger the salary or wage, the larger the bonus. Second, Livesey introduced a separate arrangement whereby to evaluate the merits of individual workers: the agreement signed by each employee terminated at a different time from all others and thus each case could be scrutinized individually. While this arrangement was introduced primarily to prevent the entire workforce from giving notice and striking at the same time, it also served for a closer evaluation of each worker's merits.

Finally and more specifically, the rules of the profit-sharing scheme allowed the directors to reserve the right to refuse permission to sign an agreement with any man who took "no interest in the welfare of the company or who is wasteful of the company's property, or careless, or negligent in the performance of his duty." Although the agreement, in principle, promised the worker 12 month job security, it obliged the company to keep this promise only if the worker 'shall remain sober, honest, industrious, and able to do the work allotted to him.'[41] Under such conditions, the elimination of disloyal and indifferent workers was a simple matter.

Perhaps the most significant contribution of the South Metropolitan scheme was its transition from simple profit-sharing to co-partnership. It was to become a landmark of its kind: whenever co-partnership was discussed, the South Metropolitan scheme was referred to. Except for the system introduced at William Thomson and Son, a woollen manufacturer in Huddersfield, the South Metropolitan scheme was the most progressive to be found anywhere. Above all, it was notable because, being in so large a company, it affected so many. It seemed to prove that co-partnership and worker participation were feasible even in large-scale firms. To understand how this transformation from profit-sharing to co-partnership took place, we should first look at the changes in Livesey's thinking.

Livesey's original perspective did not go beyond the simpler notion of profit-sharing; the idea of co-partnership was to develop only gradually in his mind. The evolution of his ideas thus consisted of several stages. In the first, he was still resisting the idea of co-partnership. As early as 1892, he told the Royal Commission on Labour, on which he also served as a commissioner, that he had thought of allowing employees to sit on the board, but "the time has not come for it yet." There could be advantages in it but there were also practical difficulties and therefore he did not see any way to it.[42] By the time the Commission turned in its final report in 1894, however, he had added a memorandum in which he presented his view on the next step after profit-sharing, that is, making the employees shareholders and giving them a proper role in the responsibilities of management.[43]

The first step in this direction came in 1894, when Livesey specified in the profit-sharing agreement that one half of the total bonus should be invested in the company's ordinary stock. In this stage, however, Livesey still viewed profit-sharing as a prerequisite to the establishment of co-partnership. Thus, when William Lever, in 1901, attacked the profit-sharing system and advocated what he called "prosperity-sharing," Livesey vigorously defended profit-sharing, asserting that "the goal is partnership...and the only way I can see for its attainment is by means of profit-sharing."[44]

Livesey, however, eventually came to feel that "profit-sharing does harm and very little good," and concluded that only co-partnership would provide a genuine solution.[45] Profit-sharing gave the worker job security and the employer strike security, but Livesey saw in this no creation of a deep common interest between employer and employee. Security against strikes was not enough; an identity of interest ought to be created. Therefore, Livesey concluded that profit-sharing did not go far enough and that it was at best only a half-way house on the road to a total identification of interest between employer and employee.. Indeed, it stopped "half-way between a pension and partnership."[46]

What, then, made Livesey hit on the idea of co-partnership? The immediate and obvious explanation was Livesey's recognition of co-partnership as the best means of enlisting employee loyalty. As was referred to in Chapter III, a workingman shareholder at the Taff Vale Railway, who held L 5 of the company stock and refused to join his fellow workers in striking, gave him the idea. Making the worker a shareholder seemed to offer many advantages. First of all, it was expected that by becoming a shareholder, the worker would learn something of the risks and the ups and downs of capital, and that his view of things would thereby be enlarged. He would learn that there were two sides to the question of labor and that labor was not, as the socialists claimed, the only factor in producing profits and creating wealth. It would help the workman to better understand the economic aspects of business, and make him look at the employer's side of industrial questions as well as his own.[47]

However, the essence of co-partnership was, in a phrase, the closer linking of the employee's destiny with that of the company. Livesey had learned from the stokers' strike that kind feeling and friendly sentiments on the part of the employer would not by themselves keep his workmen loyal. He never forgot the strike of the winter of 1889 when the stokers of the company, "almost to a man, mainly old servants and many near the pension age, at the bidding of the union, left their work never to return."[49] This was all the more inexplicable in view of the fact that Livesey's company was one of the pioneers in providing workers with various welfare benfits. Now he realized that something more than simple welfare provisions would be necessary to bind the men to the company. He repeatedly claimed that the solution to an industrial war was industrial co-operation, and criticized arbitration and conciliation for falling short of the object of industrial peace on the grounds that they only accentuated the antagonism by stressing the difference between capital and labor. Conciliation and arbitration were paliatives at best; what was needed was "the union of capital and labor."[50]

Moreover, co-partnership seemed to Livesey an inevitable historical development--indeed the fulfillment of the prophecy by the Italian revolutionary Mazzini: that the laborer, who was originally a slave, then a serf, now a hireling, must ultimately become a partner.[51] Livesey was deeply impressed by Mazzini's insight and frequently cited this phrase. Believing strongly in it, Livesey not only viewed the wage system as transitional, but partnership in some form as the final stage in industrial organization: partnership in profit and loss, in responsibility, and in management. He believed that the worker could render hearty, interested, intelligent service, but felt that mere day wages would not pay for it, because present wages were "the wages of mediocrity."[52]

Livesey admitted that the unrest of the present time was largely due to unequal distribution of property but dismissed socialism as utterly unacceptable. He was a member of the Anti-Socialist Union and vigorously attacked socialism publicly and privately:

> Socialism is not the way to make the poor richer. Under Socialism, every man is to be the servant of the state and there would be no freedom under it and freedom is what man wants and on which he thrives best.[53]

He admired co-partnership because it seemed the best antidote to socialism by its power to transform the "have nots" into the "haves." He was deeply concerned with the rise of the Labour Party. In his letter congratulating Lord Robert Cecil after the 1906 election, Livesey predicted that the old parties would submerge and "the struggle would be between the 'have nots' and the 'haves.'" He would like to see a more equitable distribution of property but "not in the socialist way."[54]

Livesey was shrewd enough to recognize the importance of labor management in harmonizing capital and labor. Yet, in spite of his proclaimed desire for "identity of interest," the relationship he wanted was one based on paternalism, on the relationship of what Macaulay described as the great man and the poor. He longed for "brave days of old," when "the great man helped the poor, and the poor man loved the great."[55] Livesey spent all his life in close touch with his workmen. He was born and grew up in premises adjoining the gasworks and they were in fact his playground. He had known the men from their childhood, either through Sunday school or temperance work. "We were very happy before the strike," he recalled. "I knew the men and when I came into the office I knew every man by name."[56] When the union came, one foreman said to Livesey: "You know, sir, the workmen are totally different to what they were in your early days."[57]

Livesey saw the workmen as children who had been accustomed to acting under orders for many generations, and who therefore needed leaders. Their "natural leaders" were "employers who might have neglected that duty with ...the result that working men have been moved by the men who control the trade unions."[58] Indeed, even after the strike he did not cease to be a paternalistic employer to the men who had deserted him. He tried to provide the strikers with work; a magnanimous response under the circumstances. In the same spirit, he informed them about another gasworkers' strike in Leeds and arranged for their work there as blacklegs.[59]

And it was the same paternalism that underlay his transformation of profit-sharing into the co-partnership system. When the profit-sharing scheme was started, saving was not compulsory, but the workmen were encouraged to leave their bonus on deposit at 4 percent interest. However, to Livesey's considerable disappointment, less than half the men did so. There were two reasons why the workers preferred their bonus in cash: first, they were not quite certain that the money they received was their own unless they made direct contact with it, and second, because they were afraid that if they left their bonus with the company and showed the company officers the amount of their savings, their wages would be reduced. Profit-sharing was, after all, an unprecedented system and the workers were not sure how it operated and how it would affect their wages. But the main reason for the cash withdrawal was that the workman, after all, needed every penny of all his earnings. Charles Booth's survey on the laboring class in London revealed that the living standard of gasworkers in East London by no means enabled them to live a comfortable life in spite of their relatively higher wages among unskilled workers.[60] Livesey, however, did not take this into consideration and warned against the withdrawal of an excessive part of the bonus.

Livesey agreed with the view that property in society was not fairly divided, yet he refused to blame only the upper classes for this disparity. He believed much of the working class's misery was its own fault, that working men might have been and "might soon become owners of a large amount of property if they did not spend their earnings on drink or worse and waste them on betting."[61] Livesey was a staunch teetotaler and actively involved himself in promoting teetotalism, serving as the treasurer of the National Temperance League. Not only did he discourage drinking among his employees, he banned betting and going to money lenders. If any information on such behavior was received, the employee concerned was excluded from the scheme.

The Co-partnership Committee and the System of Workman Directors

In spite of the heavy-handed paternalism we have just examined, the South Metropolitan scheme contained progressive features. The main body of the South Metropolitan scheme was carefully thought out and consisted of three parts: first, the profit-sharing bonus and later the cumulative stock under co-partnership; second, the co-parnership committee; third, worker representation in management through workman directors. The co-partnership committee, the system of employee representation, was an especially important aspect of the South Metropolitan scheme. The committee was originally composed of 36 members: 18 nominated by the directors and 18 elected by the workers. As of 1898, the 18 nominees included the chairman, 4 engineers, 1 clerk, 3 superintendents, and the foremen of 6 stations; the workers' representatives were elected in a proportion consistent with the number of workers at each station.[62]

In 1910, the number of co-partnership committee members was increased from 36 to 54 and it was provided that "candidates must hold and continue to hold while in office on the committee not less than L 25 of stock, and they must have been not less than 5 years in the company's service."[63] This provision all too obviously favored those who had substantial service, tended to be loyal, and maintained a respectable company nest egg.

The committee's chief function was to administer the scheme, but through its subcommittees it also dealt with the accident fund, the provident fund, and when war came, the war fund. Yet, the committee's greatest contribution was made not in administering the scheme but in reducing friction between management and workers. Charles Carpenter, the successor of George Livesey, described the co-partnership committee as follows:

> The committee is, in fact, a small scale parliament of labor, with business-like habits and a directness of action which would credit to its purpose. With it in operation, no one need conceal a grievance until it festers, and nor keep back any idea for greater unity of effort.64

Yet in the final analysis, apart from its human relations value and its symbolic significance as an example of worker democracy, the co-partnership committee played a minor role. Apart from helping to administer the scheme, its principal business was largely a matter of conducting such welfare programs as the ambulance service and the widows and orphans' society. It was never to handle any of the wages, for example.[65] The excuse for this was of course that the workers were represented on the board of directors, which assumed the supreme authority for such questions. But in fact did the system of workman directors meet such a claim? Let us see.

In 1894, an arrangement was made to the effect that half the bonus should be reserved for buying company stock under each employee's name as well as in the name of the collective body of workmen. In 1896, the company sponsered a bill that would empower the stock-holding employees to elect directors from their own class when the aggregate amount of stock held by the employees exceeded L 40,000 in nominal value. When this total was reached in 1898, the act was implemented, and one vote was given to every L 10 value of shares.[66]

The requirements for a workman director were extremely demanding: the candidate ought to have been continuously in the company's employment not less than 14 years, and ought to have held not less than L 120 company stock accumulated under the co-partnership scheme. Furhther as the aggregate holding of stock by the employees increased, so did the minimum requirement for stock held by a candidate:[67]

Aggregate Holding		Candidate's Holding	
	L 200,000		L 120
	300,000		140
	400,000		160
	500,000		180
One-third of capital or more			200

The extreme difficulty of meeting the requirements can be seen in the number of men eligible: in 1906, out of some 8,000 workers, only 14 were possible candidates for the role of workman director.[68]

What was that role exactly? Charles Carpenter stated publicly that the employee directors would exert a "very real and mighty influence on the policy of the company in regard to the employees with their intimate knowledge and experience."[69] But in reality, that influence was more marginal than mighty. First of all, workman directors were always in a minority on the board and thus their voting power was slight. Secondly, they were expected to make their contribution only in the area of labor policy, a role so limited it could have been more practicably handled by the system of joint committee or council. Even Carpenter, on a different occasion, was to admit that the workers' influence on the prosperity of the company was "greater by their work in the co-partnership committee than by work in the board room."[70]

Neither were the workers overwhelmingly enthusiastic for worker directors. In 1900, for instance, the total number of employees at six stations was 2,852, but only 1,865--65 percent--participated in the election of the workman directors. In 1906, not one of the 14 workers eligible chose to run, and the one incumbent worker director maintained his seat in an uncontested election.[71] Therefore, it is clear that in spite of all the propaganda, worker participation at South Metropolitan was meager. The most significant feature of the co-partnership system remained its material benefits.

Material Benefits under co-partnership and Employee Loyalty

The financial gain of the worker under the system was considerable. As shown in the table below, the company failed to pay a bonus of less than 7.5 percent on wages and salaries only on rare occasions. In 1920, the total stock held by the co-partners stood at L 422,000. As the employees in the same year ranged between 7,925 and 9,734, of whom 8,200 were qualified to participate, the average holding of each worker stood at L 51.[72]

From the worker's standpoint, this was a considerable amount. J. W. Higgins, a stoker, was proud to have even L 7 in 1892, two years after the scheme was started. It was for him a considerable addition to wages, "I think no man ought to turn against it, no working man at all," he asserted to the Royal Commission on Labour. "I think it is a benefit to them."[73] One anonymous employee of the company sent a letter to the London Daily Chronicle in 1899 and explained how much his position had improved since the scheme was initiated:

> Ten years ago, when it was started, I had a wife and family, and consequently it was difficult for me to save...I had not a penny, and doubtless that could have been my position today if Mr.Livesey had taken no more notice of the welfare of his employees than some other employers.74

His position was fortunate indeed: he had sold some of his

Table 7.1 Co-partnership Bonuses and Employee Shareholdings

Year	N of employees	Bonus	% of bonus on wages	Shares and deposits held by employees
1895		13,538 L	6 %	L
1896		17,417	7.5	
1897		18,562	7.5	
1898	3,664	19,296	7.5	
1899		21,028	8.25	
1900	4,988	24,305		
1901		10,357		
1902		8,288		
1903		22,887		
1904	4,598	34,341	9.75	264,000
1905	5,050	42,000	9.75	264,000
1906	5,000	43,962	9.75	309,000
1907	5,200	45,590	9.75	327,367
1908	5,146	36,426	7.5	363,367
1909	5,369	37,122	7.5	382,424
1910	5,459	41,133	8.25	401,038
1911	5,403	43,043	8.25	423.721
1912	5,951	45,350	8.25	439,065
1913	6,225	48,348	8.25	444,392
1914	6,303	49,189	8.25	450,683
1917	8,578	28,621	3.75	402,500
1918	8,500	Nil	Nil	412,800
1919	7,667	Nil	Nil	342,385
1920	9,200	Nil	Nil	355,640

Source: SMGC, "Proprietors' Minute Book", 1894-1920; Clarke, Nicholls, and Coombs, _The Proof of the Pudding_ (London: 1919).

stock in 1899, which had been accumulated through the bonus and valued at L 40, and with that and a loan from the company's building society had bought a house and still kept stock of L 65. "So you see this scheme gives me capital. Using it carefully, I am able to greatly better my position still further--namely, my bonus at present is L 20 and my saving through the building society about L 20." To him, it was "beyond the dreams of avarice, without co-partnership."[75] Quite obviously, then, the co-partnership bonus provided a way for the worker to elevate his material circumstances. Some of the employees with sufficient savings were able to sell stock and leave the company to found businesses of their own.

Although significant to the individual worker, the aggregate shares held by the employees never reached more than one sixteenth of the total capital. In order to obtain majority control on the board of directors, the workers would have had to hold more than half the shares and each worker would have had to possess an average of about L 500.[76] But of course the acquisition of stock amounting to L 500 through the co-partnership bonus would have required an eternity.

If the workers' holding was small in proportion to total holdings, however, it was by no means negligible in absolute terms. In 1907, for instance, the value of employee stock and other deposit with the company amounted to L 348,000. This was equal to the capital invested in the three largest gas companies in Essex-Chelmsford, Colchester, and Southend. In other words, had they chosen to become entrepreneurs, the South Metropolitan employees could in theory have purchased these companies and run them for themselves.[77]

What did the workers give to the company in exchange for these benefits? Loyalty certainly, and to a degree, greater efficiency. And it was, that loyalty that George Livesey wanted above all else from co-partnership. He was concerned with saving money and improving productivity, of course, but loyalty was paramount if only because it was what the union hated to see. In fact, Livesey simply refused to acknowledge labor organization once the strike was history. No member of the Gasworkers Union was employed, and every worker was required to renounce membership before being accepted into the profit-sharing scheme--a practice that continued until 1902. Asked by the Labour Commission in 1892 if he believed in workers' organizations, he promptly replied, "No, certainly not." He dismissed any future relationship with the Gasworkers Union: "Not with these Socialists, for that is what they are--they are all Socialists."[78]

He openly admitted that his profit-sharing scheme was "an anti-union motive, no doubt." It was to "protect ourselves against the union by attaching the men to the company."[79] He viewed trade unionism to be incompatible with profit-sharing. "The two things are directly opposed. Trade unions are antagonistic to the employer; they are the union versus the employer; in our case it is the union of the man with the employer."[80] He believed that the success of profit-sharing would eventually remove undermine any need there might be for trade unions. "Industrial salvation would not come through the trade unions," he firmly believed, "but through co-operation between employer and employee."[81]

Trade unionism in the South Metropolitan was virtually destroyed. Union members who were taken back after the strike either had to leave the union or to conceal their membership. Will Thorne himself admitted in 1892 that the union had insufficient power to intervene in the company's affairs. On several occasions, the company dismissed union members immediately upon receiving negative information about them from co-workers.[82] Livesey not only banished the Gasworkers Union from his company but vigorously supported the anti-union movement in general. He was described by Collison, the leader of the Free Labour Association, the strikebreaking organization, as "one of the best friends Free Labour has ever possessed in this country."[83] He donated generously to the Association and threw a feast for those attending its annual meeting.

Only one year after the profit-sharing scheme had been started, Livesey could report to the shareholders that for the purpose of "attaching the men to the company" it had produced the desired effect.[84] Meanwhile after the defeat at the South Metropolitan, the Gasworkers Union also experienced serious setbacks in other London gas companies. Thus one observer noted that trade unionism appeared nonexistent in the gasworks, and that the union had insufficient members in any of the London gas companies to contest management policy.[85]

By the time Livesey introduced a similar scheme at the South Suburban Company, of which he was also chairman, he was able to rely on his employees' loyalty to such a degree that he could tell them that they were free to accept or reject the scheme.[86] On this occasion, Will Thorne came down to the South Suburban gasworks and inquired about it, but did not dare advise the men not to sign the agreement.

Indeed the union had become so weak at the South Metropolitan that Livesey was no longer concerned. At the same time, the union, which had once alarmed employers with its militancy, now adopted a moderate approach. Nevertheless, the clause in the profit-sharing agreement disqualifying members of the Gasworkers Union from participation in the scheme remained in force until 1902; it was then abolished at the request of the Labour Co-partnership Association, which had been deeply concerned over criticism of profit-sharing as a tactic against trade unions. Much of the criticism indeed derived from the practices of the South Metropolitan. However, the real reason for Livesey's decision to abolish the offensive clause was that the clause was no longer necessary. In 1894, A. Browne, chief engineer at Rotherhith station, observed the strongly marked difference between 1889 and 1894: in 1889, there had been a little hesitation over the non-union clause in the case of some workers but the hesitation had now "entirely passed away."[87]

Therefore, Livesey could assert to the Royal Commission on the Trade Disputes that insofar as the South Metropolitan and the South Suburban were concerned, a strike was "unthinkable and impossible...Unionists are not excluded but they are simply ignored."[88] Livesey never inquired into a worker's union membership for the simple reason that he considered it senseless to belong to a union. The worker now had something better.

The South Metropolitan employees indeed had few complaints to make. They were paid the full trade union wage rates under the eight-hour shift, and in those works where the 12 hour shift was applied, the workmen were paid proportionately more. They also enjoyed extensive welfare programs: pension, sick fund, paid holidays, etc. Above all, the 12 month agreement was particularly appreciated by the men. Livesey, after being challenged by A. Mundella, an "enlightened" employer who opposed the signing of the agreement with its intention of binding the men, proposed that the agreement be abolished. "The eagerness with which they all urged me not to interfere with the agreement in any way was almost pathetic," he maintained.[89] Charles Carpenter, the chief engineer, also testified that if they were not allowed to sign the agreement, the employees would be "highly aggrieved."[90]

This seems particularly ironical when we recall that the major objection of the Gasworkers Union to the profit-sharing plan had been precisely the 12-month contract, which they viewed as an attempt to "bind the workers hand and foot."[91] Indeed Will Thorne had claimed that the strike was simply a protest against the 12 month agreement. A former worker at the Greenwich station, however, sharply contradicted Thorne's claim and blamed the union leaders for striking "to crush profit-sharing whilst in the bud and before the men would fully see its many advantages."

> I never heard that objection raised myself. No sensible man would for a moment hesitate to sign such an agreement as I signed at East Greenwich. A few agitators scattered about the yard...and in the retort houses...and that caused all the trouble. They were men who belong to that class that are never satisfied with their own lot and endeavouring to make their fellows as discontented as themselves.92

Obviously, job security for a fixed period was of great value to the workman, whose trade was basically seasonal and who did not possess the sort of skill that would be in demand no matter what.

The relationship between the company and its employees could not have been better. One of the frequent employee letters of gratitude to Livesey read as follows:

> We have derived great benefits from your profit-sharing system and think it is one of the best methods ever started to bring master and men together. We would be extremely pleased to see it adopted in every firm throughout the country and that is our true and honest opinion.[93]

Every year a grand dinner party was given to co-partners and their wives at the Crystal Palace in which extravagant compliments were paid to the employers. One worker asserted what seemed to be the general view--that workers did not need union under profit-sharing and co-partnership because they had future security.[94]

Material benefits under co-partnership seem to have banished normal worker concerns. "Sleeping or waking, we are growing richer. Could anything be better?" they asked. They admitted that they gave "very little thought to matters outside those of the company." What they obtained from the observation of other workers was only an idea of "the advantages under which we work."[95] The Workman's Times blamed the South Metropolitan employees for having sold "their birthright for a mess of pottage," but the workers were indifferent to such complaints.[96] The fact that they were "co-partners" of the company also made them proud and self-respecting. "We have changed; we have been more careful," they claimed. "We have something to look for; we have shares in this great company."[97] They echoed the belief in the unitary ideology apparently planted in their mind by their employers. "If you honestly work for the company's advancement we automatically work for our own advancement because _we are the company_, or at least a very important limb of it."(Emphasis added.) "Capital and labor are frequently referred to as though there is something antagonistic between the two; but they are really complementary and should combine on terms fair to both."[98]

This closely resembles the typical statement of almost any employer. For them, the terms made between their employers and themselves seemed perfectly fair, and they were glad that the prediction of the "Socialists" in the bleak winter of 1889 failed to materialize. Notwithstanding the "dirty water that has been thrown on it by those so-called Socialists," one workman proclaimed, "co-partnership will stand as a monument to the greatness and intelligence of our employees."[99]

Another worker, wanted to see the spread of co-partnership all over the country so that "there will be little fear of trade disputes or the Socialist movement." H. T. Manley, a worker at the Old Kent Road station asserted that "the co-partnership scheme has given us peace.(Hear, hear). We never have strikes--we never think of it."[100] Joseph Newbold, a workman director, urged his fellow workers to avoid being swept away by the agitator:

> Seeing that we have such a heritage left us--a heritage that has lifted us from mere wage earners into shareholders--let us see to it that we are not made the tools of agitators, who would like to capture us because they see that if co-partnership should become more general their occupation as agitators would be gone. Let us not sell our great heritage for a mess of pottage...but each realize our individual responsibility and duty.[101]

A great deal of rhetoric was uttered, to be sure. But the reality also points to harmonious labor relations at the South Metropolitan. Its employees became non-union workers after the 1889 strike, and gladly remained so. Although Livesey withdrew the non-union clause from the profit-sharing agreement in 1902, and allowed "reasonable" unions such as old craft unions to survive, he never compromised with the "Socialist" Gasworkers Union. Neither were his employees attracted to the Gasworkers Union: the union had no followings at the South Metropolitan. And since the gasworkers constituted the majority of its employees, the South Metropolitan remained an essentially non-union company.

One barometer of worker loyalty is the absence of

strikes. After 1889, strikes were nonexistent at the South Metropolitan until the General Strike of 1926 when a mere 50 employees out of 8,000 left work. Even those 50 men, who responded to the unions' strike call, stressed that they had no grievance against the company: simply put, they were among that tiny fraction whose loyalty to their unions was stronger than their allegiance to the company.[102]

The loyalty of the South Metropolitan employees was also exhibited in the way they accepted the dilution of labor. The employment of women in the gasworks during the first World War, including the retorts and purifying plants, was strenuously resisted by most gasworkers. The South Metropolitan employees, however, did not raise any objection to dilution, and indeed, the South Metropolitan was known to employ the highest proportion of women workers at any gasworks. The same cordial attitude was demonstrated when the co-partnership scheme was hurt by the war economy. The higher cost of coal increased the cost of production; and consequently, the bonus disappeared, yet the South Metropolitan worker accepted the situation calmly. The lack of a bonus in fact persisted for several years, but during that time the employees still showed no sign of discontent. To be sure, the company continued to pay extra money apart from the sliding scale arrangement that existed under profit-sharing and the employee shareholders still received dividends on their stock. Therefore, the absence of a bonus did not mean the absolute disappearance of extra income.

Nevertheless the understanding and support of the employees were remarkable under the circumstances.

The Effect of Co-partnership on Efficiency

Now let us turn to the question of efficiency. It must be noted again that efficiency was by no means the primary concern of George Livesey, even though co-partnership seemed to increase it. Efficiency can be achieved in many ways, of course, but most directly, it can be achieved either by introducing improved technology and machinery or by increasing labor productivity. The South Metropolitan achieved greater efficiency in both ways. By winning employee loyalty, the company could utilize extensive labor saving machinery and thus greatly increase productivity. At the same time, the bonus inspired the workmen to perform with greater diligence and greater care, eliminating, or at least, curtailing previous wasteful practices.

The cost of production in the gas industry was determined to a large extent by the price of coal, yet labor expenses were also an important cost element. Until the emergence of the Gasworkers Union in 1889, the notion reducing expenses by replacing workers with machinery was not a concern for most gas employers. As early as 1860, machines for the drawing and charging of retorts had been invented, but the trouble and expense had prevented them from being widely used since manual labor was docile and satisfactory. The cost of carbonizing wages in the Gas Light and Coke Company, for instance, had been 2s. 6d. per ton of coal prior to 1889. After the union's demand for the eight-hour day and Sunday double time were conceded, the cost of carbonizing had risen to 3s. 6d. a ton.[103] At the South Metropolitan, the eight-hour day had increased the carbonizing wages 25 percent, from 2s. 7d. per ton of coal to 3s. 7d. Other demands by the workers caused the total cost of retort house to labor increase 45 percent, or L 40,000 a year. As a result, the profits of the South Metropolitan had dropped from 8.91 percent in 1889 to 6.3 percent in 1890.[104]

Now the adoption of profit-sharing reduced the cost of carbonizing tremendously: it decreased to 2s. 2d. by 1901. One reason for this was the workers' greater diligence and economy. Under the system, the employees had the strongest possible interest in reducing the cost of production and thereby increasing the company's profits. This was because the whole of the surplus profits were applied in reducing the price of gas, a reduction that automatically increased the employees' bonuses. The workmen now became more careful with their tools and materials. When coal was spilt, they were reported to have complained to the offender, "That will go against our profit-sharing."[105] It was not surprising, then,to see these workers act like foremen to each other and to report that "so and so is a loafer and a disgrace to profit-sharing."[106] Thanks to the worker's greater care, accidents decreased considerably, in fact by almost 40 percent after the system was introduced.[107]

The cost of carbonizing at the South Metropolitan was much cheaper than at other non-profit-sharing companies; and observers argued, not surprisingly, that the non-union workers at the South Metropolitan worked more efficiently than the union workers elsewhere. The South Metropolitan was promoted as the best example of non-union efficiency in a series of the *Times*'s articles on the union practice of restricted output that were geared towards anti-union public opinion. The articles pointed out that while non-union stokers at the South Metropolitan drew 50 retorts an hour, the unionists at other gas companies using similar machinery kept it to 40.[108]

The statistics of two London gas companies seem to support this allegation. In 1881, the gas price of the South Metropolitan was 2s. 10d. per 1,000 cubic feet, whereas that of the Gas Light and Coke was 3s. 2d. By 1898 the gap had widened: 2s. 3d. as against 3s. per 1,000 cubic feet.[109]

Several factors contributed to an absolute difference in the cost of production. The GLCC had to carry its gas for a longer distance than did the South Metropolitan and therefore had to use more exhaust power in pumping gas.[110] However, the most important factor in reducing the cost of production seems to have been new machinery, which the South Metropolitan made extensive use of. Although the company was not particularly concerned with reducing labor cost, it now saw an opportunity to introduce new systems of carbonizing whereby "a large amount of labor will be unnecessary, now that the union was destroyed."[111] The adoption of machinery at the South Metropolitan became so extensive by 1905 that Charles Carpenter, then chief engineer, testified before the special committee of the Charity Organization Society, that "a good deal of our carbonizing work, which was at one time done wholly, or nearly wholly, by hand, is now done nearly wholly by machinery."[112] Already in 1892, Livesey reported that between 1889 and 1892, the introduction of new machines allowed for a 60 percent reduction in the workforce employed in carbonizing an equivalent amount of coal.[113] And this trend became stronger as time went on. The number of workers employed in the retort house declined from over 2,000 in 1889 to 1,250 by 1907, even as the company was doubling gas production.[114]

Subsequently, the proportion of retort house men, once the nucleus of the gasworkers, to the total workforce declined considerably. In 1889, at least 67 percent of all the men employed in the winter were actually engaged in the retort house; in 1907, only 20 percent. The passion for labor saving methods, Livesey confessed, was "crazy." It was so because the saving in retort house wages came to only about 2d. per 1,000 cubic feet of gas sold. Of this, about half was absorbed by interest on the cost of, and maintenance on the machinery. In short, the saving by the machine was so small that gas managers would not have thought it worthwhile to introduce it except for a more important purpose--securing independence from the workers.[115]

Understandably, the critics of profit-sharing saw the South Metropolitan scheme as a typical case of an employer manipulating the workforce for its own ends. Ramsay Macdonald, for one, asserted:

> The South Metropolitan bound its men to itself in precisely the same way as the proverbial man bound his donkey to his will by hanging a carrot in front of the animal's nose. Hoping ever to reach the carrot, the donkey romped home, and the driver's end was cheaply accomplished.[116]

Harry Quelch made an estimate of cost reduction under the co-partership system at the South Metropolitan. By his account, worker productivity increased by 14 percent and thus allowed the company, in theory at least, to discharge one out of seven workers. If the six remaining men received 2s. additional pay as bonus, then, since 20s. was the entire wage of a dismissed man, the employer would save 8s. Thus, Quelch concluded that profit-sharing in any form, while appearing to increase labor's share of the product, "really reduces it and ensures a greater expenditure for a smaller remuneration...and proportionally increases the number of the unemployed."[117]

The extensive use of machinery indeed curtailed the number of workers required to produce the same amount of gas, but there was another consideration: insofar as the company was expanding, it could always absorb the extra labor force. The company in fact did so until the early days of the twentieth century by which time the gas industry's expansion halted. After that, the higher productivity brought about by machinery caused a serious unemployment problem. Livesey himself admitted that labor-saving machinery had driven the men out of jobs and worried that those who lost jobs were in great danger of drifting into the ranks of paupers. Yet, he blamed the Gasworkers Union for leaving the gas companies no option but to adopt machinery to displace workers.[118]

Livesey was personally responsible for the results of the South Metropolitan scheme. Without his dominating personality, persistent paternalism, and unbroken determination, the scheme would not have developed as it did. In commenting on Livesey's dominant position, John

Burns suggested in 1907 that as soon as Livesey was gone, the system would end at the South Metropolitan and the profit-sharing movement in the gas industry would be halted.[119]

Contrary to Burns's prediction, the South Metropolitan scheme not only survived its founder's absence but prospered. The respect and admiration Livesey inspired in his employees was shown by the thousands of workers who marched in his funeral procession on a rainy October day. In his enlogy, S.Y Shoubridge, a gas employer paid Livesey high praise: "Thousands of tongues at the works of the South Metropolitan and South Suburban Companies blessed him for his efforts for their advancement by means of the co-partnership; and thousands yet unborn would live to bless his name or the great benefits which would result from it."[120]

The Progress of Co-partnership in the Gas Industry

John Burns was wrong not only in his prediction about the South Metropolitan but about the further development of co-partnership in the gas industry: profit-sharing, in fact, would not be in its heyday in this industry until around 1908. The fact that it took place only then is curious because the gas industry enjoyed especially favorable circumstances for the success of profit-sharing and co-partnership. Even before Livesey's conversion to it, employers were preaching the merits of the system at a gas engineers' meeting in 1881.[121] Now we turn to examine what those favorable conditions were.

In the first place, the gas industry enjoyed local monopoly. The use of gas for public utility commenced in the early nineteenth century, the first chartered gas company appearing on the scene in 1812. In 1860, the first major step towards eliminating competition was taken. The Metropolis Gas Act granted the London companies a virtual monopoly in their respective areas of supply, and subsequently this arrangement was extended to the entire country. In addition to monopoly status, the gas industry enjoyed an unlimited expansion until approximately 1910. The gas sold per authorized undertaking increased from 129,000 cubic feet to 224,000 cubic feet between 1882 and 1909, and during this period, the number of undertakings doubled, rising from 400 to 826. At the same time, the total output trebled from 66,614 million cubic feet to 198,923 million cubic feet per year.[122] The gasworks were expanding along with the city population, a new district springing into existence and soon after a new gasworks being created. Amalgamation was a persistent phenomenon in the gas industry, largely for reasons of cost reduction.

The third favorable condition for the gas industry vis-a-vis profit-sharing was that the industry never experienced losses: it was a monopoly and therefore a company could always pass along its losses to its consumers. The success of profit-sharing schemes was a corollary of this arrangement. At the same time, the business cycle did not affect the industry in the same way it affected other industries. Demand was constant in the gas indutry. Although there were the inevitable seasonal fluctuations between the summer and winter months, there was nothing like the irregular intense business cycle of boom and slump.

Finally, the gas price was based on a sliding scale. By statutory requirement, surplus profits were used to reduce the price so that the consumer could indirectly benefit. Both the maximum dividend to shareholders and the maximum price of gas were fixed by law. As a result, since the companies had no real claim on the surplus profits, they had no serious reluctance when it came to using them for the benefit of their employees.

The internal situation of the gas companies also favored profit-sharing. First of all, most workers at the gasworks were paid on a time basis, which made the matter of determining the size of the bonus relatively simple. (Only the unloading and handling of coal involved piecework.) At the same time, the gas companies had established, from the early days, a fairly centralized management structure. Hiring and firing were largely handled not by foremen but by management, and the payment was made directly by the payroll office--this at a time when such customs as the foreman taking money from the employer and paying the men, or even buying them spirits at public houses, were still common in many industries. In the South Metropolitan, the system of centralized payment was already in place in the 1880s. Understandably, then, these internal and external circumstances contributed greatly to the development and success of the gas industry's schemes and particularly to that of the South Metropolitan.

This is not to imply that the gas industry was immune to industrial problems. The tendency for profits to fluctuate certainly existed, because the price of gas largely depended on the price of coal, over which the gas industry had no control. Also, competition with other utility sources, such as electricity and oil, became keener. The South Metropolitan, for instance, had to compete with five electric supply companies and four municipal suppliers.[123] But there was no competition between gas companies. The favorable conditions just discussed were indeed exceptional in the British economic structure in the years 1880-1920. Generally, it was a time in which small-scale, family-oriented firms struggled for survival in the free market system.

In spite of favorable conditions in the industry and Livesey's strenuous efforts, no noticeable step was taken until after his death to incorporate co-partnership throughout the industry. The other companies' reluctance suddenly disappeared in 1908, when no fewer than 12 gas companies introduced the system. By 1912, 33 gas concerns, which manufactured 49 percent of the total gas produced in the United Kingdom, introduced profit-sharing. Why this sudden change?

There were no discernible changes in the industry itself around 1908. Business was conducted as usual with no serious labor trouble reported. The only distinctive feature was Livesey's increased propaganda, as he vigorously championed co-partnership in various meetings and public lectures. The papers he read in December 1907 and August 1908 provoked much discussion and great public interest. He died in the following October, and his death precipitated wide public discussion of his co-partnership scheme--what might be considered a proper tribute to a great man in the industry. At the GLCC shareholders' meeting in early 1909, when it was decided to adopt co-partnership, one voiced his company's determination: "As Sir George has shown us the way, we will do our best to follow it."[124]

Around the same time, Sir Christopher Furness, a captain of industry, announced the introduction of co-partnership in his shipbuilding works at Hartlepool. In early 1909, William Lever introduced a co-partnership scheme to the already well-known Port Sunlight soapworks.

The enthusiasm among leading businessmen, then, seems to have been behind the sudden burgeoning of profit-sharing and co-partnership in the gas industry. By the time of Livesey's death, a great obstacle to profit-sharing had been removed: trade unions, especially the Gasworkers Union, no longer pressed for opposition to it. Given the impressive material benefits which the union alone could not procure for its members, union leaders discretely retreated from their once outspoken criticism.

The highwater mark in the enthusiasm for profit-sharing was the GLCC's decision to introduce the system, since the company was the largest gas undertaking in the world, employing some 10,000 workers. The motives of the GLCC are interesting because of the peculiar relationship between the company and the South Metropolitan. Even though the GLCC and the South Metropolitan had different local monopolies, north and south of the Thames respectively, the GLCC maintained a keen interest in the business of the South Metropolitan.

There had been personal antagonism between Livesey and the directors of the GLCC and the latter publicly labeled Livesey "the uncompromising opponent of combination among workmen."[125] The antagonism of the GLCC management towards Livesey was understandable: the GLCC, with its higher gas prices and subsequent lower dividends than those of the South Metropolitan, was criticized by both shareholders and consumers. The shareholders and consumers attributed the higher gas price to inefficient management and the lack of a co-partnership system in the GLCC, although there were quite different reasons for the higher price, as we have already seen. Understandably, while Livesey was alive, the GLCC management was reluctant to be seen as a copycat follower of the South Metropolitan, which adopting co-partnership would have made it appear to be. After all, Livesey was the successful inventor of the system as practiced in the gas industry. With Livesey's death, the directors of the GLCC were free to adopt his method.

The GLCC employees were delighted with the decision. Their enthusiasm is clearly demonstrated by the fact that only 19 out of some 8,500 employees failed to sign the co-partnership agreement.[126] Letters from officers and workers were sent to the directors expressing their gratitude and asserting that they would do everything they could "to repay the shareholders."[127] With the GLCC joining the profit-sharing companies, all London gas concerns were run under the system: the South Suburban having practiced it since 1894. The whole gas supply industry of London--an organization second only to the railways in terms of the number of employees--was now based upon co-partnership principles.

Profit-sharing in the gas industry prospered. By the time nationalization took place in 1949, about 58 gas companies were practicing profit-sharing and co-partnership schemes, paying out L 400,000 annually to 52,000 employees.[128] The favorable conditions in the industry undoubtedly facilitated this large scale application of the system, yet perhaps the real reason lay in the fact that one of the most vigorous propagandists of the system happened to be a gas employer, and that the industry happened to encounter one of the most militant new trade unions. Without George Livesey and without the labor movement around the year 1889, profit-sharing would not have obtained the hold it did in the gas industry. It was an interesting example of how a dominant individual could change the contour of a company and even an industry, and how pressure from militant trade unionism transformed paternalistic employer practices into calculated labor relations based on industrial welfare.

Notes to Chapter VII

1.

Retort house men included coal-porter, coal-wheelers, coke-spreaders, firemen, and stokers, while yardmen and outsidemen comprised bricklayers, plasters, smiths, and a host of general laborers. For the composition of the workforce in the gas industry, see Charity Organization Society, Special Committee on Unskilled Labour, Minutes of Evidence, Charles Carpenter's testimony Q.828-969 (London: 1905); Political and Economic Planning, Report on the Gas Industry in Great Britain (London: 1939); F. Poppelwell, "The Gas Industry" in Seasonal Trades ed. Sidney Webb and A. Freeman (London: Constable, 1912); Trevor Williams, A History of the British Gas Industry (Oxford: Oxford Univ. Press, 1981).

2.

In Charles Booth's survey of the East London working class, 5,847 males were reported under the heading of gasworkers, of whom 5,577 were adults. C. Booth, Life and Labour of the People in London 2nd series, vol.3 (London: Macmillan, 1903), p.456.

3.

Eric Hobsbawm, "British Gas Workers 1873-1914" in Labouring Men: Studies in the History of Labour (Garden City, N.Y.: Doubleday, 1967).

4.

Indeed, gaswork and brickmaking were interchangeable in terms of time, for brickmaking was slack during the winter, and gaswork had slack season in the summer; as a result the composition of the workforce in the two was largely identical.

5.

Charity Organization Society, Minutes of Evidence, Q.911.

6.

S. Everard, The History of the Gas Light and Coke Company, 1812-1949 (London: Benn, 1949), p.117.

7.

Institute of Gas Engineers, Transactions, (1887), p.37. (Hereafter IGE).

8.
W. T. Layton, *The Early Years of the South Metropolitan Gas Company, 1833-1871* (London: Spottiswoode, Ballantyne, 1920); A. Holden, *The Co-partnership Scheme of the South Metropolitan Gas Company* (London: 1947). Many of the workers served the company for over 15 years, and even the Gaswokers Union admitted that the men, previous the the strike, were "loyal in their desire to serve the company faithfully and well," as their length of service so often demonstrated. See *Daily News*, Dec. 6, 1889.

9.
South Metropolitan Gas Company, *Co-partnership*, Oct. 1921, p.236.

10.
See Hobsbawm, "The Gas Workers," pp.190-2; Sidney and Beatrice Webb, Unpublished Trade Union Collection, Section A, vol.42, folios 299, 320, at the British Library of Political and Economic Science.

11.
H. Clegg, A. Fox, and A. F. Thompson, *A History of British Trade Unions since 1889* vol.1 (Oxford: Oxford University Press, 1964), p.90.

12.
The socialist element of the union acted strongly in cities such as Leeds where a small band of socialists took the initial steps to organize the men. See Ben Turner, *About Myself, 1863-1930* (London: H.Toulmin, 1930), p.79.

13.
Sidney and Beatrice Webb, *The History of Trade Unionism* (London: Longmans Green, 1920: rpt. Augustus M. Kelly, 1973), p.406.

14.
National Union of Gasworkers and General Labourers of Great Britain and Ireland, *Rule*, 1890 in the Webb Collections.

15.
No demand for higher wages at the formation of the union indicates their relative satisfaction with wages.

16.
General and Municipal Workers Union, *Souvenir History, 40 years, 1889-1929*, (London: 1929), pp.5, 16.

17.
Royal Commission on Labour, Group C, *Minutes of Evidence* Cd. 6894-ix (1893-4), Q. 26790. (Hereafter RC on

Labour).

18\. RC on Labour, Q. 26789; John Burns, _Speech delivered by John Burns on the Liverpool Congress_ (London: Green, McAllan and Feilden, 1890).

19\. RC on Labour, Q.26823-8.

20\. RC on Labour, Q.26828.

21\. RC on Labour, Q.26835.

22\. _Ratepayers' Chronicle and Parish Parliament_, Jan. 4, 1890.

23\. _Economic Journal_, "Successful Profit-sharing," 9 (1899), p.587.

24\. The accounts of the proposed profit-sharing scheme and the subsequent strike are based on Livesey's testimony to the RC on Labour; Thorne's testimony to he RC on Labour; Will Thorne, _My Life's Battle_ (London: George Newnes, 1925); _Commonweal_; _East London Observer_; _Daily News_; _Labour Elector_; _Ratepayers' Chronicle and Parish Parliament_; _Times_.

25\. RC on Labour, Q.27079-81.

26\. _Commonweal_, Dec.14, 1889, p.398.

27\. _Labour Elector_, Nov.23, 1889, p.328.

28\. SMGC, "Directors' Minute Book," Dec. 24, 1889.

29\. _Reynolds's Newspapers_, Dec. 8, 1889.

30\. Yvonne A. Kapp, _Eleanor Marx_, vol 2 _The Crowded Years 1884-1898_ (London: Virago, 1976), p.361.

31.
Karl Marx and Friedrich Engels, Articles on Britain (Moscow: Progress Publishers, 1971), p.523.

32.
Commonweal, Dec. 21,1889, p.406; Dec. 28, 1889, p.414; Justice, Jan. 1, 15, Feb.15, 1890.

33.
Reynolds's Newspaper, Jan. 5, 1890.

34.
Memorandum by the Gasworkers Union (London: 1890).

35.
SMGC, "Directors' Report" Dec. 1889, p. 5; IGE, Transactions (1892), p.346.

36.
RC on Labour, Q.26702.

37.
RC on Labour, Q.24639; South London Press, Dec. 28, 1889.

38.
Harry Quelch, The Co-partnership Snare (London: Twentieth Century, 1912), p.11.

39.
National Union of Boot and Shoe Operatives, Monthly Report (Leicester), Feb. 1890.

40.
Ministry of Labour, Report on Profit-sharing and Labour Co-partnership in the U.K., Cd. 544 (1920), p.iii. (Hereafter Report, 1920).

41.
SMGC, "Profit-sharing Agreement" in Report, 1920, p.179.

42.
RC on Labour, Q.27042-3.

43.
RC on Labour, Final Report, App.I. Memorandom by G. Livesey on Profit-sharing, p.154; Livesey "Profit-sharing--A Vindication," Economic Review, 2 (Oct. 1901), p.412.

44.
Livesey, "Vindication", p.421.

45.
Royal Commission on Poor Laws, Minutes of Evidence Cd. 5066 (1910), Q.83143.

46.
George Livesey, "Another Step in Promoting the Union o Capital and Labour," IGE, Transactions (1897), p.145.

47.
Livesey, "Vindication", p.411.

48.
George Livesey, The Profit-sharing Scheme of the South Metropolitan Gas Company: The History and Results (London: 1899), p.10.

49.
Livesey, "Co-partnership," p.54.

50.
Livesey, "Vindication," p.413.

51.
Livesey, "Co-partnership," p.57; SMGC, Co-partnership, 1 (1904), p.99.

52.
Livesey, "Vindication," p.412; SMGC, Co-partnership, 1904, p.99.

53.
SMGC, Co-partnership, 1 (1904), p.99; 5 (1908), p.194.

54.
Livesey's letter to Robert Cecil, Cecil Papers, British Museum Add. Mss. 51158, f.54-5.

55.
RC on Poor Laws, Q.83136 (49).

56.
RC on Poor Laws, Q.83136 (1).

57.
RC on Poor Laws, Q.83170.

58.
Times, Dec. 31, 1901, 13c. Livesey himself must have neglected his duty if we follow his argument since his own employees had been moved by the union leaders.

59.
Times, May 12, 1890, 7f; *People's Press*, July 12, 1890; RC on Labour, Q.24943-4.

60.
Charles Booth, *Life and Labour*, pp.456-8. Booth's survey, for instance, discovered that in 44.5 percent of the gaworkers' housholds two or more persons were living in a room.

61.
SMGC, *Co-partnership*, 1 (1907), p.3.

62.
Livesey, *Profit-sharing of the SMGC*, App. A. p.23.

63.
In 1918, the number was again increased to 82, so as to include representatives of the large number of women workers who had been taken on during the war. *Report*, 1920, p.57.

64.
Charles Carpenter, *Industrial Co-partnership* (London: Labour Co-partnership Association, 1921), p.47.

65.
However, the committee seems to have assumed wider functions as time went on. We can find that even wage questions were discussed in the committee meetings in the post-war years. SMGC, *Co-partnership*, 5 (1918), p.176.

66.
The number of employee directors was confined to three: two to manual workers and one to salaried officiers. As a result the employee directors remained a minority but they occupied a proportionally excessive part because the employee-shareholders held only some 7 percent of the total shares, and yet elected three out of ten directors.

67.
Report, 1920, p.53.

68.
SMGC, "Directors Minute Book," Oct. 10, 1906.

69.
Report, (1920), p.53.

70.
Carpenter, *Industrial Co-partnership* (London: Co-partnership Publishers, 1921), p.45.

71.
SMGC, "Directors' Minute Book," Oct. 10, 1906.

72.
The different numbers of employees were due to winter men, the qualification for whom to participate was three month continuous employment.

73.
RC on Labour, Q.24319.

74.
London Daily Chronicle, Sep. 29, 1899. Quoted in Livesey, *The Profit-sharing Scheme of the SMGC*, p.20.

75.
Quoted in Livesey, *The Profit-sharing scheme of the SMGC*, p.20.

76.
Labour Co-partnership, Nov. 1922, p.156.

77.
Labour Co-partnership, Jan. 1908, p.14.

78.
RC on Labour, Q.27010, 277058.

79.
RC on Trade Dispute, Q. 4569.

80.
Livesey, "The Failure of the Wages System of Payment and the Remedy--Profit-sharing," IGE, *Transactions* (1892), p.161.

81.
Livesey, "Vindication," p.417.

82.
RC on Labour, Q.26981.

83.
W. Collison, *The Apostle of Free Labour* (London: Hurst and Blackett, 1913), p.96.

84.
SMGC, "Proprietors' Report," Dec. 1890.

85.
Times, Dec. 28, 1901, 8e.

86. Livesey, _The Profit-sharing Scheme of the SMGC_

87. IGE, _Transactions_, (1894), p.47.

88. RC on Trade Dispute and Trade Combinations, _Minutes of Evidence_, Cd. 2826 (1907), Q.4333; RC on Poor Laws, Q.83173. Even before 1902, trade unions existed among some tradesmen and yardsmen. Amos Mann, the organizing secretary of the Labour Co-partnership Association, visited the South Metropolitan in 1913 to find out if the prevalent criticism on the company was valid--the criticism that the company did not allow the trade unions among the emplyees and that their bonus was simply the compensation for lower wages than union rates. Mann's finding was that many of the workers belonged to the unions. _Labour Co-partnership_, Aug. 1913, p.98.

89. Livesey, "Vindication," p.415.

90. IGE, _Transactions_, (1908), p.72.

91. Will Thorne's testimony, RC on Labour, Q. 24632.

92. RC on Labour, Q26872.

93. "Discussion on the Union of Capital and Labour," IGE, _Transactions_, (1897), pp.152-3.

94. _Times_, Oct. 10, 1899, 11e.

95. SMGC, _Co-partnership_, 1 (1904), p.150.

96. _The Workman's Times_, Feb. 27, 1891.

97. SMGC, _Co-partnership_, 5 (1908), p.200.

98. SMGC, _Co-partnership_, 5 (1908), p.199.

99.
SMGC, Co-partnership, 1 (1904), pp.149-50.

100.
SMGC, Co-partnership, 1 (1904), p.167.

101.
SMGC, Co-partnership, 8 (1911), p.53.

102.
SMGC, "Directors' Minute Book," May 12, 1926.

103.
S. Everard, The History of the Gas Light Coke Company (London: Benn, 1949), pp.260, 284.

104.
SMGC, "Directors' Minute Book," Feb. 18, 1890; The Workman's Times, Jan. 2, 1892.

105.
RC on Labour, Q.26961.

106.
C.O.S., Q.938.

107.
C.O.S., Q.959.

108.
The Crisis of Industry, essays published in The Times. These essays were published as book form later. Edwin Pratt, Trade Unionism and British Industry (London: J. Murray, 1904), pp.63-4.

109.
Everard, The History, p.284.

110.
Times, Dec. 28, 1901, 10e.

111.
Livesey, "Co-partnership," IGE, Transactions (1908), p.58.

112.
C.O.S., Q. 947.

113.
RC on Labour, Q.26983-5.

114.
RC on Poor Laws, Q.83136 (44).

115.
RC on Poor Laws, Q.83136 (50).

116.
James Ramsay Macdonald, _Socialism and Society_ (London: Independent Labour Party, 1908), pp.132-3.

117.
Quelch, _The Co-partnership Snare_, p.12.

118.
Livesey, "Co-partnership," p.55.

119.
SMGC, _Co-partnership_, 4 (1907), p.100.

120.
IGE, _Transactions_, (1908), p.66.

121.
T. Travers, "A Means for Reducing the Labouring Force in Gas-works", IGE, _Transactions_, (1882).

122.
PEP, _The Gas Industry_, pp.45-7.

123.
Carpenter, _Industrial Co-partnership_, p.26.

124.
Gas Light and Coke Company, _Report of Proceedings of the half-yearly Meetings_, Feb. 1909, p.7.

125.
GLCC, _Reply of the Directors to the Criticism which Mr. George Livesey addressed to the General Meeting of the Proprietors_ (London: 1898), p.10.

126.
GLCC, "Minutes of Proceedings of the Court of the Directors," July 19, 1909.

127.
GLCC, "Minutes," July 19, 1909; Jan. 29, 1909.

128.
During the war the gas industry suffered from the high prices of raw materials and wages. The profit-sharing bonuses vanished altogether in a majority of cases. However, only 2 out of 38 schemes were abandoned during the war. _Report_, 1920, P.29; Trevor Williams, _A History_, p.49.

Chapter VIII. The Co-partnership Scheme of Lever Brothers: the Pursuit of Efficiency

The remarkable program initiated by Lever Brothers, one of the biggest corporation on earth, was representative of co-partnership schemes that aimed at greater efficiency. This scheme, whose announced goal was increased efficiency, was inaugurated by William Lever, the company's founder and one of the most energetic and colorful men in the annals of British industry. The son of a small trademen, he would spend the last six years of his life as Viscount Leverhulme.

The co-partnership scheme Lever instituted in 1909 continued until his death in 1925, after which time it was neglected and yet survived until 1929, when the company, Lever Brothers, was amalgamated with a Dutch corporation to become Unilever. The scheme was one of the two most widely publicized profit-sharing and co-partnership schemes in England; the other, of course, was that of the South Metropolitan Gas Company. Lever's innovation attracted great attention not only because of the company's prominence in British industry and the sizable number of employees involved, but also because the company was already noted for its generous welfare services and the model village of Port Sunlight. Finally, but most significantly, the scheme was discussed far and wide because it was the creation of William Lever, the man described by one historian as "the most remarkable character who has ever played a part in British business."[1]

Before exploring his co-partnership, it is logical to examine William Lever's economic philosophy and his concept of management, for his famous co-partnership scheme must be understood against the background of his pursuit of efficiency and human relations management. Moreover, the influence of Lever's preaching on business efficiency and industrial welfare were as impressive as the great corporation he had built. Lever was well aware of the weakness and relative unprofitability of contemporary management methods that relied upon the cheapest labor working the longest hours in the most unhealthy conditions. He believed in the high-wage economy and the human touch in management. "Every increase of wages gives increased power of consumption to labor," he preached, "and consequently a larger production for the manufacturer, with a cheaper cost of production and the possibility of increasing profits."[2] For him, the healthy, contented worker was the most productive worker, and the biggest problem the employer faced was to obtain a permanent, efficient staff made up of such workers.[3]

The first step in Lever's plan to produce a healthy, contented workforce was the construction of a model village, the famous Port Sunlight, near Liverpool.

Housing facilities by employers were not unprecedented in British firms for the purpose of recruiting and controling the workforce, as recent studies on employers' social policy have pointed out.[4] Port Sunlight, however, was based upon neither of these motives. It is true that a new village had to be built around the factory when Lever Brothers moved its works from Warrington, yet there was no reason that new living quarters had to be a model village. Recruiting presented no problem in soap manufacturing, where the bulk of the workforce was unskilled. At the same time, because Port Sunlight was located near such industrial centers as Liverpool and Birkenhead, sufficient workers must have been always available.

Port Sunlight, therefore, can be described as an example of philanthropic benevolence, although that does not reflect the entire picture. Lever's model village and the co-partnership scheme were an interesting combination of philanthropy and calculated management policy. Indeed, Lever repeatedly asserted that he did not believe in philanthropy: there was no room for philanthropy in business, he insisted; business had to be conducted on sound economic principles. There would be "no worse friend to labor than the benevolent, philanthropic employer who carried on his business in a loose, lax manner showing kindness to his employees, for his business would be soon compelled to close."[5]

However, his remark must not be taken at face value. No matter how strongly he would have protested against it, his motives were at least in part philanthropic--he could have produced the same goods without constructing an expensive model village for his workforce. Lever, certainly, did not want to present himself as a benevolent employer. In any case, "we must remember there is no sentiment in business and no room for any fads," he told the employees in his dedication speech at Port Sunlight in 1890. "Any arrangement that is made must benefit the masters as well as the men, or it won't last."[6]

Lever was shrewd enough to realize that, without efficient management, philanthropy could not be a permanent solution to the industrial problems. He was among the first British employers to recognize the importance of the distinctive function of management. As we have seen, British employers were generally reluctant to adopt the methods of modern management, and remained so until well after the turn of the century. It was not until the first world war, for instance, that Frederick Taylor's scientific management was given interest in British industry. The very nature of Lever's industry, soap manufacturing, was probably instrumental in helping Lever formulate his management policy. The soap industry was basically a salesman's business and was founded on new methods of marketing unlike other chemical industries, which were founded on technical innovation.[7] However, the most important factor that shaped Lever's managerial ideology was his personal background.

William Lever was born in Bolton in Lancashire on September 19th, 1851. James Lever, William's father, was a native of Bolton. He was apprenticed to a Bolton grocer at the age of 14, then went to Manchester to take charge of a new branch grocery shop. After ten years in Manchester, James Lever returned to Bolton and opened a new grocery shop in 1842, which by the time William entered the family business in 1867, had become a thriving wholesale concern. Among the first jobs that William had to learn was the cutting and wrapping of soap, which in those days came to the wholesale grocer in long three-pound bars from the maker and was then cut into lengths and weights to suit the retailor's customer. Soon, however, he began to assist his father, by introducing reforms in his father's bookeeping system and in other business decisions. William's service proved so valuable that the prudent James Lever took his son into partnership at a salary of 800 pounds a year.[8]

The younger Lever was not a man simply for the grocery business, however. By 1884, Lever had come to the conclusion that he had exploited the potentiality of the business to the full, and consequently began to look for a new one. His thoughts understandably turned back to soap--the wrapping of soap having been his first occupation when he was apprenticed to his father. If the rising standard of living enabled people to buy more butter and eggs, why not more soap? Lever purchsed a small soap concern and launched his own business.[9]

Lever believed in individualist Liberalism, and never gave up individualism throughout his life. Significantly, his hero was Samuel Smiles, the staunch propagandist of self-help style individualism, and he made it a habit to present Smiles' Self-Help, to young chaps. "I know," he wrote later, "that people nowadays are inclined to scoff at Smiles and his gospel of self-help, but my advice to the young man of the present generation is to act on the principles taught in Smiles' philosophy."[10]

Everything Smiles preached fit in with Lever's temper; unremitting effort, relentless perseverance, and endless ambition. Lever was indeed a perect example of what the philosophy of self-help could produce. He started his soap business with L 4,000 he managed to borrow from his father. When he died in 1925, the capital employed at Lever Brothers with 151 associated companies stood at nearly L 57 million--an enormous sum for that time.

It is misleading, however, to attribute the success of William Lever entirely to himself. The social and economic conditions of the time also provided him with a favorable background. Soap is a consumer good that is marketable only when the general standard of living improves--as it did. The increase in the national consumption of soap in the nineteenth century corresponded to the degree to which the standard of living progressed. National consumption of soap, estimated at about 24,000 tons in 1801, rose steadily until the 1830s; between 1831 and 1841, there was a sharp increase--from about 47,000 to 75,000 tons. By 1861, England was probably producing rather more than 100,000 tons of soap a year. Meanwhile, the excise tax, which was levied at the rate of 3 d. a pound, was repealed in 1853, making soap an everyday commodity. Production was further expanded in the 60s and 70s. Between 1861 and 1891, the annual per capita had nearly doubled--from 8 to 15.4 pounds.[11]

Even with this remarkable expansion, Lever was not content. He wanted to create the market, not simply fill up the existing one or wait for a market to develop. Lever was among the pioneer businessmen who made use of advertising to great effect. The first thing was to find a name for the product that would have an immediate appeal to the consumer. After a long perusal, Lever hit upon the name, "Sunlight." The next step was to find an equally appealing slogan. Hence the famous catch line: "Why does a woman look old sooner than a man?"[12]

Lever's business philosophy consisted of several distinctive features. First, he was a vigorous opponent of socialism. Second, instead of the labor theory of value, he developed what may be called the "management theory of value," placing management in the core of the production of wealth. Third, he acknowledged the importance of the human factor in industry. Finally and most significantly, he believed in efficiency. It was at the very center of his economic thought and he regarded it as the best solution to the problems of the capitalist system. Co-partnership entered here as the best means of promoting efficiency. Now we will explore these features in detail.

Lever declared the labor theory of value to be "a great fallacy," and one 'that "has done the greatest possible harm."[13] He praised capital and advised labor to realize the identity of interest between capital and labor. "Where capital is lowest, wages are the lowest," he pointed out. The working man who thought the capitalist was his natural enemy did not understand the situation. To Lever, the wealth and comfort of Victorian England were produced by capital; capital that was employed on sanitation and on improving productive machinery. He even claimed that capital was "servant to labor," and was "the best friend of every worker in the country." "If you conscript wealth," he warned, "you kill the goose that lays the golden egg."[14]

Lever's entrepeneurial conviction naturally led him to total rejection of the labor theory of value. Lever, like Livesey, was a staunch anti-socialist. Like Livesey, he was a member of the Anti-Socialist Union, and devoted time and effort relentlessly to prove what he saw as the unworkability and absurdity of socialism. His belief in capitalism and the wage system never changed. He repeatedly asserted that the wage system had stood the test of the time; "it is not the product of a past stage of society, as was slavery or serfdom; it is no arbitrary system, artificial in character or devised in the interests of the employer."[15] The wage system was for him a convenient system, logical and practicable, and a great advance over all previous systems not because it was an ideal system but because it was the most workable. Although he conceded the malperformance of capitalism in certain aspects and the maldistribution of wealth in society, Lever rejected the suggestion that simple change of the ownership of industry would solve the fundamental problem. After all, for Lever, the socialist claim that labor was the only source of wealth was as ridiculous as saying that music played by the violinist was the violinist's. Capital and labor were interdependent sources; on top of them lay management, which was indispensible for the success of business. "It is you and I together who produce the money," he asserted to his employees.[16]

His own experience proved his point. When he took over a company that was almost bankrupt and revived it, nothing had changed except the addition of one factor--Lever himself. There was no more capital than before; labor consisted of the same workers. Therefore the sole source of the eventual success of the company lay in Lever himself. Where could the socialist labor theory of value fit in?

Thus it was "the successful management of labor, and only the successful management of labor that can produce any wealth."[17] Socialism would be a misfortune to his countrymen, he said to the Anti-Socialist Union, and particularly "to the working men, because without stimulus of individual rewards there would be less prosperity."[18]

If he was not quite right in asserting that the wealth of any one class could not be increased simply by diminishing that of another, it was certainly a valuable insight to see that successful management meant efficiency and efficiecy meant increased wealth. Lever stressed the priority of the increase of wealth to a more equal distribution, for the mere fact of equal distribution could hardly increase the total amount of wealth. We may call Lever's theory the principle of "Bigger pie before a bigger piece." These arguments coalesced around the concept of efficiency. Since Lever found the only solution in the increase of wealth, the next question was how to achieve it. His answer, of course: become more efficient. The purpose of business, for him, was to make and increase profits, which could best be done by increasing the quantity and the quality of the product. "It cannot be done by working a greater or less number of hours," he maintained, "it can only be done by making men in every way more efficient."[19]

However, Lever disagreed with scientific management on the ground that it was designed to increase the profits and advantages of the employer at the expense of the employee. At the same time, he criticized the sort of managerial practice which he viewed as being totally associated with the idea of control: the whole idea associated with management is that of control, in the name of "boss." But workmen had grown, he observed, and developed, and were "no longer blindly consenting to be "bossed" or controlled as if they were children."[20]

He believed that good management should not merely control the employee; rather it must seek to attain voluntary effort from the employee. Lever had insightful recognition of the importance of the human touch in good management. He once observed that whereas the greatest achievements of the nineteenth century lay in the field of mechanical invention and in the discovery of new forms of power and energy, the primary problem to be solved by the twentieth century would be the human one--the man behind the machine rather than the machine itself.[21] Thus, in Lever's view, the worker ought to be the master of machines, not vice versa. At the same time the value of machinery and technology was fully appreciated, and Lever was very quick to introduce new machines.

If efficiency was the chief goal for Lever in his early conduct of business, it became more and more an obsession in later years. He wrote in 1923, two years before he died, that he had "only one absorbing thought, namely my own efficiency."[22] In order to pursue the utmost efficiency, Lever developed a managerial hierarchy consisting of departmental and general councils. In 1899 he introduced a system of committees intended to make each manager and department head take a personal interest and at the same time be conscious of his power to influence the business by taking part in these committees. This "diffused management" was the result of his belief that a big industry could not be managed entirely from the top. In 1903, he added to this system of committees the council, on which the chairman of each committee sat as a member and of which the general works manager was the chairman.[23]

The Port Sunlight village and other comprehensive welfare provisions were another way of achieving efficiency. The first sod being cut in 1888, the village was a pioneer of such ventures in England. It was a model village not only in terms of health and sanitation but in artistic quality. "No two blocks are alike," one observer wrote. "Some are old English in style with diamond lattice eaves and solid oak doors, others have verandahs; some are treated with beams and plaster work, others with terracotta mouldings; some are of stone, others of brick." None had less than three bedrooms and most cottages had bathrooms. The Liverpool Fabian Society, after visiting the village, admired its cottages as "models of what the houses of the workers might be under Socialism." One visitor said he felt as if he had left towns of the Devil and had suddenly entered the garden of Eden.[24]

The death rate and child mortality figures for Port Sunlight show the sanitary quality of the village.

Table 8.1 The Death Rate and Child Mortality

	Average Death Rate per 1,000	Infantile Mortality per 1,000
All England and Wales	16	149
Liverpool	20	140
Port Sunlight	9	70

Source: W. L. George, Labour and Housing at Port Sunlight, pp. 152-3.

Hospitals, Sunday and day schools, and a free library were eatablished as were old age pensions, paid holidays, scholarship for the employees' children, and train and tramway service for the girls who did not live in the village. A concert hall and dining room, named for William Gladstone, was opened by the grand old man himself in 1891. The women employees were taught sewing, dancing, and cooking. The men could join bowling, cricket, tennis, football, and quoits clubs. There were also allotment gardens. The education in Port Sunlight was free; in 1898, 500 children were being taught. On Sundays, the central hall was used for services. Following Lever's liberal religious convictions, Anglican, Wesleyan, Primitive and

Methodist, Congregationalist, and occasionally Presbyterian services took place on a rotating basis.[25]

The employees' benefit fund was started in 1904; it was non-contributory and there was no deduction from wages. The management of the fund was run by eight trustees, four from the company and four representing the employees. Through this fund, an old age pension was given to employees, who retired at the age of 65 in the case of men, and at 60 in the case of women. The fund also provided pensions to those who were compelled to retire owing to ill-health or accident, and to the widows of the employees. Interestingly, like other benefits of Lever Brothers, the trust deed of the employees' benefit fund did not specify the amount that the company should pay in; the contribution was voluntary and might be stopped at any time, stating only that there be "a sum sufficient to place the fund on a sound financial basis."[26]

While he provided all these excellent welfare services, Lever did not conceive of enlightened industrial relations as largely a question of canteens, model village, free libraries and so on. In his opinion, it was much more a question of wages and hours and working conditions in the factory. The extensive use of labor-saving machinery to reduce human toil was a corollary of such ideas of efficiency and welfare work. When 10 or 12 hour day was the normal practice in British industry, Lever Brothers already established the eight-hour system, and furthermore, Lever had evolved the idea of a six-hour day by the end of the first World War. Under the six-hour system, he reasoned, the 72 hour week (two 36 hour shifts) would be established, which would produce more goods than the eight-hour day-48 hour week. The only reason for his failure to establish a six-hour day was trade unions' opposition which saw it as contradicting their rules.

But higher wages, shorter hours, and employee benefits were, of course, only part of the forms of Lever's drive for efficiency. Perhaps the most distinctive feature of all was the co-partnership scheme. One cannot exactly state why and how Lever caught the idea of co-partnership. He once said to his audience, "If you asked me where I first met with the idea of co-partnership, I would have to answer with the Lancashire man who was asked when he first met his wife, and who replied, 'I did not meet her, she overtook me.'"[27]

It is unclear what payment system Lever Brothers employed in the early days. One can only presume that the direct incentive system, such as piecework, was not extensively applied in soap manufacturing generally, for the nature of the manufacturing rendered payment by results inappropriate. One study in 1938 revealed that in the parent chemical industry, 91 percent of the workforce were paid by time wages and only 9 percent were paid on a piecework basis.[28] It can be speculated, therefore, that the difficulties of employing a direct incentive system may have obliged Lever to develop another system with which to promote efficiency. At the same time, the idea of co-partnership suited his unitary philosophy and human relations management. Lever, as we have seen, repudiated scientific management which seemed to him to basically drive people at a greater speed; that was not his idea of achieving efficiency. Instead he relied on the "human touch" managemnet. "If you are willing to take the same keen interest in this business," he appealed to his employees, "and exert yourself in it as if it were your own, and to improve the quality and to increase the quantity, to save and economize raw material and the tools, then I will give you a share in the prosperity."[29]

The idea of profit-sharing "overtook" Lever as early as 1888. He studied the existing profit-sharing schemes closly, particularly that of the Maison Leclaire in Paris which was the first such system. Lever's conclusion was that profit-sharing was not satisfactory. The report of the Board of Trade on profit-sharing published in 1894 confirmed him in this belief, for it showed that 51 out of 152 schemes, including those of co-operative societies, that had been introduced in the previous 65 years had been discontinued by 1894. Furthermore, the report showed that the average duration of the existing schemes was only five years and ten months. On the basis of these findings, Lever concluded that profit-sharing was not worth trying. Instead, he invented "prosperity-sharing," a concept slightly revised from profit-sharing. Then, why was profit-sharing unsuccessful?

Lever felt the defect in profit-sharing was that it did not include loss-sharing, thus was not effective in binding the employee to the employer. Moreover, the bonus disappeared altogether in bad trade years, which naturally caused the employee to complain and criticize the employer. Under the prosperity-sharing system, by contrast, the employee did not know the details of the business, and the employer had free hand in conferring benefits. Prosperity-sharing simply meant that the employer provided the employee with benefits without actual contract or agreement. In the bad years, the employer had nothing to explain or apologize for because he was not obliged to share profits one year or the next. Further the employees had no say in the matter. Yet the actual difference between profit-sharing and prosperity-sharing was subtle; but the latter was clearly more paternalistic in nature.

The Port Sunlight village was the result of Lever's idea of prosperity-sharing. Lever himself explained it as follows:

> If I were to follow the usual mode of profit-sharing, I would send my workmen and workgirls to the cash office at the end of the year, and say to them; "You are going to receive eight pounds each; you have earned this money. It belongs to you. Take it and make whatever use

> you like of your money." Instead of that, I told them, "Eight pounds is an amount which is soon spent, and it will not do you much good if you send it down your throats in the form of bottles of whiskey, bags of sweets, or fat geese for Christmas. On the other hand, if you leave this money with me, I shall use it to provide for you everything which makes life pleasant-viz. nice houses, comfortable homes, and healthy recreations."[30]

These remarks clearly reveal the paternalism involved in Lever's venture. William Ashley indeed observed that the Port Sunlight scheme was "a curiously patriarchal character for modern times."[31] Paternalism can be seen in many aspects of the village life. During the winter weekly dances, for instance, where every girl employed at the works was invited twice, girls over 18 were asked to submit the names of men to the social department, which issued invitations to them unless there be reasons to refuse them. Girls under 18 were provided with partners by the company.

"The whole village was dominated by a spirit of soap," Angus Watson, once an employee of Lever and a great admirer, wrote. "All of its occupants were employed in the industry; not only were they engaged in it all day, but it was a constant source of conversation at night...The chairman, the managers, and the workpeople alike were caught up with the fever of the progress of this great enterprise; there was little time to talk or think of anything else."[32] A minister at Port Sunlight confessed to Watson, "I sometimes feel that I am intended to be an advertisement for Sunlight soap more than for the kingdom of God."[33] "No man of an independent turn of mind," wrote the secretary of the Bolton branch of the Engineers' Union to Lever, "can breathe for long the atmosphere of Port Sunlight."[34]

This last remark seems an exaggeration. Although it was indeed a kind of twentieth-cetury feudalism of his own, as Charles Wilson put it, the Port Sunlight experiment was a bold venture, a conception with vision, imagination and a genuine concern for human welfare. W. L. George, son of Henry George, concluded with sober confidence after conducting a comprehensive investigation on Port Sunlight: "The rock upon which Port Sunlight might split does not loom very large on the horizon; I mean paternalism--a danger which is always to be feared by social schemes conceived and conducted by a man or a very small group..."[35]

Interestingly, Lever's criticism of profit-sharing and his elaboration of prosperity-sharing invited Livesey's counterattack, and the two giant figures in British industry pursued their arguments in the pages of the Economic Review. Lever concentrated his argument on the scheme of the South Metropolitan Gas Company, and ironically criticized the paternalistic character of Livesey's scheme.[36]

By 1909, however, Lever had realized the

shortcomings of prosperity-sharing and embarked on discovering a new system to replace it. A major reason for this probably lay in the first business setback Lever was to experience in 1906. The soap business had run into difficulties by this time. The standard of living, which had been rising from the late 1860s until the 90s, and had been a ladder of success for the soap makers, now was checked, and there were even signs of a fall in real wages. Soap, still on the margin of necessity, might well be the first commodity a household would cut. Since the 1880s, soap and advertising had gone hand in hand. To Lever and his imitators, a market was the size they chose to make it. Lever's idea of a cure of this sluggish trade was to reduce not only advertising but also excessive competition among makers by joint action. Thus he came to consider a combine of soap manufacturers and justified it on the ground that a combine aimed at providing "a cheaper product...a more abundant product...and a better product."[37]

The major economies which Lever envisaged from the amalgamation were in reduced advertising and selling expenses. But there was a further economy the combined buying of raw materials. By September of 1906, major soap companies, including Crosfield's, Edward Cook's of London, and Richmond and Jones of Liverpool, agreed to join the combine. But there were setbacks. The first was at the hands of the *Daily Mail*, which discovered that one of the objects of the combine was to lessen the cost of advertising. The paper promptly condemned the "Soap Trust" and advised readers which soap to buy and which to avoid. The attack of the Northcliffe newspapers was successful. Sales in November were 60 percent below those for the same month in the previous year. Soon the frenzied competition of the pre-trust days returned in an even more severe form.

Lever was not the type to put up with such humiliation. In July 1907 he went into action against the Northcliffe press on the charge of libel. Even before the case opened, Lord Northcliffe conceded that he had overstepped and offered Lever public apology. But Lever refused to accept it and the battle was on. In the end, Lever Brothers received L 91,000 in compensation, which was enormous by contemporary standards. Yet even so large a reward failed to make up for the disastrous effects of the press campaign. Nowhere was the impact of the 1906 crisis more serious than on Lever's own trade. Sunlight soap had suffered its first setback. Lever Brothers' credit had been seriously shaken by the crisis. Buildings under construction at Port Sunlight had to be stopped. "We could not get 1 d. of cash," Lever wrote of this period later.[38] By the end of 1909, Lever calculated his losses at over half a million despite the amount received for damages. Although profits from the associated companies that had been established all over the world were sufficient to balance Lever's losses, the problem of the increased prices, which were the greatest element in soap makers' costs, were driven upwards by the margarine makers, who needed much the same oils and fats.[39]

It appears that the co-partnership scheme was designed in this context. By 1909 Lever had evolved new schemes for new lines of business. He needed a new system which would create a new bond and greater efficiency for reconstructing business. Since the system of payment by results was inapplicable to soap manufacturing, he had to devise an entirely different system. That system was co-partnership. "In my opinion," he told his employees in 1909, "ordinary profit-sharing has been proved and found wanting. Prosperity-sharing is very good, but does not go far enough." Also there was a question of providing a more comprehensive welfare system than Port Sunlight village, because the company, through acquisition, had employees in factories other than Port Sunlight. Since Port Sunlight was the main establishment under prosperity-sharing, and could not afford to subsidize the growing number of employees, it was necessary to devise a new system to reestablish solidarity between Lever and his employees and to promote efficiency.

The co-partnership scheme of Lever Brothers was a peculiar one. In fact, it was not co-partnership in the real sense. As a judge of the case Lever's employees versus the Amalgamated Society of Carpenters and Joiners put it, it was "extremely difficult to see how the workers at Port

Sunlight could be considered co-partners at all."[40] The co-partnership motto of Lever Brothers was "Waste not, want not" which indicates the objects of the system--namely economy and efficiency. At the same time, it was believed that the worry and cares of management would be relieved for working with a body of partners must be infinitely better than working with simple wage earners.

Lever laid down essential conditions for the success of co-partnership as follows:

> (1) Co-partnership must not degenerate into charity or philanthropy; (2) the objct must be to increase efficiency, resulting in increased prosperity for all--not for the man on the top only, but for all; (3) It must maintain the supremacy of management; (4) Co-partnership must not result in the weakening of management, but on the other hand, labor must be free to work out its own ideas--free from the tyranies of victimization if it expresses its views...;(9) The control must rest with those who find the capital.41

The chief peculiarity of the co-partnership scheme of Lever Brothers was that co-partnership certificates did not carry market value unlike other companies' shareholding provisions, and therefore left the bearer without the traditional right and responsibility of the shareholder. Lever deliberately created certificates that would have no value whatsoever in the market, but would bring the holder a nominal annual dividend. The certificates were blank paper unless Lever himself consented to declare a dividend. In the South Metropolitan scheme, as we have seen, the employee received ordinary shares and was entitled to the same rights as a shareholder. Why, then, did Lever create such a unique scheme?

The reason lies primarily in his unwillingness to allow the working man to participate in management. Lever was an autocrat by temperament, and could not stand any contradiction from those who served under him or with him.[42] He was also an adventurer who believed that the business was his personal creation and that the risk of loss should fall upon him and him alone. It was his early hope to own the entire ordinary shares of the company so that he could maintain absolute control to carry out whatever ventures he chose. Already in 1902, he purchased the last segment of ordinary shares from his brother, partner of Lever Brothers. He allotted other shareholders preference shares, which entitled the owner to receive a fixed dividend at a certain rate before any dividend at all was paid to the ordinary shareholders, but carried neither liability nor responsibility.

Lever did not believe in industrial democracy or the ability of the worker to manage, thus his co-partnership was designed in such a way as to give the worker no share in control. "Just as taxation and representation must go together," he asserted, "so it seems to me loss-bearing and control must go together."[43] To expect that a man could be selected out of the works by his mates to sit straight away on a board was to him an utterly futile expectation. Supreme management must always be in the hands of trained men. He was certain that if the decision-making was left to labor, the business must suffer losses, and that in all well-organized industries, some must work with their hands and others with their hands.[44]

Second, the co-partnership scheme of Lever Brothers was distinctive in its discriminatory nature. Not only the selection of the co-partners but the allocation of certificates were based on discriminatory principles. The sheme also favored managerial staff in a marked way--an indication of Lever's conviction of the importance of management. Even the basis of success in co-partnership was, for him, improvement in management. In the first place, not all the employees were allowed to participate in the scheme. It was a merit system in a word. The co-partners were selected among those who were considered "desirable partners" and who had "a clear record of at least five years' faithful and loyal services with the company."[45] The selection of the co-partners and the allocation of certificates were left to the discretion of the co-partnership trust composed of the directors of the company and finally decided by Lever himself. The bonus was a monetary award based on individual merit, individual efficiency and individual loyalty. Lever was discontented with the practice of collective barganing under which all the workers received a uniform wage for a uniform number of hours. He saw it as unfair on the ground that the work renderd by each individual worker was not uniform and never could be. In this context, co-partnership was introduced to provide payment in addition to salary or wages.

The co-partnership trust stipulated that the system of allotment was based upon value of service; the very "slacker and ne'r-do-weel" received nil, the "apathetic" from 5 percent to 10 percent, and the "enthusiastic, appreciative, and responsive" above 10 percent, with special allotment for special services and helpful suggestions.[46] If any report came in on any man having committed any act of "insubordination, any neglect of duty or any minor offenses," he would forfeit any allotment he would otherwise have received during the year. On the other hand, if any excellent report came in, he received more, and if any man rendered the company exceptional service, he received still more so that there was always elasticity.[47]

When there were strikes, non-strikers were rewarded with more certificates whereas strikers found their certificates cancelled. In 1920, after the clerks and the warehouse workers' strike, special services during the strike were acknowledged by issuing certificates to even those who were not yet officially eligible.

In the second place, Lever's scheme was

discriminatory not only in the selection of co-partners but in the allotment of certificates among different levels of employees. It was decidedly favorable to the managerial staff against manual workers. The employees were divided into four groups--directors; management and foremen; salesmen; and the work staff. Each group was allowed to hold a quarter of the total amount of certificates collectively. Let us compare the number of the directors with that of the workers. The first partnership certificates were distributed to 7 directors, 125 managerial staff, 103 salesmen. and 806 work staff--for a total of 1,041 co-partners.[48] Thus with seven directors holding 25 percent of the total, the average amount of each director's certificates was 115 times as great as that of the average worker. For that matter, the foreman might have six and half times as much as the worker.

Lever justified this discrimination on the ground that the directors had "the greatest power...to influence the success of the business." The management and the salesmen were also said to have great power to influence success; the workman supposedly did not. Yet Lever boasted that they were still given equal power in the aggregate.[49] There was a maximum limit of certificates that each co-partner class was allowed to hold except for the director class. Only the directors were allowed to receive certificates not exceeding the limits from time to time fixed by the holder of the majority ordinary shares i.e.,

Lever. Lever never fixed this limit for the directors, and the records of the company reveal the tremendous amount of certificates held by the directors. This was the logical result of Lever's preference for managerial staff. Although he constantly asserted that all Lever Brothers' employees were in the same boat, he reminded the employees: "Let us each in our own different positions jointly make the profits."[50]

Even the company's holiday policy distinguished among classes of employees. Paid holidays were introduced in Lever Brothers in 1905, when such a thing was virtually unknown in British firms. They permitted employees to take one to four weeks. However, the length of vacation differed according to the employee's status on the principle that "those who work with their heads require a longer rest than those who work with their hands."[51]

The third novelty of the co-partnership scheme of Lever Brothers was the absolute separation of the partnership certificates from the profits of the company or the employees' earnings. The dividend on certificates, of course, depended upon profits earned, but under the operation of the scheme, certificates could still be issued even in a bad trade year, although there would be no dividend. In this way the gap between good and bad years was brilliantly bridged without pressure on the company to weaken its commercial position by excessive distribution.

The last, but not the least peculiarity of Lever's scheme was its explicit aim of binding the fortune of the employee to that of the company. The partnership certificates brought their holder a dividend 5 percent smaller than the dividend to the ordinary shareholders. This was deliberate and was intended to make each co-partner realize that "if there is no dividend for the ordinary shareholder, he knows that there is nothing for him either." Nothing could have been more effective in making the co-partner employee aware of his dependence upon his employer. Also, the co-partner was reminded that "only during his lifetime and during the lifetime of the profit-earning capacity of the business, the certificates are worthy any more than the paper they are printed on." If the business ceased to be profitable, the value of the certificates would disappear. Therefore, they were "all in one platform--we are all in the same boat."[52]

The co-partner was required to sign an agreement before being accepted promising that he:

> will not waste time, labor, material or money in the discharge of my duties, but will loyally and faithfully further the interests of Lever Brothers Ltd., its associated companies, and my co-partners, to the best of my skill and ability...53

The bonus under the scheme was simply a monetary gift for

this loyalty and faithful service. The employer was to give some money out of his own pocket and the employee was to receive whatever was given to him. "You are taking something from the ordinary shareholder, that is myself;...I can give more, I can give less, I can give none," he said to his employees.[54]

Lever strenuously rejected the claim that the worker had a right to profits: "Labor has no claim on anything but its wages. That is the beginning and the end of the contract."[55] He believed the wage contract to be the fairest and most appropriate contract between capital and labor. According to him, workers made a bargain with employers in exactly the same way as they made it with their grocer and butcher when they fix the price for butcher's meat and grocer's.

But there was more in it than that for "we are dealing humanity; we are not dealing with machines." However, it was not a question of right, but a question of "relationship between humanity, between flesh and blood and human sympathy."[56] Co-partnership, he thought, came as a final touch to the wage system--something like the spire on the cathedral to crown the earnings of the wage system and point to something better.[57]

The Holdings of Partnership Certificates among Employee Classes

The first distribution of partnership certificates in 1909 was quite generous. As we have seen, the first certificates were distributed at the nominal amount of L 116,064 to 7 directors, 125 managerial staff and foremen, 103 salesmen, and the 806 member of work staff. The allotment was made retrospetively to make the year 1901 the starting date of the scheme. Thus the person who had been in the company's employment for eight years (i.e. from 1901 to 1909) would receive an amount approximately equal to a year's salary or wage in scrip. In other words, each co-partner received approximately a year's salary or wage as certificates in the first distribution. In addition to partnership certificates, partnership preferential certificates, bearing a fixed dividend of 5 percent, later raised to 8 percent, were created to allow co-partners who had retired or been forced to leave by accident or illness to convert their certificates to preferential certificates.

How uneven were the holdings of partnership certificates among different classes of employees? The remaining company records do not reveal the exact allotment of certificates in each year. Yet it can be estimated. In 1912, for example, there were 1,874 co-partners, and certificates had been issued in the amount of L 350,000.

The dividend on the partnership certificates was 10 percent; that on the ordinary shares, 15 percent; and the amount to be divided was some L 40,000. The average dividend can be calculated at L 20 per head; but with higher dividends for the higher ranks, the ordinary employee must have received far smaller dividends.

In the year 1929, to take another example, 13 directors owned 177,358 certificates whereas the rest of the co-partners held 1,391,621 certificates altogether. The actual amount to be divided in that year was L 119,116 3 s. 7 d. The following table shows the average amount of money the director would receive compared with that the employee of the rest classes would be paid.

le 8.2 The number of co-partners and their certificates

	co-partners	of certificates	per head	dividend	per head
ctors	13	177,358 L	13,643 L	13,500 L	1,000 L
rest	10,674	1,391,621	130	105,500	10
l	10,187	1,568,979		119,000	

ce: "Leverhulme Corresponence," 1389D, November 23, 1929.

Considering the further uneven distribution among the rest of the co-partners, namely between managers and foremen, salesmen, and the work staff, the average worker's dividend must have been much smaller than L 10.

The calculation becomes more complicated if we take into consideration the bonus on the preferred ordinary shares. The dividends were paid in cash for the first several years, but after 1913, they were paid in 5 percent cumulative "A" preferred ordinary shares, which the holder could sell at any time for cash at par value if he wanted. So long as the original co-partner held these "A" preferred ordinary shares he received a further bonus of the same rate of interest enjoyed by the ordinary shareholder. The fixed rate of dividend on the preferred ordinary shares was raised to 8 percent in 1923.

Now let us examine a more specific case. In 1929 there were 13 directors of whom 4 held particularly huge number of 8 percent preferred ordinary shares:[58]

James Furguson.....................6,600 shares
G.Long.............................24,226
C.R.Baker...........................3,600
C.W.Barnish........................23,800

Let us calculate the amount of money a director received as dividend on preferred ordinary shares and bonus in a certain year. There was no dividend declared in 1925 and 1926 and no further distribution of partnership certificates was made. Thus it would not be inaccurate to assume that the co-partners held approximately the same amount of certificates and preferred ordinary shares in 1924 as they did in 1929. In the case of G.Long, the money he received as 8 percent dividend on his 24,226 shares amounted to some L 1,938. In addition to this, he received the bonus of 8 percent on the same shares which would give another L 1,938.[59] As a result, he would earn approximately L 71 14 s. per week in addition to his regular salary.

Not all the directors held such huge amount of shares: only four directors out of thirteen did. Nevertheless, this enormous shareholding by several directors must have left smaller room for other co-partners. The company records also reveal huge shareholdings by chairmen and directors of the associated companies, who were also co-partners.[60] Having that in mind, we turn to examine the money distributed to the rest of the co-partners, who numbered 17,025 in 1924. The total amount paid as dividend on certificates and bonus on preferred ordinary shares stood at L 219,588 15 s. 5 d. in that year. Thus the average sum per head can be calculated at approximately L 12 18 s. If we consider the portion to the directors and other privileged co-partners such as chairmen of the associated companies, and allow further differences between classes, many of the work staff must have received far less than L 12 18 s.

However, the long-serving artisans appear to have received a considerable amount too. In 1921, for instance, the average amount of certificates held by carpenters and joiners of Lever Brothers stood at L 95 per head and each of them received some L 20 as dividend and bonus in that year.[61] The major victim of Lever's discriminatory policy was the unskilled female workers who occupied a bulk of the workforce. A disadvantage was given from the outset of the scheme due to the minimum age of the qualifying co-partner at 25, and the minimum period of employment at 5 years.[62] It was not easy for girls to meet these conditions. As a result, of 806 co-partners of the workstaff class who were admitted to the scheme in the first year, only 87 were women, and there were only 12 women co-partners in the managerial class which numbered 125.[63]

Most of the profit-sharing and co-partnership schemes were destined to be discriminatory to the extent that the bonus was paid on the basis of salaries and wages, thus allowing the higher wage earners a larger bonus. Lever's scheme was, however, practiced beyond this unavoidable discrimination. To be sure, Lever's aim was not the establishment of an egalitarian system. He used the scheme to promote the efficiency of each employee, and to him, the efficiency of directors and managerial staff was more crucial than that of the workforce, the bulk of whom were unskilled young women.

Trade Unionism under the Co-partnership System

Now we turn to the delicate question of trade

unionism under the co-partnership system of Lever Brothers. In Chapter V, the relationship of trade unionism to profit-sharing was discussed and it was argued that trade unions were not as great a barrier to the development of the movement. Here, we will see if such an argument can be justified in the case of Lever's co-partnership scheme.

Any profit-sharing or co-partnership scheme would naturally try to enforce solidarity between employer and employee, avoiding the antagonistic relationship between capital and labor, and otherwise prohibiting opposition on the part of employees. In principle, Lever was not against trade unionism, although he was an individualist by nature: "I am just as loyal and true to every man in my employment, whether trade unionist or not--I make no distinction no more than a father would between his boys and girls. I have no quarrel with the unions; I believe in organized labor."[64]

Lever Brothers was indeed one of the few firms that enjoyed a fairly smooth relationship with trade unions. It is more remarkable, considering the number of the unions represented in the works--namely 30, with their different rules. Lever repeatedly asserted that if he had been a working man, he would have joined a union. However, he criticized many trade union practices, particularly ca'canny and strikes, which he considered diametrically opposed to the pursuit of efficiency. "All employers must abandon their idea that low wages mean cheap production and high profits," he insisted, "and workman must equally abandon his idea that limited production means more labor employed and at higher wages."[65] "Men have had to strike many times," Lever told his employees, "to obtain justice when strike for justice seemed to be the last and only weapon remaining." However, he warned, at the same time, that the business could not be carried on in a state of warfare, which was what a strike was.[66]

It may be wrong to say that Lever was a supporter of trade unionism. It would be closer to the truth to say that Lever had realized that trade unionism would continue and thus it would be useless to fight it. He thus decided to co-exist and compete with them in a spirit of fair play. Co-parntership was a weapon in the battle for worker loyalty and efficiency against trade unions and their seemingly wrong practices.

One can only guess at the degree of organization among Lever Brothers employees. The company was said to negotiate with some thirty trade unions at one point, including the General Warehouse Workers Union as well as organizations of carpenters, joiners, electricians, and stonemasons. It can be speculated that trade unionism may have been weak since the bulk of the employees were unskilled laborers, with many young women. Tradesmen in Lever's employment, on the other hand, appear to have been highly organized. Regardless of the degree of organization,

Lever's employees enjoyed the best conditions they could have expected. They received trade union rates or higher; they worked eight hours when a ten or twelve-hour day was the normal practice in industry. They enjoyed every facility of Port Sunlight village as well as numerous other benefits. On top of everything else, Lever's employees received a bonus that was an absolutely free gift from the employer. It was not surprising therefore that the co-partnership scheme of Lever Brothers, unlike so many other schemes, was blessed by trade union officials.

An official of the Electricians Union who was invited to the first distribution of dividend on partnership certificates declared that the shceme was "what I or any other sensible man, calls socialism," and it was the "mutual interest and sincerity and conscience with which master and workman, employer and employee, have to work together, that is dwelt upon tonight." Another trade union official from printers union expressed the wish that there would be more employers to bring about a better understanding with their employees, and wished the co-partnership scheme much success and future prosperity.[67]

Lever's acknowledgement of the validity of trade unionism, however, did not automatically lead to his acquiescence of strikes and other union practices. One objection Lever raised against profit-sharing was that it could not prevent strikes--for profit-sharing provided no binding loyalty of the employee to the employer. Co-partnership was believed to cure this shortcoming by combining loss-sharing with profit-sharing. Lever was so convinced of the effect of co-partnership as to boast that he would not dismiss a worker who struck: "If he gets more money out of a strike than out of co-partnership, he would be a fool to be a co-partner.' the workman had 'the fullest liberty to strike or not."

Generous and progressive as these words sound, the position of Lever's employees was not so simple a matter. The Co-partnership Trust Deed stipulated that "if the holder is guilty of neglect of duty, dishonesty, intemperance, immorality, wilful misconduct, flagrant inefficiency, disloyalty to his employers or any breach of his undertaking," his certificates were liable to be cancelled.[68] The Trust Deed also required continuous service of the employee for qualification as a co-partner. Strikes obviously belong to the category of "wilful misconduct" or "disloyalty to his employers" as well as representing a break of continuous service. This clause was, as we shall see, used in all strikes to punish strikers. Now the exact circumstances under which strikes took place ought to be examined, as well as the way in which the company reacted to them.

It must be noted, first of all, that there were only three strikes during the duration of the scheme, and none of them was caused by disputes between the company and the employees. Not only that but they were either sympathy strikes expressing solidarity with workers in other companies or a strike brought by one union against another. It is also interesting to note that no matter what the causes were, Lever's policy was consistant, applying the same principle of "no strike at Lever Brothers."

The first strike that took place in the Port Sunlight oil mill in 1911 was a sympathy strike as a part of a local strike, and involved only a small number of Lever's employees. Lever did not much bother himself over it, and was willing to "let bygones be bygones." Nevertheless he considered the affair both an opportunity to define the relationship of co-partners to the company in case of strikes and to establish a precedent. The result was that co-partnership certificates were granted in recognition of help given during the strike in the following year. Because of the small number involved, the 1911 strike had no significant effect either upon the co-partership scheme or labor relations at Lever Brothers.

Another sympathetic strike on the part of Port Sunlight electricians in 1918, however, proved more serious. In September that year, there was a strike of electricians in the Mersey district because a non-union foreman had been employed at a munitions factory. Naturally, Lever's employees were also called out. The strike was settled by the foreman joining the union and both sides agreed that there would be no victimization. Lever Brothers, however, decided not to include those who took part in the strike in the next distribution of partnership certificates. Furthermore, the company also decided to withhold the dividends on the strikers' existing certificates. Walter Citrine, then secretary of the Liverpool and Birkenhead district of the Electricians' Trade Union, was requested by the members to ask Lever to reconsider.

Citrine found Lever "a sprightly, fresh-complexioned fellow, small of stature but sturdy" and having "keen, restless eyes," and one who "would have attracted notice in most places."[69] Citrine, who was to become the general secretary of the TUC, was far from Lever's equal at this point. Citrine confessed that Lever's discourse was so closely reasoned that he almost convinced Citrine, forced the latter to fall into a complete defeat on every material point, and made him lose confidence completely. Lever's argument was basically that it was those who were at work, not those who were on strike, that made the co-partnership dividends and profits, and thus it was not fair to treat them equally. He agreed to concede in certain cases when the workmen were forced to strike by an employer's refusal to arbitrate. Before resorting to a strike, however, Lever urged workers to turn to discussion and to seek a peaceful solution.[70] However, it ought to be noted that Lever's argument does not apply in sympathy strikes, for in such cases the employer and the employees of Lever Brothers could hardly settle a dispute that had originated in another firm.

Trade unions watched the case with keen interest, for the outcome would affect the members of many other unions. While the electricians eventually lost their partnership certificates, Lever permitted a full inquiry on the co-partnership scheme. It was conducted by a committee comprising of directors of the company and union officials under the chairmanship of W.A.Appleton, general secretary of the General Federation of Trades Unions. The 1918 strike, while it did not originate at Lever Brothers, indicates the growth of tension between the firm and trade unions. The trade union movement of the post-war era became increasingly militant and class-conscious, and this attitude was to cause disturbances in the smooth functioning of Lever' co-partnership system.

The greatest challenge to this smooth functioning was brought about by a large-scale strike at Port Sunlight in the summer of 1920. It ought to be noted that the strike did not result from any grievance against the company, but rather from a conflict between two unions over the issue of the right to organize. The strike was a quarrel between two unions for the right to be recognized as the "official negotiating body" in a word. The largest union at Port Sunlight was the National Warehouse and General Workers

Union, which had sizable number of both clerical and manual workers. During the war, several hundreds of the clerical staff left the union to join a new union, the Liverpool Shipping Clerks Guild, which recruited clerks only. Long before the end of the war, the laborers' wages had overtaken the clerks', for the former's wages had shot up during the war; the salaries of the clerks had not. By June 1918, the lowest wage for an unskilled laborer was 54 s. whereas the lowest wage for a clerk was 48 s. per week.[71] In early 1920, both unions wanted to obtain pay increase for the clerks.

Lever told the two unions to first reach agreement among themselves and then meet him for negotiation. The unions, however, could not settle their differences; the NWGU claimed the sole right to represent the clerical workers, a claim that was rejected by the Clerks Guild. Lever again suggested arbitration, but the two unions could not agree upon the composition of arbitrators. As a result, the NWGU called a strike, the first large-scale strike in the history of Port Sunlight.

At the outset, the union called out only the clerks, who numbered some 1,050 at Port Sunlight and Liverpool headquarters. It was demanded that the company discharge those who remained at work, which, of course, the company refused to do. The union then called out its members in the work section, which increased the total number of strikers to about 6,000.[72] The usual rhetoric was heard. Beardworth, local secretary of the NWGU, declared that the strikers were "up against one of the biggest combinations of capitalists in the country," but insisted they would prove themselves stronger than any such combines. He also told his audience that some people thought co-parnership and that sort of thing should be allowed to rob them of their rights as trade unionists, but they would not have their loyalty bought in that way.[73]

No matter what the rhetoric of the union leadership declared, it did not represent the opinions and feelings of the rank and file. A workman had observed in December 1918 that he had yet to find "the man or woman at Port Sunlight who wants to strike."[74] This appears to have been true in the summer of 1920 too, Many of the employees did not want to come out on strike in the first place. Union rules stipulated that a vote by ballot should be taken before any strike and that one week's notice should also be given. These rules were conveniently ignored in the callng out of both the clerks and the work staff. No ballot was taken, the decision being made by a mere show of hands at meetings where many of the members were not even present. Nor was notice of one week given. Thus the majority of union members did not know, as one of them complained, that they were on strike until they saw the pickets and the placards of the sandwichmen.[75]

The leadership found itself defied during the

strike. Not only did many members initially resist the union's decision to come out, but more and more strikers went back to work each day. They were protected by the company, which transported them in vans and trains straight into the yard. It was said that some of the pickets boarded a train at Woodside station in order to chat with and persuade some of the workers to join the strikers. "Unfortunately for them," the story goes, "it was one of the specials which ran direct into the yard...the pickets accepted their fate and returned to the desks they had deserted."[76]

The rank and file strikers could find no justification for the strike. One of them challenged the union leadership in the fight with the Clerks Guild, insisting that working people had "a pefect right to choose their own representatives," and that the strike had nothing to do with Lord Leverhulme (he was raised to the first viscount Leverhulme in 1920). A member at the union meeting asked the officials if it was not possible "to come to an amicable settlement as reasonable men and women. Lord Leverhulme had never rebuffed trade unions." Another suggestion was made that "the union executive should take steps to reopen negotiation with the firm and, if possible, to take joint action with the Guild."[77] Since the strike had clearly been started and was being prolonged by an arbitrary union leadership, the rank and file were understandably disenchanted.

For the Port Sunlight employees who had not experienced serious disturbances, the strike was an occasion of entertainment. One striker asserted that they had "managed to conduct (the strike) on picnic lines."[78] When the work staff were called out, the young women "strikers" obligingly threw custards, pies, and sandwiches to the clerks who remained at work. A local newspaper reported, with what may well have been understatement, that "generally the crowd were quite good humoured."[79]

The strikers even asked the strike committee to provide free cinema shows during the wet weather in addition to the usual band performance.[80] The village was decribed as in holiday aspect, "the girls having discoarded their work dress for outdoor attire." A newspaper reporter observed, that there was "little evidence of the seriousness of the position in regard to the immediate prosperity of the industry."[81]

It is not surprising, then, to find the strikers demanding the "reinstatement of every member in his old position, not only as regards actual working but...co-partnership, pensions, and rewards for long and faithful service."[82] For them, the strike in no way represented opposition to their employer. When they heard that the company would cancel their partnership certificates, they naturally asked that the decision be reconsidered. When their request was refused, the nature of the strike changed from a dispute between two unions to a confrontation between the Warehouse workers Union and Lever Brothers. At the same time, the issue became the full reinstatement of strikers with the full benefits of co-partnership. The company promised employment to the strikers and other benefits such as paid holidays, but made it clear that their partnership certificates would be cancelled. The reason: violation of the terms of the co-partnership trust deed. Although the Joint Industrial Council in Soap and Candle Trades, which had been established in the line of the Whitley Council report after the war, was held at the request of the union and recommended full reinstatement, the company refused to alter its position.

What did Lever himself feel? Not surprisingly, he was deeply hurt, having been convinced that his firm would never see an internal strike. To his pained surprise, all he had done for his employees was not enough to prevent them from striking. Even if the strike was not personally directed against him, he could not accept the employees' behavior. One union official interpreted Lever's attitude as "How dare you strike against a firm of our class?"[83]

Lever's attitude was unbending. Even the directors thought the decision of cancelling certificates too harsh, considering the number of those involved, but nothing could change Lever's mind. Thus, 1,447 employees who remained on strike until the end, lost their scrips. The certificates of those who had returned to work while the strike was on progress, were left unharmed. The rhetoric nevertheless persisted on the part of the union leadership, who declared that "We are consequently not inclined to put up a trade union fight for the retention of co-partnership, the general opinion being that an improvement in wages will have a more permanent and independent value to the whole of the workers." No matter what the leadership rhetoric said, the 1,447 employees who lost their certificates, lost a valuable bonus. Considering that the average bonus among the work staff amounted to L 12 in 1920, and that annual earnings were not much over L 100, those 1,447 employees probably lost more than 10 percent of their take-home pay because of a strike they never wanted.

Did Lever's employees expect the penalty after the strike? Apparently not. They seem to have taken at face value Lever's statement that the workman had every right to strike. They also seem to have relied on the fact that the dispute was not directed against him. Most significantly, they did not think they had violated the spirit of the co-partnership scheme, because they were still loyal to their benevolent but difficult employer. Nevertheless, it does seem that Lever's employees should have known that by going on strike, their interest as co-partners in the business would almost certainly be terminated. That, after all, had been the consistent policy of the company in previous strikes. As one non-striker put it: "If the employee was not short of intelligence, he would expect to lose his shares if he decided to strike. That is the opinion of co-partners who are still at work." He regreted to see persons in strike who "have hitherto been outspoken in their praise of the scheme in its entirety."[85]

The Conflict with the Amalgamated Society of Carpenters and Joiners

The strike of the clerks and warehouse union certainly left a mark on the labor relations of Lever Brothers and on the co-parnerhsip scheme, but it did not cause a serious break in the relationship between Lever and the union. More serious event in the context of the co-partnership scheme and its relations to trade unionism took place when the Amalgamated Society of Carpenters and Joiners raised a direct confrontation to Lever's scheme. In October 1919, the executive of the ASCJ decided to expel from their ranks any member who continued to receive benefits from profit-sharing or the bonus system.

The premium bonus system and other forms of payment by results had been gradually taking hold in British industry in the last decades of the nineteenth and the early twentieth centuries, and much resistance and cry against such systems were heard. Despite the general assumption that both workers and unions objected to piecework, however, Sidney Webb pointed out that a majority of unions in Britain insisted upon piecework and the average workman preferred working on a piece basis. He also discovered that not all the employers were eager to adopt this system of remuneration. To take only two examples: the London printing firms, in the early ninteenth century, replaced piecework with payment by time, and the biggest strike ever in the boot and shoe industry was caused by the employers' attempt to abandon piecework for timework.[86]

As the ASCJ viewed the matter, at least in 1919, such a system of remuneration was against the spirit of trade unionism, tending to make the workers "greedy and apt to outstep the bonds of trade union rules."[87] Why did the ASCJ suddenly decide to resist co-partnership in which they had acquiesced for decades? First of all, the economic realities of the time played a part. The post-war boom had begun to lose momentum by the fall of 1919 and the union had paid large sums in unemployment benefits even while some of its more fortunate members were working under the payment by result system. Also, the fear that payment by results would concentrate work in the hands of a smaller number and deprive many others of any work at all still persisted. But more significantly, general post-war labor militancy, particularly the claim for workers' control appears to have made the union rethink its position on co-partnership. The ASCJ had not objected to its members' participation in Lever's scheme, but now it insisted that "the greatest mistake that the Union has ever made was when they allowed Lever Brothers carpenters and joiners to join the scheme in 1909."[88]

The ASCJ had grounds on which to act: its rule already stipulated the right to expel any member for "working in a co-partnership system when such system makes provision for operation holding only a minority of the shares in the concern."[89] And obviously, not only did the workers hold a minority of shares, they also had no voice in decision making in Lever Brothers. "To real co-partnership which involves joint control, we have no objection," the union concluded, "but as practiced today, it is merely a bonus on production, which is payment by results; in other words, piecework."[90]

Lever had no intention of establishing joint control, but he did suggest a possible solution. He offered to add dividends on partnership certificates to weekly wages, instead of distributing them annually, if such a device should suit the union's rule. This, of course, the union rejectd.

As a result, 49 co-partner carpenters and joiners at Lever Brothers had to decide whether they would remain co-partners or members of a union for they could not remain both. A mass meeting of employees was held at Port Sunlight on November 20, and there was harsh criticism of the union leadership. One speaker declared that the workers did not expect more than "improvement of conditions and wages from the unions," and thus would not accept the union's opposition; after all, co-partnership was an "excellent means of achieving their objects."[91] T. D. Stevens, workman, asserted simply and forcefully that so long as the standard wage was given, "a trade union had no right to rob the worker of whatever extra the employer chose to give" (applause). It was insisted that this was perhaps the "first time on record that a trade union has refused to take as much money as the employer chose to give." (laughter and applause).[92] The meeting passed a unanimous resolution that,

> This meeting of co-partners employed by Messrs. Lever Brothers emphatically protest against the action of the ASCJ...Our co-partnership recognizes the just right of labor to receive a share of the profits which they have helped to make, and any attempt to prevent co-partners particularly in the benefits...is diametrically opposed to the truest principles of trade unionism. We also pledge ourselves to resist by all means in our power any interference with our liberty as a free people.93

This was not merely a reaction of the workers in Port Sunlight. Local officials of the ASCJ saw the situation differently from the executive and sent a petition asking for reconsideration.

> That we, the members of the above branch, protest against the expulsion of the members of our society employed at Port Sunlight for participating in Messrs. Lever Brothers' co-partnership scheme, as directed by the executive council circular of November 8,1919, as the object of trade unions is to obtain a just and equitable share of the profits earned to be paid to the workers, and we respectfully submit to the executive council that this case should be reconsidered in order that these workmen may be retained as members of our society.

The petition did not stop in requesting the reversal of the executive's decision. It further criticized "this tyrannical action" of the executive and demanded that if the rules of the union justified the action, the rules which "applies in this case be deleted as soon as possible."[94]

The carpenters and joiners of Lever Brothers, though prepared to sacrifice their union membership, were aware of what expulsion could mean in an increasingly closed-shop labor market, and so decided to bring the case to court. Their action is even more interesting for carpenters and joiners of other firms overwhelmingly sacrificed benefits banned by the union executive.[95] The financial expenses were met by the company but the joiners lost the case. The court ruled that a trade union which was not a legal entity could not be sued.

The economic benefits at stake were by no means

negligible. All the joiners had been in Lever's employment at least 13 years (one for 31 years), and many of them over 20 years. Their co-partnership certificates stood at L 4,656 as of 1920, and their holding of preferred ordinary shares was calculated at L 57 8 s. on average. The total account of partnership benefits to the 49 joiners was as follows.

Table 8.3 The joiners' holding of partnership certificates in 1921

Holding of partnership certificates	L 4,656			L 95		
Partnership dividend	698	8s	0d	14	5s	0d
Holding of 5 % preferred ordinary shares	2,812	15	0	57	8	1
Bonus paid on preferred ordinary shares	326	2	9	6	13	1

Source: Leverhulme Correspondence, 1313A, April 1, 1921

From the table, it can be calculated that in 1921, the ordinary co-partner joiner of Lever Brothers received about L 20 18s. as a dividend on his partnership certificates and bonus on 5 percent preferred ordinary shares. For the workman who received L 20 extra a year in addition to his full or higher union rate wages, it was unthinkable to give up this monetary advantage. Thus it is not surprising to hear Ashley, one of the plaintiffs, declare that he would "fight the union to my last penny."[96]

Lever, however, disappointed at the court decision, decided he would no longer continue the financial support. It was the joiners themselves who decided to take the case to the appeal court on their own financial responsibility. At a meeting on May 4, 1921, the co-partner joiners resolved that they would sell their preferred ordinary shares as a way of raising the necessary funds. Only 3 out of 49 joiners refused to join the resolution, stating: "While we have no objection to the action of the appeal, we feel that by signing our names to agree to finance the appeal, we would jeoperdize our position in the Society, as according to the rule, we are liable to be expelled."[97] But the others pressed on. Moved by their determination, Lever granted further financial assistance.

We find the feelings of the rank and file vividly expressed in a joiner's letter to a local newspaper. He takes issue with a union official's remark that "Once a man becomes a proprietor he ceases to be a member of his trade union." He finds this contradicting another statement that "a man shall not work on a co-partnership system when such a system makes provision for the operatives holding only a minority of the shares in the concern." "According to the above statement," he reasoned, "we have to be thrown out either way. If we become the majority shareholders, we become proprietors and are therefore not eligble. If we take part in the scheme and are minority shareholders only, we are thrown out. Surely he does not expect to have both ends of the stick."[98] Surely it appears that the ASCJ was determined to crash Lever's co-partnership scheme.

The cases brought by Lever's employees against the ASCJ and the General Union of Operative Carpenters and Joiners eventually went to the House of Lords and resulted in a victory for the plaintiffs. The court finding stated that since there was no clear definition of a "co-partnership" system, and neither was there a provision in the scheme of Lever Brothers to keep the workmen holding a minority of shares, the plaintiffs were right in saying that they had done nothing in violation of the rule of the unions. Therefore, "an injunction must be granted to restrain the defendents from acting upon the threat to expel them."[99] The case against the GUOCJ was also decided in favor of the plaintiff on the ground that the Lever Brothers scheme could not possibly be called premium bonus system.

The victorious joiners of Lever Brothers held a meeting and passed a resolution of gratitude:

> That this meeting of joiner co-partners of Lever Brothers Ltd. tender to the Right Honourable Lord Leverhulme and the Honourable W. Hulme Lever their most grateful thanks for the generous and prompt assistance rendered by them to the co-partner joiners in their strenuous fights against the recent trade union actions.

> Recognizing as the joiners do, the disastrous effect the first verdict would have had to them, had it not been repealed, the joiners are doubly sensible of the great and incalculable assistance generouly rendered which will ever be remembered by them with gratitude and esteem.[100]

Lever called "absurd" the view that co-partnership was an opponent of trade unionism. He acknowledged the role of the unions in the questions of uniformity of wages, hours, and conditions of employment, for he believed that there ought to be uniformiy in these matters to prevent employers from "sweating" labor.[101] Lever's recognition of the rights of trade unionism was qualfied endorsement, however. On the one hand, he thought it just to give the workman freedom to choose as to organizational membership. It is interesting, thus, that Lever Brothers encouraged the organization among its employees around the end of the war. It was a managerial judgment against ideological conviction on the part of Lever as the size of the firm grew larger. The company encouraged the unions in every way, and even provided facilities for shop stewards collecting the weekly contribution.[102] Yet he had watched the development of trade unionism around the turn of the century with little sympathy. Trade unions, to his mind, should restrict their activities to industrial matters and stay out of politics.

The co-partnership scheme of Lever Brothers was born following a long history of various welfare services for the employees, and therefore did not cause initial suspicion and antagonism among the unions. That is the reason that Lever's scheme was started with their blessing. Gradually, however, the unions became uncomfortable with Lever's venture and looked upon it with increasing concern. Lever was more eager to keep good terms with the unions than vice versa. He even invited their opinions on the co-partnership scheme. He knew perfectly well that co-partnershiip could never become a genuine alternative to trade unionism, and decided to keep the two compatible.

At the same time, Lever seemed to have nothing to fear because wages and working conditions of his firms could not be better. In no case did an employee of Lever Brothers receive less than the union rate of pay. They also admitted that Lever's employees often worked far shorter than trade union rules called for. The overall opinion of the employees was that they had no right to expect more. Moreover, they received a bonus that they had "no earthly claim for," as one of the employees insisted. They recognized that Lever Brothers could cancel the whole scheme tommorrow, and yet "still be complying with the very highest demands of trade unions."[103]

Lever's generosity towards the unions stemmed from the recognition of this great advantage he was holding. He generously let the unions exist and compete with the various welfare services he provided, for he was convinced that victory would be his in case of an inevitable battle, if he did not want to see it happen in actuality. After all, his chief concern was efficiency. If the unions responded to his call for efficiency, why not tolerate them? However, when they were on his way to this goal, the spirit of challenge arose within him and made him fight.

Trade unions were obviously aware of their weak position. They looked upon the practices in Lever Brothers with gloomy eyes but did not dare confront him. The main factor behind their toleration seems to have been their loyalty to members, for they knew that the rank and file members liked it. Thus the unions did not attempt to obstruct the scheme; they only gave it a "cold shoulder," as Lever put it.[104] They did attempt to intervene in one occasion when Lever established a health insurance as a part of co-partnership benefits. The unions raised objection because a medical check-up was required under such a scheme while union rules prohibited members from taking one. The matter was eventually settled because it was not the insurance plan per se but the conditions for being admitted to the plan, particularly the medical check-up with its "lowering down the trousers," that the unions opposed.[105]

However, his experience with the unions over the years rendered Lever to take an increasingly severe attitude. The interference of the ASCJ with the co-partnership scheme was decidedly a major event to drive him to such an attitude. At the height of confrontation with the union, he withdrew the previous assertion that if he had been a working man, he would have joined a union, and proclaimed that "If I were a working man today, I would decline to be a member of any union that had...men with Bolshevik tendencies, and who desire to rule the country not by the ballot box, but by holding up the public to ransom like brigands and highwaymen...at any point of the road they might get the opportunity."[106]

Now let us return to the initial question that we had raised before we examined the relationship between Lever's co-partnership scheme and trade unionism: namely, if trade unions were a main cause of the failure of the profit-sharing movement. In case of Lever Brothers, it was not true. In the first place, trade unions did not object to the scheme at its initiation. Some of them even blessed it. When they grew uncomfortable with the scheme, they nevertheless acquiesced it probably because they took into consideration the welfare and opinions of members who were apparently eager for such benefits. In both cases of the Electricians Trade Union and the National Warehouse Workers Union, the unions, on behalf of members, petitioned to Lever for the continuation of co-partnership benefits to their members. As for the Amalgamated Society of Carpenters and Joiners, their attempt to obstruct the scheme failed because of the rank and file's defiance. The members even decided to sacrifice the union membership for the sake of co-partnership benefits and fought the union leadership to the bitter end. Based on these findings, it can be concluded that trade unionism was not a strong barrier to the co-partnership scheme of Lever Brothers. There was always tension between the two, but the unions failed to present themselves as a powerful oppositional force to check the scheme.

The Results of the Scheme: Loyalty and Productivity

Now we must examine whether the scheme produced the results Lever had expected. And before evaluating the results, we should identify the founder's motives for the results can only be judged against the objectives the scheme was intended to achieve. As discussed previously, a recent study on worker participation argues that the history of profit-sharing proves what the author calls the instability thesis, namely that employers took the initiative in offering profit-sharing only when industrial relations stability was in danger.[107] Lever's case, however, does not bear out this thesis. In 1909, the year of the initiation of the scheme, Lever had no trouble whatsoever with the employees. It was not industrial unrest but a desire for efficiency that prompted Lever to act as he did. Lever wanted to exchange material benefits for worker efficiency. At the same time, he realized that the cost of efficiency could not be calculated purely in economic terms. He set out to earn his employees' loyalty as well.

"The first qualities I look for in an employee are loyalty, integrity, and industry," he once stated. "If with these qualities are coupled with ability, ambition, alertness and quickness of perception, he is additionally attractive."[108] Loyalty was especially important to Lever; he felt that when it was obtained, the directors and managers would be free of the worries of everyday details and could devote more time to more complex problems. Thus, it was again efficiency that was laid behind the desire for loyalty.

Did, then, the co-partnership scheme have any impact on increasing labor productivity and employee loyalty as Lever had hoped? Let us first turn to productivity. As there is no easy way to assess this factor objectively, we must rely upon subjective evaluation, particularly that of Lever himself. In his earlier years, Lever's paramount consideration was long emloyee service. He felt that above all else, efficiency was the result of continuity. Thus his enthusiasm for welfare provisions, which all but guaranteed long service. As W. L. George observed, "It was rare a regularly employed left Port Sunlight of his own free will."[109]

The co-partnership system, without doubt,

tremendously lowered labor turnover. Even before the scheme was yet to be established, the employees' long service in Port Sunlight was noted. It is all the more significant when we consider that Port Sunlight was close to two great employment centers, Liverpool and Birkenhead, and that unemployment was not prevalent in the district. The fact that Port Sunlight workers did not leave on their own suggests a high degree of job satisfaction.

The nature of the soapmaking industry also helped this low turnover. The industry did not require high skill, and machinery was used to the utmost possibility. The greatest requirement for the worker was long period of experience and service to get to know the special ways and have an inkling of their secrets. The worker who did not possess special skill, thus a high market value, was likely to desire a stable employment in a particular firm. The low turnover of Lever's employees was a result of mutual consideration.

The numbers of the staff did not vary much more than 10 percent, even that much variation being largely accounted for by some hundreds of casual workers. The turnover among regular employees was well below 10 percent, as the following table shows.

Table 8.4 Turnover among the co-partner employees

Year	Number of co-partners	Number of co-partners leaving	Percentage
1909	1,041	19	2 %
1910	1,126	44	4
1911	1,761	74	4.5
1912	1,874	58	3
1913	1,984	58	3
1914	2,731	33	1.5
1915	3,416	29	6
1916	4,206	187	4.5
1917	4,921	151	3
1918	5,881	393	7
1919	7,082	121	2
1920	8,050	1,868*	23*
1921	10,989	389	8.5
1922	15,239	298	2
1923	16,214	1,646	10
1924	17,025	1,449	8.5

* This is due to the strikers who numbered 1,447: excluding them, the balance is 421, and the percentage stands at 5.5 percent.

Source: "Leverhulme Correspondence," 1398D, August 22, 1929

The above is the account of the co-partners who left the scheme each year. If we exclude the turnover after 1923 when the company discharged a large numbr for reorganization, and exclude the 1,447 strikers in 1920, we get 3.7 percent on average. We may assume that the overall labor turnover including that of non-co-partners would be no more than this or slightly higher.

An obvious way to encourage long service was to establish long-service awards and the figures of this awards also prove long service of Lever's employees. In 1922, although the company had been estabished at Port

Sulight only for 32 years, 332 employees received awards for 25 years' service, and 1,844 for 15 years' service. In 1924, 584 employees had served the company for 25 years, and 2,434 for 15 years.[110]

This long service, however, did not promote as great a record of efficiency as Lever had expected. The great increase in the workforce had not been accompanied by any proportionate increase in output. By the time the company was forced to undertake a reorganization in 1920--due to the slump and also the failure of Lever's expansion policy--the fact had become clear even to Lever. "If a man had been with us and thought his position was one in which he could come-aday, go-aday, God send Sunday, with his eyes on the clock and that was quite enough." He realized that there were "too many inefficient men, too many highly paid men, too many elderly men, and men past their work..."[111] What a different observation from his earlier conviction that repetition and long service would guarantee efficiency!

The company was overstaffed because it had rehired former employees who had served in the war, while retaining those who were hired during the war years. Reorganization was inevitable. Whatever pain it may have caused, reorganization was followed by a remarkable increase in productivity. In 1927 Port Sunlight was producing the same volume of goods it had produced in 1921 with 4,000 fewer workers. Between 1921 and 1923, the number of man-hours required to produce and pack a ton of soap fell from 115 to 61. At the same time, the cost per ton fell, during one week of 1923, from L 10 1s. to L 3 22s.[112]

What produced this huge increase in productivity? It was not, as Lever hoped, hearty, voluntary co-operation. Nor was it an increase in the bonus. It was something far more basic. He noted the psychological effect on the others: "I am confident that this has produced a state of fear in the minds of the remainders; if they were not efficient, their turn would come next..."[113]

From efficiency we turn to loyalty. If Lever's pursuit of efficiency had failed, effort to earn loyalty through co-partneship appears to have succeeded. As we have seen, there were only three strikes during the life of the scheme, and two of them did not originate with the company. The strike in 1920 was simply a dispute between two unions and had nothing to do with animosity against the company. Moreover, the strike was not desired by the workpeople; it was imposed by the union leadership. As the strike went on, the conflict between the leadership and the rank and file became increasingly apparent. Although the Daily Herald defined the strike as "a fight between one of the biggest of the organizations of capital and the workers," and predicted that "the workers are going to win," the workers saw the situation in a different light.[114]

Understandably, some of Lever's employees suffered as a result of their divided loyalty. Although one of them frankly confessed that, "I want to be faithful both to the union and the employers," it was to be proved impossible to be both.[115] This was to be particularly apparent in the carpenters and joiners' action. The employees had a deep trust in Lever. When the dispute began, the members of the Warehouse Workers Union expressed the belief that the misunderstanding was the fault of the directors; saying that they felt "if Lord Leverhulme himself knew the real facts, he would never have allowed things to come to this pass."[116] Nevertheless, some of the employees refused to participate in the scheme even though they were qualified. Lever called them "conscientious objectors," and did not put pressure on them.[117]

Lever's employees, on the whole, saw no contradiction between co-partnership and trade unionism: trade unions had to do with wages and working hours and conditions of employment, whereas co-partnership went beyond that realm. One employee declared that "co-partnership is the big brother of trade unions," and proclaimed that "the only fault of co-partnership is that it put trade unions out of date."[118]

The following conversation between Lever and his trade unionist employees shows how Lever's employees conceived the issue that co-partnership and employees' benefits interfered with the solidarity of labor.

> A employee: If you go anywhere outside Port Sunlight, you have to do your best and only get your wages, but in Port Sunlight you get a little extra in co-partnership, so it is worth trying for.
>
> Leverhulme: That is my opinion also.
>
> B employee: That is the spirit we all share.[119]

The division between union officials and the rank and file arose from different perception of what co-partnership meant. To the union leadership it represented a threat to union solidarity and loyalty; it was a dangerous rival for the workers' affection. To the workers, it was a very agreeable wage supplement. All a worker normally wanted from his union was a decent wage rate and reasonable work rules, and of course, welfare provisions. One trade unionist employee at Port Sunlight put the reason for joining trade unions bluntly: because it provided out-of-work pay, sick pay, and superannuation allowance, and also gave a better chance to find employment.[120] Thus the rank and file found nothing wrong with Lever's straightforward invitation: "If you do your best for me, I'll make you a co-partner and give you a share in the profits."

Clearly, Lever's employees considered themselves fortunate and privileged, and interpreted the unions' objections as an act of jealousy. They were proud to belong to Lever Brothers, to be "co-partners" of so large and famous a company. They boasted that they had "the finest craftsmen of all kinds in the world," and proclaimed that "the best men are bound to go for the best terms." Why should men who were less fortunate try to "rob these men of benefits given them for faithful service?"[121]

They saw the unions as running roughshod over their members. Again and again, Lever's employees complained that the unions simply did not want to understand co-partnership, and argued that a trade union that would force a strike without "some greater cause than we have had at Port Sunlight is no longer the protector of our interests." If the co-partnership scheme, which had the effect of raising wages each year, was "an enemy of trade unions, then the more enemies of this kind we have, the better."[122]

The employees who lost their partnership certificates after the 1920 strike were not long in attempting to reclaim them. As soon as they thought the atmosphere of bad feeling had dissipated, they applied for reinstatement. The implication of their reinstatement appeal, of course, was that they had simply made a mistake and were acknowledging it. The company naturally used this occasion for propaganda against the trade unions. At the co-parters' meeting at the end of 1921, when the "prodigal sons" were officially readmitted as co-partners, they adopted a resolution which read:

> We, the reinstated and admitted co-partners, desire to express to the Right Honourable Lord Leverhulme and the Honorouble William Hulme Lever, our grateful thanks for reinstatment and admission in the co-partnership scheme. Furthermore, we take this opportunity of assuring...of our fixed determination at all times to carry out the principles of co-partnershp as true and loyal employees of the company.123

They went on to assert that co-partnership was a means of promoting happiness. They knew that because they were "very unhappy without it last year," and pledged to prove their "loyalty in the future." They assured Lever that he would have "no more assiduous workers than those whom you have admitted to co-partnership tonight." Lever, in a graceful and seemingly magnanimous address, told the employees that, after hearing the very noble words in the resolution, he no longer regretted the strike. Indeed, he felt that the strike had drawn them closer together.[124]

Did Lever really want to let bygones be bygones? Never. When the company embarked on reorganization and discharging after the 1920 strike, he insisted that no one who had been loyal during the strike should be dismissed. But the directors and his own son pointed out that, if strikers were the only ones discharged, the unions would consider it victimization. Lever's response was anger and contempt. Across a page of the policy council minutes he wrote: "All a myth. Simply the words of timidity--without the courage of rabbits. We do not intend to victimize a single trade unionist...I will face anything and everything rather than allow any injury to be suffered by loyal members of staff."[125]

Lever also instructed secretary of the company to put a note in each of striker's record whether he was involved in the previous strikes, so that the fact should be taken into consideration in alloting certificates.[126] Another incident is of particular interest to see Lever's feeling. In 1923, L. Fildes, secretary of Lever Brothers, wrote to Lever about a warehouse man at Port Sunlight who had been discharged when the warehouse was closed down. When he was rehired at Lever House in London in 1922, he requested that he be reinstated as a co-partner. Fildes imprudently suggested that Lever give him not only former holding of certificates but an allotment for 1922. Lever furiously scrawled on the edge of the letter asking "by whom the warehouse man had been reengaged," and ordered, "Report fully." Then he remarked: "He should not have been. Did he disclose his previous connection? I am shocked to read he was reengaged and wish case fully investigated and reported on to me."[127]

Here we can see clear contradiction between Lever's public statements and day to day decision. In two occasions of 1921 and 1922, as we have seen, Lever readmitted former co-partners who had lost their certificates and were still employed at the company. But it appears that he never forgot or forgave them. This is a grim picture of a man once generous and straightforward, yet it accords with the impression of Lever gained of him by many who knew him in his later years: the impression of a driving tyrant, prone to find fault with his subordinates, yet possessed still of a fighting spirit which compelled their profound admiration.[128]

Regardless of whether Lever's co-partnership scheme produced the expected results internally, the scheme was extolled as a great success by the public. For one thing, Lever never failed to divide bonus that was lower than 10 percent on partership certificates. However, the material success of the scheme was likely to depend upon the prosperity of the company, not vice versa. The business in which the scheme was introduced was an exceptionally sucessful one. Lever Brothers occupied 70 percent of the total production of soap in Britain and 50 percent of the whole market. Perhaps what he said of Leclaire, the father of profit-sharing, and his employees could equally apply to Lever and his co-partners: "Leclaire owes nothing of his success to his adoption of co-partership or to his workmen. It is the workmen who owed everything to this man, who, from the humblest beginnings and uneducated raised himself by the practice of good management and self-denial to what he became."[129]

What was the total amount Lever gave away to his employees under the co-partnership scheme? Before we consider that question, we should recall that even before the co-partnership system began, he had given a large sum of money to Port Sunlight village through various welfare provisions. But if we look at the spending only since the scheme was started until one year before Lever died, the total sum for those 16 years reached L 2,002,940. The bonus rate, which was 5 percent less than the dividend on the ordinary shares, never went below 5 percent and was quite often in excess of 10 percent. Moreover, it was frequently supplemented by a bonus to those who held the originally allotted amount in preferred ordinary shares. The year 1921 is particularly interesting because the sum of money given to the employees, L 219,715, almost equaled what Lever himself was receiving, L 228,000, on his ordinary shares. If Lever had not given it away, it was his to put into his own pocket. The company paid even separation allowances to the families of the employees who were serving the war, the amount of which reached over L 150,000. An employee serving in the war wrote to him saying "One cannot wonder at the prosperity and success of such a noble-minded employer."[130]

The following table shows the extraordinary spending of money under the co-partnership scheme. The percentage of the shares held by the co-partners, however, was much smaller than the impression the absolute sum would give. In 1921, for example, the share capital held by the co-partners through preferred ordinary shares was L 718,666 when the capital of Lever Brothers stood at L 46,769,079. The employees' shareholding constituted approximately 1.5 percent of the total capital of the company. This may have been inevitable in such a world-wide, highly capitalized corporation. At any rate, the small proportion of employees' shareholding was never given attention, and the enormous amount of the money given away was sufficient to impress the co-partners as well as outsiders.

Table 8.5 The co-partnership bonuses

Year	Amount of certificates issued	Number of co-partners	Dividends on partnership certificates			Dividends on ordinary shares	
	L		L	s.	d.	%	L
1909	116,064	1,046	7,379	2	0	15	150,000
1910	215,248	1,139	18,670	4	0		
1911	307,886	1,761	39,958	13	5	15	150,000
1912	305,216	1,874	40,068	11	11	15	150,000
1913	402,332	1,984	41,272	6	5	15	228,493
1914	442,694	2,731	24,094	16	4	10	200,000
1915	509,213	3,416	70,209	0	5	10	200,000
1916	610,213	4,206	42,946	18	3	10	200,000
1917	751,536	4,921	130,834	0	2	15	300,000
1918	920,833	5,881	206,143	8	2	17.5	350,000
1919		7,082	271,299	6	2	17.5	355,638
1920		8,050	276,854	11	8	20	456,000
1921		10,989	219,715	3	9	10	228,000
1922		15,239	196,478	15	8	10	233,917
1923		16,214	197,427	1	10	10	240,000
1924		17,025	219,588	15	5	10	240,000
			2,002,934				

Source: <u>Progress</u>, 1909-1925; Lever Brothers, <u>Reports and Accounts</u>, 1909-1925.

The Mixed Motives of Lever: Efficiency and Sentimental Benevolence

The co-partnership scheme of Lever Brothers was a result of Lever's enlightened management philosophy; at the same time, it was an outgrowth of philanthropy, no mattter how strongly he protested against it. If a despotic one, Lever was one of the best kind of benevolent employers. Brought up in Bolton, which was once a quiet, peaceful rural area but drastically transformed into an industrial town in the nineteenth century and which Frederic Engels described as the worst of the Lancashire industrial towns after Preston and Oldham, he witnessed the miserable life of the working class.[131]

> Why should we not recognize that it is a right and proper human aspiration for a workman to desire an increase in wages? Those who, like myself, have been born and bred in a Lancashire manufacturing town, have listened, between five and half-past in the morning, whilst lying in bed, to the patter of the clogs of people going down the street on the way to the mills, and have heard the same patter between five and six o'clock in the evening when the workpeople have come back. Some of you, like myself, may remember the condition of the workers in the late 50s, when...you could only see two patterns of legs--the knock-kneed and the bow-legged. This was the result of immature youths being forced to work long and laborious hours in the vitiated atmosphere of mills and foundries...[132]

He spoke to the House of Lords. To be sure, this benevolence was combined with the calculation that healthy body and contended mind could produce the superior worker. And sadly, his obsession with efficiency grew more severe as he approached the last days of his life.

The co-partnership scheme was very much the creation of Lever's peculiar personality, and Lever took a great pride in and cherished his own creation. His correspondence and the company records reveal how closely and deeply he was involved with every details of the scheme. "The eyes of the world were fixed more intently on Port Sunlight than any other part of the United Kingdom," he said, "so it was for the employees and not for me to prove whether Lever Brothers were working on right lines."[133]

The correspondence beween Lever and the secretary of the company also reveals his intimate knowledge of his employees. One thing he truly wanted to establsh was personal contact with his employees. Enjoying such power and wealth, Lever was basically a sentimentallist, and wanted to be thought of with affection by his employees. "I trust my co-partners," he confessed, "I always feel that if I were to lose trust and confidence in those who are working with me at Port Sunlight, everything of value for me in the business would have ceased to exist; I would be left without any motive or incentive to carry me on."[134] Port Sunlight was an attempt, in Lever's own words, "to socialize and Christianize business relations and get back again in the office, factory and workshop to that close family brotherhood that existed in the good old days of hand labor."[135]

Lever repeatedly asserted his belief that "efficiency depends upon personal contact." Contact between Lever and the employees was frequent in Port Sunlight. He lived near the village before he moved to London, and used to be chairman of various village institutions. But since it was impossible to get in personal touch with all the employees who numbered over 40,000 by the early 1920s, he hoped co-partnership would provide such a contact. He still managed to know many of the employees personally, in spite of the growing size. A journalist observed that Lever seemed to know half of the children when he walked through Port Sulight with Lever.[136] Angus Watson accompanied Lever in the trip to America and recorded how an ex-female employee at Port Sunlight was greeted by Lever in the middle of an important meeting with American businessmen. This woman who was now married and living in New Jersey read about Lever's visit to New York and came up "in the hope of getting a glimpse of him. The conference is brought to an end at once; the blushing visitor is ushered into his room...and for half an hour she is kept amused with the latest news from her old village. It is many years since her old chief has seen her, but he immediately recalls her family and her years of service with the company," Watson wrote.[137]

The co-partnership scheme of Lever Brothers was left to die gradually after Lever's death in 1925, his successors having no great interest in such a system. Moreover, co-partnership had become difficult to apply to the needs of such a world-wide corporation with varied component elements. The size of employees grew simply too enormous to be embraced by the spirit of co-partnership. The total number of the employees of Lever Brothers and its associated companies stood at over 85,000 and that of the co-partners at over 17,000.

	Number of co-partners (1925)[138]
Lever Brothers Ltd...........	5,372
Home Associated companies....	8,518
Overseas companies...........	3,135
	17,025

Now the attempt to combine greater productivity and the larger earnings on the part of the worker had to cease and the two problems were tackled separately.

When revived interest in profit-sharing and co-partnership due to the introduction of such schemes by ICI and Courtaulds pressed Unilever to consider the readoption of the system in the 1950s, the directors of the company decided to stay away from it.

> The board had the matter continuously under review and many years' experience of schemes of this kind has convinced them that the employee's best interests were served by his participation in the prosperity of the business taking the form of the best possible working conditions which could be created, rather than a direct financial interest in the profits...It had always been the Company's policy to review salaries and wages as favorably as possible and to provide a high standard of welfare and other amenities.[139]

What a different observation it is from Lever's conviction that "High wages, bonuses, pension, or piecework, apart from a system of co-partnership can alone bring no solution of labor difficulties. Only the true spirit of co-partnership can tend in this direction, and by combining the democratic with the individualistic attributes of human nature, will result not only in higher total earnings but greater efficiency."[140]

Lever, certainly, was an exceptional figure in British industry. His enlightened management and progressive labor policy, combined with benevolent concern for welfare of the worker, left long-lasting marks on the British industrial scene. It is ever more significant because he initiated them when industrial relations were still in infancy and when very few employers pursued the effort to combine efficiency and prosperity of the business on the one hand and welfare and humanity on the other. To be sure, he was despotic and tyrannical, but he was an enlightened despot. Without Lever, as Charles Wilson put it, the whole structure of the British industry and the section of British world economic interests might have been a very different picture.[141] And without Lever, the profit-sharing and co-partnership movement might have lacked a great color and vitality, and welfare capitalism would have taken a much slower pace.

Notes to Chapter VIII

1. W. J. Reader, "Personality, Strategy and Structure: Some Consequences of Strong Minds", in *Management Strategy and Business Development*, ed. L. Hannah (London: Macmillan, 1976), p.109.

2. William Lever, *The Six-hour Day and Other Industrial Questions* (London: George Allen and Unwin, 1918), p.320.

3. Lever, *The Six-hour Day*, p.247.

4. Jo Melling, *Housing, Social Policy and the State* (London: Croom Helm, 1979).

5. Lever, *The Six-hour Day*, p.64.

6. The second Viscount Leverhulme, *Viscount Leverhulme by His Son* (London: George Allen and Unwin, 1927), p.54.

7. W. J. Reader, *Imperial Chemical Industries: A History* (London: Oxford Univ. Press, 1975), vol. 2, p.235.

8. Charles Wilson, *The History of Unilever*, (London: Cassel, 1954), vo. 1, pp.23-4.

9. Lever Brothers started as a partnership between William Lever and his brother, James. It became a private company in 1890 and in 1894 a public one, under William Lever's chairmanship, James, his father, and P. J. Winser as directors.

10. Wilson, *The History*, p.24.

11. Wilson, *The History*, p.9.

12. Wilson, *The History*, p.39.

13. Lever, *The Six-hour Day*, p.39.

14. Liverpool Incorporated Chamber of Commerce, *Monthly Journal*, Mar. 1921.

15. *Progress: the Magazine of Lever Brothers*, Dec. 1912.

16. *Progress*, Aug. 1913.

17. Lever, *The Six-hour Day*, p.13; Aneurin William, *Co-partnership and Profit-sharing* (London: William and Norgate, 1913), p.109.

18. *Anti-Socialist*, April 1909.

19. Lever, *The Six-hour Day*, p.67.

20. Lever, *The Six-hour Day*, p.251.

21. Leverhulme, *Viscount Leverhulme*, p.198.

22. Wilson, *The History*, p.291.

23. *Progress*, April 1909.

24. *Labour Chronicle*, Aug. 1, 1896; W. L. George, *Labour and Housing at Port Sunlight* (London: Alston Rivers, 1909), p.189.

25. M. P. Brocklebank, "A Visit to Port Sunlight", *Economic Rev.*, 8 (1898), p.527.

26. George, *Labour and Housing*, p.52.

27.
Lever, The Six-hour Day, p.112.

28.
N. C. Hunt, Methods of Wage Payment in British Industry (London: Sir Isaac Pitman, 1959), p.31.

29.
Progress, Dec 1912.

30.
Wilson, The History, pp.146-7. The village was run by the committee which was selected from the villagers. The rents were lower than in neighboring industrial towns such as Liverpool, and the income from the rents comprised only a quarter of the whole expenditure, the rest being met by the company under the profit-sharing scheme. Lever laid down the objects of Port Sunlight as follows: to establish friendly relations between capital and labor; to get the men to do their best work, to make the men's comfort depend on the firm's prosperity; to put capital in the right by treating the men as well as possible, leaving it to their conscientious reply.

31.
George, Labour and Housing, p.112.

32.
A. Watson, My Life: An Autobiography (London: Ivor Nicholson and Watson, 1937), p.137.

33.
Watson, My Life, p.138; Wilson, The History, p.150.

34.
Wilson, The History, p.151.

35.
Lever, "Prosperity-sharing vs Profit-sharing in Relation to Workshop Management," Economic Review, 11 (Jan. 1901), pp.47-64; "Prosperity-sharing: Rejoinder," Economic Review, 11 (July 1901), pp.316-21; G. Livesey, "Profit-sharing: A Vindication," Economic Review, 11 (Oct. 1901), pp.410-21. There was rivalry between Lever Brothers and the South Metropolitan in terms of the co-partnership system as they were the two most well-known schemes. The house magazines of both companies occasionally printed sharp criticism on each other.

36.
Wilson, The History, p.75.

37.
Wilson, The History, p.119.

38.
Reader, Imperial Chemical Industries, p.235.

39.
Engineering World, Sep. 9, 1920.

40.
Lever, The Six-hour Day, p.71.

41.
Lever, The Six-hour Day, pp.95-6.

42.
Lloyd George, for one, remarked on this aspect of Lever's personality. He is reported to have said of Lever that "He could not work with other men." Quoted in W. P. Jolly, Lord Leverhulme: A Biography (London: Constable, 1976), p.73.

43.
Lever, The Six-hour Day, p.69; Labour Co-partnership, Jan. 1910, p.18.

44.
Lever, The Six-hour Day, p.89.

45.
Progress, April, 1909; Lever Brothers, "Co-partnership Trust Deed" at Unilever House, London.

46.
Lever Brothers, "Co-partnership Trust Deed."

47.
Jolly, Lord Leverhulme, p.92.

48.
"Leverhulme Correspondene," 1389D, Aug. 22, 1929. (Hereafter correspondence).

49.
Progress, April 1909.

50.
Lever, The Six-hour Day, p.85.

51.
Progress, Jan. 1909.

52.
Lever, *The Six-hour Day*, p.84.

53.
"Co-partnership Trust Deed."

54.
Progrerss, April 1909.

55.
"Correspondence," 1321, Nov. 22, 1916.

56.
Progress, Aug. 1913.

57.
"Correspondence," 1321, Nov. 10, 1915.

58.
"Correspondence," 1389, May 27, 1929.

59.
Remember that as long as the original co-partner was holding the preferred ordinary shares allotted to him, he received additional bonus.

60.
"Correspondence," 1389, passim.

61.
"Corrrespondence," 1313A, April 1, 1921.

62.
These qualificaions were reduced to 24 and 4 years respectively in 1916. In 1920, Lever again reduced the age limit of the employee co-partner to 21 and the service years to 1.

63.
"Co-partnership Trust Deed," 1909.

64.
Progress, Aug. 1913.

65.
Progress, April 1913; Wilson, *The Hisotry*, p.294.

66.
Progress, Jan. 1920.

67.
Progress, Feb. 1912.

68. "Co-partnership Trust Deed."

69. Walter Citrine, _Men and Work: An Autobiography_ (London: Hutchison, 1964), p.55.

70. _Progress_, Jan. 1920.

71. Wilson, _The Hisotry_, p.223.

72. The strike was entirely confined to the laboring element--soapmakers, packers, sorters and fillers--all the skilled workers and motor-van men being at work. No support came from tradesmen.

73. _Liverpool Daily Post_, June 8, 1920; _Liverpool Echo_, June 8, 1920.

74. _Progress_, Dec. 1918.

75. _Liverpool Echo_, June 11, 1920.

76. _Liverpool Daily Post_, June 11, 1920.

77. _Liverpool Daily Post_, May 28, 1920.

78. _Liverpool Daily Post_, June 18, 1920.

79. _Liverpool Echo_, June 19, 1920.

80. _Times_, June 12, 1920, 6e.

81. _Liverpool Daily Post_, June 10, 1920.

82. _Liverpool Daily Post_, June 12, 1920.

83. _Liverpool Daily Post_, June 15, 1920.

84. *Liverpool Daily Post*, June 19, 1920.

85. *Liverpool Echo*, June 16, 1920.

86. Sidney Webb, *The Works Manager Today* (London: 1918; rpt. N.Y.: Arno, 19790, pp.56-7.

87. *Liverpool Daily Post*, Oct. 23, 1919.

88. "Corrrespondence," 1313, Feb. 4, 1920.

89. *Labour Co-partnership*, July, 1921, p.83.

90. *Labour Co-partnership*, Feb. 1920, p.21.

91. *Liverpool Daily Post*, Nov. 21, 1919.

92. *Liverpool Daily Post*, Nov. 21, 1919.

93. *Liverpool Daily Post*; *Liverpool Echo*; *Times*, Nov. 21, 1919, 10f.

94. ASCJ. *Journal*, Jan. 1920.

95. *Liverpool Daily Post*, June 24, 1920.

96. "Correspondence," 1313, April 21, 1921.

97. "Correspondence," 1313A, May 4, 5, 1921.

98. *Liverpool Daily Post*, Nov.27, 1919.

99. *Progress*, April, 1921.

100. "Correspondence," 1313A, June 21, 1921.

101. "Correspondence," 1321, Nov. 11, 1915.

102. *Liverpool Daily Post*, June 2, 1920.

103. *Liverpool Echo*, June 16, 1920.

104. Unilever, CPCOP 50.

105. Unilever, CPCOP 49, 50.

106. *Bolton Evening News*, Oct. 9, 1919.

107. A. Ramsay, "Cycles of Control: Worker Participation in Sociological and Historical Perspective," *Sociology*, 2 (Sep. 1977).

108. Leverhulme, *Viscount Leverhulme*, p.244.

109. George, *Labour and Housing*, p.58.

110. *Progress*, Jan. 1924.

111. Wilson, *The History*, p.276.

112. Wilson, "Management and Policy in Large-scale Enterprise," in *Essays in British Business History* ed. B. Supple (Oxford: Clarendon, 1977), p. 133.

113. Wilson, *The History*, p.292.

114. *Daily Herald*, June 10, 1920.

115. Unilever, CPCOP 49.

116. *Liverpool Daily Post*, June 2, 1920.

117.
"Correspondence," 1313, Aug. 6, 1919.

118.
Progress, Dec. 1919.

119.
Unilever, CPCOP 49.

120.
Unilever, CPCOP 49.

121.
Progress, Dec. 1918; Liverpool Daily Post, Nov. 21, 1919.

122.
Progress, Dec. 1918.

123.
Progress, Feb. 1922.

124.
Progress, Feb. 1922.

125.
Wilson, The History, p.276.

126.
"Correspondence," 1389, Oct. 13, 1900.

127.
"Correspondence," 1389, Jan. 11, 1923.

128.
Wilson, The History, p.293.

129.
Lever, "Prosperity-sharing vs Profit-sharing," p.58.

130.
A. C. Menzies, Modern Men of Mark (London: H. Jenkins, 1921), p.173.

131.
Wilson, The History, p.21.

132.
Leverhulme, Viscount Leverhulme, p.234.

133.
Unilever, CPCOP 38.

134\.
Menzies, <u>Men of Mark</u>, p.162.

135\.
<u>Birkenhead News</u>, Quoted in George, <u>Labour and Housing</u>, p.5.

136\.
<u>Progress</u>, July 1925.

137\.
Watson, <u>My Life</u>, p.219.

138\.
"Correspondence," 1389, Aug. 2, 1929.

139\.
Unilever, "Special Committee Minutes," July 21, 1954. I owe Howard Gospel for this information.

140\.
Lever, <u>The Six-hour Day</u>, p.121.

141\.
Wilson, <u>The History</u>, p.291.

Chapter IX. The Assessment

If we look at the history of profit-sharing, the first thing that strikes us is the high rate of abandoned schemes. Out of 380 schemes started since 1865, only 182 existed in 1919. It is undoubtedly a high proportion, yet the abandonment must not be identified with failure. The fact that a scheme was abandoned was no proof of a failure for in many cases abandonment was due to various circumstances such as the death of the employer or the termination of the business, none of which could be properly attributed to the operation of the system.

As shown in the table below, the cause directly derived from the system itself stood only at 35, 44, 46 percent, in the years 1894, 1912, and 1920. Thus, the actual rate of failures was not as great as the percentage of abandoned schemes suggested. When William Wallace made an investigation into profit-sharing in 1920 at the request of Seebohm Rowntree, he found that only 36 percent of the firms that had terminated profit-sharing plans considered that the scheme had failed.[1] Moreover, the mere fact of survival was no proof of success. In many schemes, employers and workers remained lukewarm in the matter after a certain period lapsed, and many schemes were continued simply because there was no particular reason to terminate it.

Table 9.1 The Causes of Abandonment

	1894		1912		1920	
	N	%	N	%	N	%
Altered circumstances: death of employer, sale of business etc.	5	10	30	18	39	20
Finalcial Reasons: losses, liquidation, etc.	23	45	54	33	52	26
Dissatisfaction with the scheme: apathy of employee, dissatisfaction of employer	18	35	71	44	91	46
Unknown or difficult to distinguish	5	10	8	5	16	8
	51	100	163	100	198	100

Source: Report on Profit-sharing and Labour Co-partnership Cd. 7458 (1894), p.136; Cd.6490 (1912), pp.14-5, 114; Cd.544 (1920), pp.12-3.

What seems more significant is the rather high rate of failure due to financial reasons. In 1894, for instance, more schemes were terminated because there were no profits to divide than any other reasons. The failure to profit was by no means exceptional in reality of the late Victorian and the Edwardian economies. In 1891, for instance, the Reverend A. Anstey of Leicester traced the fortunes of 105 firms in hosiery trade in the previous 28 years: 54 had closed down for lack of profits; 13 had sold the business;

no information was obtained on 21 firms; and only 17 were known still in business.[2]

Profit-sharing firms as well as non-profit-sharing concerns evenly failed to prosper. It is evident that profit-sharing was not a particularly effective remedy for unprofitable business, and notwithstanding the earlier belief that profit-sharing would bring about prosperity, the firms with instituted profit-sharing system followed the same financial fluctuations as others.

However, the need still remains to explain why the system, which seemed so simple and yet promising, failed to expand further. Profit-sharing could have played a significant role in a society with no state insurance and inadequate welfare provisions, as was the case in nineteenth and early twentieth century Britain. The limits of the development of profit-sharing were largely due to the employers' reluctance, as discussed in Chapter IV. However, there was a more fundamental obstacle to it: the unfavorable response from employers coincided with an unfavorable climate for profit-sharing created by the structure of the British economy. These structural impediments can be summed up as, first, the decline of the British economy as a whole; second, the heavy dependence of its economy on export and world trade; and finally, the persistence of archaic patterns in British firms. Although the peculiarity of the British industrial structure ought not to be exaggerated, some factors undoubtedly led the

British economy to a distinct way in the years 1880-1920.

Inappropriate Industries and Occupations for Profit-sharing

Before examining the peculiar conditions of the British experiment, we ought to look at the unfavorable climate for profit-sharing that commonly existed in all economies. There are certain industries and occupations in which profit-sharing cannot be applied, or if it can, in which it will not produce the desired effect and therefore unattractive. Profit-sharing is normally improper, obviously, for nationalized industries. The late nineteenth century witnessed the municipalization of many industries, particularly such public utilities as gas and water, and the impediments to introducing profit-sharing to them were pointed out. It was believed that in public sector of industry, the cost of profit-sharing would be simply transferred to the public. Unlike a profit-sharing scheme in privately owned firms where the transfer of wealth was made between employer and employee, such a scheme based on municipal profits or municipal charges might "degenerate into a form of indirect taxation, while further difficulties would arise over the investments of bonus in municipal stock."[3]

Another unsuitable area--and a very large one--was

domestic service, although this particular occupation was to decline substantially in the early 20th century. At the same time, more and more people were choosing occupations and industries in which profit-sharing was difficult to put into practice. Not only were more people working in nationalized industries, in public administration, and in the professions, but more people were self-employed. Employment in local and central government, to choose only one pertinent statistics, rose from 104,000 in 1891 to 226,000 in 1911.[4]

There were also those industries in which the work was irregular and seasonal and whose very nature, then, made it impossible to establish any coherent system based on regular wages or length of service. Dockers, for example, were rarely employed full time; the gas industry's "wintermen" worked only in the winter. Food-processing concerns had a special difficulty: the bulk of the workforce consisted of young women whose service tended to terminate abruptly with marriage. In those industries, it was more realistic to introduce different provisions that disregarded length of service.

The ratio of labor costs to total costs, is extremely important in determining a firm's industrial relations policy. The higher this ratio, the more consideration the firm is likely to give to labor matters and the more likely it is to attempt to control labor costs. There were industries in which the cost of labor occupied such a comparativly minor part of the total cost that any attempt to reduce it through ruling out profit-sharing was unnecessary. To be sure, profit-sharing is most likely to work in an industry where the ratio of labor cost is high. In such industries as steel and oil, labor costs were very low compared to capital costs and therefore other factors such as market conditions and advertising were considered more significant than the cost of labor.[5] Profit-sharing would have hardly attracted employer's interest in these industries.

Peculiar Circumstances of the British Economy

Examining the general obstacles to the development of profit-sharing to which all economies were subject, we now turn to peculiar circumstances of the British economy. First of all, the basic prerequisite for profit-sharing is that there be profits to share. If there are not, the system naturally perishes. Unfortunately, this is precisely what happened in many profit-sharing schemes in Britain. When a company failed to make profits several years in a row, the scheme inevitably died. From 1901 to 1919, the schemes that paid no bonus to employees each year averaged 15 percent. In the period 1923-1933, the no-bonus proportion increased, ranging anywhere from 20 percent to

33.5 percent.[6] Naturally, a great many of the schemes were abandoned. Among the causes of abandonment, as we saw earlier in this Chapter, losses or diminution of profits ranged from 26 to 45 percent. No schemes were abandoned for financial reasons in the years 1901-2 or 1912-13: these were periods of good trade. On the other hand, the number of schemes abandoned for financial reasons was above the average in the bad years, 1893 and 1908-9.[7]

There have been endless arguments and hypotheses concerning how and why the decline of the British economy occurred as it did, and why the British failed to halt the decline or reestablish their position as the world's ranking industrial nation.[8] Perhaps, the primary cause was simply Britain's position as the first industrial country which predetermined the subsequent development. To quote Hobsbawm:

> Pioneer industrialization naturally took place in special conditions which could not be maintained, with methods and techniques which, however advanced and efficient at the time, could not remain the most advanced and efficient, and it created a pattern of both production and markets which could not necessarily remain the one best fitted to sustain economic growth and technical change. Yet to change from an old and obsolescent pattern to a new one was both expensive and difficult.9

For whatever reasons, the decline of the British economy was a fact, and a fact that would inevitably hurt profit-sharing--indirectly perhaps, but not insignificantly.

We now consider our second great structural obstacle: dependence on exports and consequent instability. Profit-sharing, it should be evident, requires a relatively stable business. The industries with a heavy profit-sharing abandonment rate, such as shipbuilding and engineering, were all subject to extreme fluctuations, and any prosperity in boom years in these industries was not likely to survive the testing periods of depression. Thus Benjamin Browne claimed that in engineering, returns were too low for successful profit-sharing.[10] At the same time, the British economy was heavily dependent on world trade. This could be seen in the fact that exports normally grew faster than the real national income as a whole. In such major industries as cotton, iron, and steel, which relied on overseas markets for about 40 percent of their gross production, the foreign market played an especially decisive role.[11]

The dependence on world trade made the British economy particularly vulnerable to cyclical fluctuations and this in turn made profit-sharing seem increasingly impractical. If profit-sharing was to prove its effectiveness in terms of better business results, it had to display its contributions to productivity in the profits account. This it could not always do. When market conditions overwhelmed labor's effort, the system seemed useless and without point. Market conditions were even more unpredictable and uncontrollable when industry was deeply dependent on foreign trade and under such circumstances, less room existed for recognition of the worker's contribution. All of this was clearly shown in the scheme at the Irvine's shipyards which is discussed in Chapter V. It had received the full co-operation of the trade unions and the agreements reached were satisfactory both to the employer and the workers, yet it had been started in a severe trade depression: men were working only a week or two a month in shipbuilding at the time. Despite otherwise favorable conditions, the scheme could not survive the industry's fluctuations.

Third, and finally, there was the archaic structure of British firms. To begin with, the size of British firms remained surprisingly small until the interwar years, when a substantial number of mergers took place. To be sure, the public joint-stock company had emerged after 1880, and its spread contributed to the increased size of firms. But if it would be said that a trend towards concentration existed, it was a long way from transforming the economy: the small firm employing fewer than 100 workers made up 97 percent of manufacturing concerns in 1914.[12] Here was a serious deterrent to profit-sharing indeed. As profit-sharing was still in the experimental stage in the years 1880-1920 and seemed both risky and potentially costly, it generally required a firm with substantial resources. Small firms not only feel less pressure for change, but they possess fewer resources with which to implement it.

This we can see clearly when we look at the statistics: 70 percent of the total profit-sharing schemes in operation in 1920 were those of firms which employed more than 100 workers.

Table 9.2 The size of profit-sharing firms

Having not more than 25 employees	6 %
Having between 25 and 99 employees	24
Having between 100 and 249 employees	23
Having between 250 and 999 employees	27
Having more than 1,000 employees	20
	100 %

Source: Ministry of Labour, *Report*, Cd.544 (1920), p.16.

Indeed, bigness was the general trend in profit-sharing firms. About one fifth were companies with over 1,000 employees, and of those having more than 1,000 employees, some fifteen firms had more than 2,500 employees; six had over 10,000 and one had some 70,000.

Even in relatively large undertakings, however, management remained sadly anachronistic. The chief problems of decentralized organization persisted: sub-contracting and internal contracting as well as the powerful role of the foreman. Most British firms did not have a comprehensive program for selecting and training workers.

Sub-contracting, which also implied internal contracting in nineteenth century practice, was usual throughout much of the century in the iron and steel industry, in coal-mining, and in building. Thus, as David Schloss observed in the late nineteenth century, sub-contracting was virtually ubiquitous.[13]

By means of sub-contracting, a large undertaking was able to shed most of its responsibilities for labor management. Under this form of organization the employer provided the locus of production and the machinery, supplied raw materials and arranged for the sale and distribution of the product. But the actual production was under the control of sub-contractors who hired the workers, paid them their wages, supervised the work process, and received a rate from the employer for the finished goods.[14]

The role of the nineteenth century foreman, who had existed along with sub-contractors, demonstrated a similar pattern. Not only the foreman selected, disciplined, and dismissed his workers, but he also had considerable freedom in setting pay, deciding piecework prices or allotting merit money. An employer assessed the role of the foreman in 1917: "In most works, the whole industrial life of the workman is in the hands of his foreman. The foreman chooses him from among the applicants at the works gate; often he settles what wages he shall get; no advance of wage or promotion is possible except on his initiatives; he often sets the piece-price and has the power to cut it when he wishes; and ...he almost always has unrestricted power of discharge."[15]

Profit-sharing and co-partnership were most difficult of all to apply in such industries as shipbuilding and engineering, where the work was set up on a craft basis and where workers were still largely employed indirectly. On the other hand, profit-sharing was most easily applied in industries where systematic management was already established--the chemical industry, for example, and public utilities, such as gas and electricity, with a certain degree of monopoly. Charles Carpenter testified that his company, the South Metropolitan Gas, had already established a centralized system of hiring and firing and a comprehensive payroll in the 1880s.[16] It seems obvious that the more progressive firms were likely to be large-scale and therefore in a position to develop more systematic ways to deal with problems involving organization and coordination.

It would seem that the archaic structure of British industry and the conservative practices of British management reciprocally reinforced each other. The limited perspective of the employers made them reluctant to try new management methods and the structural difficulties gave them an excuse for not attempting a more progressive approach. To be sure, these archaic practices were less in evidence by the end of the nineteenth century, yet the changes were not sufficiently influenced to transform British industry as a whole. These peculiarities of the British economy certainly did not provide profit-sharing with optimum conditions to flourish.

So far it has been argued first that, although the rate of the abandoned profit-sharing schemes was rather high, it should not be considered the failure of the system, for many of the causes of abandonment lay in factors which were not inherent in the system; second, the failure of the large-scale application of the system derived in large part from the structure of the British economy, not from defects of the system itself. In a different economic structure and circumstances, profit-sharing could have exhibited a greater potential.

A more appropriate approach to assessing the system will be done through the eyes of those who were actually involved in it. At the same time, the success or failure of profit-sharing has to be judged against the objectives which the system aimed to achieve. To the employer, the system's value lay in the improvement of productivity and labor relations; for the worker, the real question was, as Lord Robert Cecil proclaimed, whether the system materially benefited him.[17] Let us examine the worker's side first.

The Material Benefits to the Worker

It was a contemporary criticism that the profit-sharing bonus was simply delayed wages and profit-sharing firms underpaid their workers in regular wages. However, David Schloss, after a comprehensive survey on the subject, concluded that such an allegation was groundless. In only one case, the employees received lower wages than the district rate; but in this firm the employees had received the abnormally high bonus of 26.9 percent on wages, which more than compensated the gap in the regular wages. The rest of the cases, employees received the district rates or more.[18]

Another frequent criticism was made on the small amount of bonus and its seemingly negligible effect on improving worker's material circumstances. The average bonus rate on wages was around 5 percent in all profit-sharing firms, including the firms which failed to pay bonuses.[19] The critics claimed that it was illusory for a system which provided only 5 percent bonus to realize any real transfer of wealth, and attributed the smallness of bonus to the failure of the large-scale application of the system.

However, closer examination shows that the 5 percent bonus far exceeded the rate of the wage increases in the period concerned. The average money wages arose at the annual rate of 1.1 percent over 1896-1913; real wages increased by 1.94 percent annually between 1871 and 1895, and by 1.83 percent during 1895-1913.[20] Given that wages in profit-sharing firms were not lower than non-profit-sharing undertakings, the 5 percent bonus was far greater and more favorable than the increase of wages. The contemporaries did not systematically compile the annual return of wage increases or changes and apparently underestimated the size of the profit-sharing bonus.

The financial results of some successful schemes were impressive. South Metropolitan, for one, paid over L 770,000 in bonuses in 30 years up to 1920; and the employees invested more than L 500,000 in the company shares and deposits. Lever Brothers, which started co-partnership in 1909, had distributed L 700,000 by 1920. J. T. and J. Taylor, a much smaller firm than South Metropolitan or Lever Brothers, nevertheless paid over L 330,000 during 30 years under the system.

The effect of profit-sharing on productivity is a debatable question for there is no simple way to measure it. Productivity depends on various factors, including machinery, management, and working conditions. However, as discussed in chapter VI, profit-sharing does not appear to have made a substantial contribution to improved productivity. Given that profit-sharing did not increase labor productivity and thus did not create larger profits, the profit-sharing bonus was a clear addition to the normal remuneration of the employees. It was a direct transfer of income from employers and shareholders to employees. Even the TUC survey of profit-sharing conducted in 1957 admitted that the total earnings of the workers in profit-sharing firms "probably compare favorably with those in firms where similar schemes do not exist."[21]

If it is accepted that the worker was mainly concerned with the material result of the system, the system certainly satisfied his expectation. If other considerations such as the worker's desire to participate in management are to be regarded, the assessment will present a different picture. However, the workers were uninterested in taking over the business and running it for themselves. Neither did they want to become shareholders and take risk. When a co-partnership scheme did not enforce compulsory purchases of the company stock, few workers were eager to buy it and become shareholders of the company which employed them. In Clarke, Nicholls, and Coombs, London foodstuff company, the employees had several opportunities of acquiring the company's preferential shares, but they did not seem to appeal to them; as a result, the company had only 50 worker-shareholders out of 1,400 employees after almost 20 year practice of profit-sharing.[22] Aitken and Dolt, frame-makers of Edinburgh, adopted profit-sharing and wished to expand to a shareholding system, but found the majority of their employees were "against runnng the infinitesimal risk they were called upon to run."[23]

Occasionally, though, there were genuine exceptions. The worker, if he was given a full voice in management and thought himself to be a real partner, was even willing to share in losses. The workers in George Thomson's woollen factory was the case in point. In this scheme, which Ben Turner, president of the Textile Workers Union and the ILP man, called a "real co-partnership," workers owned ordinary share and were fully represented on the board, along with trade union officials and co-operative societies' representatives. The company suffered financial losses on two occasions, and the workers indeed met the losses: they paid the outside shareholders a 5 percent dividend out of their earnings, although in an equally generous response, most of the shareholders sent their money back.[24]

Most British workers, however, were uninterested in the idea of workers' control. They preferred a cash bonus to shares which implied shareholders' right and responsibility. After all, the workers needed cash money as much as possible for their daily life. Moreover, the remote dividend was not attractive to them, as one observer put it, "the very idea of owning share is a remote concept to most of shopfloor workers."[25]

Nor did the union leadership press for

participation in management. B. Pribicevic writes that within the British unions there was no evidence of socialist thought before 1910 that advocated the idea of joint or complete control of industry by the workers and their unions. When the engineers demanded a share in the control of industry in the decades after 1910, he points out, it was not for the sake of having such a share per se but out of a desire to protect their craft interests.[26] Worker's control was an extremely vague notion and subject to various interpretations according to the historic context in which it emerged, as Fraser points out.[27] However, it never represented a revolutionary assumption of the total control of industry. Traditionally the British trade unions were satisfied with industrial democracy and worker participation which could be achieved within collective bargaining.

To be sure, the unions seem to have held sufficient power to demand a certain amount of managerial control when they firmly established themselves as the body of collective bargaining. The reason they did not, Phelps Brown concluded, is simply that they did not want it. At bottom, the unions had no wish to take over the industrial system and run it themselves. Their aim was to secure for their members a fair share, and no more, of the earnings of capitalism.[28]

The ambivalence of the position of trade unionism in capitalist society is still being argued in the circle for workers' control. Richard Hyman, for one, writes: "Union is on the one hand a protest and defence against the economic and human reprivation imposed on workers by capitalist industry; on the other, a means of accommodation to the structure of capitalist industry."[29]

The workers seem to have been content with the bonus and the simple form of consultation such as profit-sharing committee, which somehow satisfied their desire for participating in decision making. Elie Halevy, the shrewd observer, had already concluded in the early 1920s that what working man wanted was "not to share the chances of gain and, with them, the risk of loss inseparable from the management of a large enterprise." They wanted "security in the forms of a stable wage and guarantee against unemployment."[26]

Profit-sharing's Benefits from the Employer's Point of View

From the worker, we turn to the employer. Here, the assessment has to be made both in terms of greater productivity and better industrial relations. As discussed in previous chapters, profit-sharing's direct impact on labor productivity was minimal. Moreover, any method which promises higher remuneration would cause an immediate stimulus of the worker. How long this stimulus lasts and to what degree this is reflected in the output and productivity are another considerations. Unfortunately, profit-sharing was not the best means to prolong this stimulus: soon after the scheme was started the initial enthusiasm tended to fade and the profit-sharing bonus became taken for granted.

Yet interestingly, the public and even the workers believed in profit-sharing's effect on greater productivity, and this belief has persisted: according to a survey by the Confederation of British Industry in 1976, 85 percent of employees thought that industry would be more productive if they had a stake in the profits.[31] If profit-sharing improved productivity at all, it was not through greater individual output but through smoother industrial relations and subsequently less labor conflict as well as fewer stoppages caused by such conflict. Therefore the more significant contribution of the system seem to have derived from creating and promoting industrial peace.

The conditions of industrial relations can be best measured by strikes or otherwise, and profit-sharing firms in general demonstrated an outstanding industrial peace. While there is no quantitative survey on strikes in profit-sharing and non-profit-sharing firms in Britain, our two case studies, South Metropolitan and Lever Brothers, revealed unbroken peace in labor-management relations under the system. In both companies, the employees displayed absolute loyalty to their employers. The 1939 survey of

American firms conducted by the U.S. Senate also discovered that firms practicing the more advanced forms of profit-sharing and co-partnership were less affected by labor trouble than others.

The rate of strikes in the firms without profit-sharing reached 23.4 percent, whereas the rate in those which had adopted such schemes remained only 9.9 percent.[32] Surely profit-sharing could not claim the sole responsibility for this result: such firms may have adopted more progressive labor policy thus the relative absence of strikes may have resulted from the general attitude of management, not from the profit-sharing scheme in particular. Yet profit-sharing was without doubt a contributing force to establish a cordial relationship, and one exuberant profit-sharing employer proclaimed that "I sometimes ask myself whether I am in a fool's paradise."[33]

The Place of Profit-sharing in the Development of Modern Management

However, the progressiveness of profit-sharing ought not to be exaggerated. In profit-sharing, both strengths and weaknesses of welfare capitalism are exhibited, although its peculiarities distinguish profit-sharing from other forms of industrial welfare. The whole debate on industrial welfare has coalesced on motivational argument. Although all arguments tend to acknowledge the place of welfare work in the context of modern management, one group emphasizes human factors in welfare work, while the other endeavours to cast it mainly in the development of capitalist modes of production and control. Thus, the former find the motivating force among the majority of welfare employers in their sense of special responsibility for dependent employees such as women and children; the latter attributes welfarism to employer strategy to discipline and retain the most important sector of the workforce, mainly skilled male workers, and to exert social control at the level of greater society.[34]

However, closer examination shows neither factor was particularly demonstrated in profit-sharing. Profit-sharing did not find its strongest advocates among the employers who were concerned with the dependent employees. The system indeed was least adaptable to firms which employed a bulk of women workers for their service tended to terminate abruptly with marriage or conception. Profit-sharing could not be based upon such irregularity of employment by its very nature.

Welfare capitalism, on David Brody's account, was an idea that management accepted an obligation for the well-being of its employees.[35] Profit-sharing was not constructed on this obligation. It was rather a bargain and a business contract that is, "If you work better and harder, I will share with you the surplus profits thus made." Profit-sharing was probably the most calculated form of industrial welfare both in terms of cost and purposes. Frequently, it was used as a system of payment by results, as was explored in Chapter VI, and when it failed to produce the immediate increase of productivity, the scheme was terminated and converted to other forms of payment by results.

Consequently, productivity and cost remained crucial factors in profit-sharing. An important factor involved in welfare work was cost. If welfarism was not widely spread in Britain, it was not only because of employers' indifference to the idea but because of the lack of resources in industries such as engineering characterized by a small firm structure which was unable to provide the capital for extensive welfare schemes, as Craig Littler points out.[36] Profit-sharing had advantages in this respect for it was less costly and required less administration than other welfare programs. Brooks, Bond, a wholesale tea blender of London, which had practiced profit-sharing since 1882 wrote: "Our system was introduced primarily for the benefits of the workers. The problem is, how to add to the earnings of labor without diminishing the profits of the employer."[37] The solution was supposed to be found in profit-sharing which allegedly created greater zeal and vigilance, economies of time and material, and therefore greater profits.

Profit-sharing in this sense was different from other humanitarian welfare provisions, and it represented the kind of welfare which claimed that "it pays." Daniel Nelson, in his study on American welfarism, argues that most of the profit-sharing companies were small firms that had otherwise shown little interest in welfare measures.[38] A similar conclusion can be made in the British context. With notable exceptions such as Lever Brothers and South Metropolitan, the majority of profit-sharing schemes were introduced in firms in which no discernable welfare plans had existed.

In most cases, profit-sharing schemes were not extended to more comprehensive welfare provisions. There were only 27 schemes which were related to welfare fund directly or indirectly: 7 cases, out of these 27, the total profit-sharing bonus was contributed to welfare fund, such as old age pension, sick fund, or death allowance. In 11 cases, the bonus was only partly devoted to welfare fund, the proportion being usually one-half or sometimes one third. In 7 cases, the fund was recruited from the share of the total bonus which was due to those employees who had not fulfilled the necessary conditions, thus were excluded from the distribution.[39]

Consequently, the preponderant type of British profit-sharing schemes was cash bonus. Straight cash bonus schemes formed 59 percent of the total profit-sharing plans in operation in 1919 if the gas companies in which distribution of company's ordinary shares became a prevalent form were excluded. The next largest group was a form, in which the bonus was paid into a savings or deposit account and could be withdrawn at short notice. If these two were added together, they constituted 71 percent of the total schemes. This shows a sharp difference from practice in other countries. In France, for instance, the usual system was that of capitalizing the bonus in order to provide a pension for the employee after retirement. However, in Britain, in firms in which pension was instituted, such funds were frequently independent from profit-sharing.[40]

The system's proponents who viewed it from the light of morality thus were not pleased with the prevalent perception of the system in terms of material gain. They complained that too much stress was being laid in the monetary side of profit-sharing. To them, the greatest advantage came from the "formation of a truer and more human relationship between shareholders, employers and the men."[41] However, to the employers, material effect of the system far exceeded any other considerations. It seems that profit-sharing received attention from the employers who were aware of the effect of welfare work, yet concerned with its cost. Of all forms of welfare programs, profit-sharing cost the least: its provision was to be made only when surplus profits were available; moreover, such surplus profits were to be produced by workers' extra diligence and efficiency. Thus profit-sharing bonus did not touch the normal turnover of the firm in theory at least, although many capitalists thought otherwise.

Profit-sharing also appeared to attract employers who sensed the limited effect of welfare work. To a painful surprise to employers, welfare work was not particularly effective either in preventing labor trouble or in raising efficiency. Employers came to realize that in order to keep the worker loyal and cooperative, shrewd calculation had to be added while still exhibiting kind feeling and friendly sentiments. Most of welfare programs did not contribute much to make the worker have a direct interest in the firm. They were too remote to be an effective incentive and not outstanding in securing employee loyalty.[42] The record of pension plans, for instance, compared with profit-sharing on preventing labor dispute proved far unfavorable, according to the U.S. Senate's survey.

Table 9.3 Strikes and turnover in U.S.companies in 1939

Form of plan	Number of plans	Strikes	Decreased turnover
Pension	86	18.6 %	25.6 %
Profit-sharng	67	0.0	47.8

Source: J. Jehring, Profit-sharing: the Capitalistic Challenge (Evanston: Profit-sharing Research Foundation, 1956), p.18

Profit-sharing, as a form of a group incentive, promised

more certain and more immediate results. It implied more effort to bind the worker to the firm and greater calculation to proportion the worker's efficiency and loyalty to the material benefits he received.

Not surprisingly, profit-sharing has been considered a system of employers' strategy to contain trade unions and retain the workforce under the employer's absolute control. Thus, R. A. Church has concluded that profit-sharing was an extension of anti-union paternalism which was characteristic to labor management in the later nineteenth century.[43] H. Gospel sums up the current assessment of profit-sharing as follows:

> Co-partnership and profit-sharing were on the whole aimed more at preserving managerial prerogatives through incorporative provisions directed especially at binding skilled labor to the firm, containing industrial conflict, and undermining the power and influence of established trade unions.[44]

The significance of anti-unionism in profit-sharing, however, has been greatly exaggerated. One of the arguments made in this dissertation is that profit-sharing's anti-union element had faded by the fitst decade of the twentieth century, after which time profit-sharing tended to establish a more progressive labor-management relations based upon union recognition. Moreover, profit-sharing revealed the least paternalism among various welfare programs due to its more businesslike arrangement, and here profit-sharing holds a possibility to persist in the post welfare capitalist era.

Indeed the advocacy of profit-sharing as the system of generating the identity of interests and preventing socialism indicates the existence of "social control." Social control and the relationship between control in the workplace and control in greater society are among the most sensitive problems which social historians have encountered in the past ten years.[45] In applying the term in historical understanding, it has been pointed out that the notion of social control contains a danger of being applied to almost any activity of the ruling elites and therefore becoming valueless, as scholars such as Gareth Stedman Jones argue. Others such as R. Hay admit the presence of social control yet still feel that "it is very clear that in the period 1880-1920 there was no single employer view on social control or on the role of welfare in relation to social control."[46]

Clearly, the employer's sphere of control reached beyond the economic realm and elements of control can be traced in social, cultural, political, and ideological aspects, as Patrick Joyce has brilliantly displayed in his study of paternalistic relations in the Lancashire factories. To make the issue more complicated, social control necessarily leads to thinking of the process of "incorporation," "accommodation," and "resistance," which in turn bring about further sophisticated debates. Moreover, the relationship between control at the level of individual employer and that at the level of class in larger society is yet to be explored.

However, if we distinguish explicit social control from unconscious and unintended motivating factors, as F. M. L. Thompson suggests, and try to avoid the danger of employing the notion in too broad a context, these notions are valuable in understanding the profit-sharing movement.[47] Profit-sharing proves not only the presence of such explicit control but also the link between the two forms of control referred above. Profit-sharing was clearly intended to intensify the employer's control in the workshop; at the same time, it was intended to operate as the best antidote for socialism and thus was an explicit strategy adopted by the ruling elites to maintain the existing basis of social and economic relationships.

To be sure, there were conscientious employers who genuinely believed in a new form of social and industrial organization. However, social control was evident implicitly or explicitly in the language of advocacy which called for "another solidarity centered around the work" against class solidarity.[48] Thus one historian of profit-sharing defines it as seeking to substitute "enterprise consciousness" for class consciousness.[49]

Table 9.4 Industries in which profit-sharing was practiced

Nature of business	N of schmes started, 1865-1919	N of schemes surviving in 1919	N of employees
Merchants, warehouse-men and retail	58	25	23,237
Metal, engineering, and shipbuilding	44	19	89,273
Paper, printing	44	17	6,708
Gas undertakings	40	36	33,528
Food and drink	34	16	7,792
Textile	25	17	24,157
Agriculture	22	8	1,267
Chemicals, soap and oil, paint, etc	22	13	16,478
Clothing	16	5	661
Building	14	3	203
Woodcutting and fur-nishing	10	1	60
Mining and quarrying	6	1	11,232
Banking and insurance	5	5	24,325
Transport	4	2	192
Electricity	2	2	303
Other business	33	12	3,634
	379	182	243,050

Source: Ministry of Labour, Report on Profit-sharing and Labour Co-partnership Cd.544 (1920), p. 15

If profit-sharing aimed at social control in the broader context, such control was not necessarily exhibited with specific intention to retain and control the strategically important work groups. As the table above shows, the system can be found even in industries where such a group did not hold particular importance. The engineering industry might have realized the necessity and scarcity of such a sector; yet the greater part of the workforce in printing and paper-making consisted in the unskilled female employees, who were equally allowed to participate in the plans. Few profit-sharing schemes deliberately separated skilled male workers from the rest of the workforce. In terms of qualification, most schemes applied standards such as age and the number of service years, but not position or gender.

The connotation of welfare capitalism is buying worker loyalty at cheap cost and thus retaining the existing economic and social relations as well as power structure. Profit-sharing undoubtedly contained such elements, and many schemes revealed such intentions. At the same time, profit-sharing and co-partnership failed to produce an enduring institution towards industrial democracy as the critics of the system have argued. For this failure, however, both the employer and the worker were responsible. The workers, did not seriously consider taking over the industry or the firm and running it by themselves. As A. Rogow suggests, the British working class probably never believed in workers' control.[50] The inertia in the progress of co-partnership thus reflects the workers' indifference toward control.

At the same time, the failure of profit-sharing's evolution to industrial democracy was not necessarily the result of employer's stubborn determination to retain their authority. The concentration of power and authority in industrial organization were probably seen as inevitable to achieve maximum industrial efficiency. Firms with profit-sharing plans in general manifested more conciliatory policy in labor management.

The fact that profit-sharing employers entertained profit-sharing committees and works councils demonstrates their relative progressiveness in comparison with other employers. Such firms tended to acknowledge trade unions and provide worker participation no mattter how elementary it may have been. Moreover, profit-sharing and co-partnership were not palliative so much as preventive, and they revealed far-sighted perspectives of employers who adopted them. It was a policy of "giving before being forced to give," and represented the attitude that Henry Ford described: "The employer must meet the employee half-way, and always be there a little ahead of time."[51] Profit-sharing was an important breakthrough from the traditional forms of industrial relations which had consisted in conflict and competition on the one hand and conciliation and arbitration on the other. It was the first attempt, apart from the workers' cooperative movement, to grant the worker the right to participate both in profits and decision making.

It is impossible to discern whether such a policy derived from their wish to wield more efficient control over the workforce or from genuine belief in industrial reorganization. If employers reluctantly pursued this road, it is the reflection of the economic development in Britain that forced the British employers to subordinate themselves to it. At any rate employers' strategy appears to have succeeded. Profit-sharing employers were shrewd in the sense that they realized that "agreeable control is better than enforced control."

The profit-sharing employers were also progressive in the sense that they acknowledged the importance of labor relations. It is indeed in the development of personnel management that profit-sharing could claim its greatest contribution as the subsequent history showed: many firms which had established profit-sharing schemes with welfare departments, such as Lever Brothers and Brunner Mond, subsequently institutionalized personnel departments.

Profit-sharing and co-partnership, in the most advanced form, were the outgrowth of more enlightened management which was occurring in workshop organization as well as labor management in the period between 1880 and

1920. Importantly, such a managerial attitude was based on the recognition that the traditional approach to the industrial problem did not provide adequate remedies. Let alone whether or not their new remedies worked out, it represented a new perspective and initiated a new phase in industrial relations practices.

Notes to Chapter IX

1. William Wallace, Prescription for Partnership (London: Sir Isaac Pitman, 1959), pp.21-6.

2. Cited in P. L. Payne, British Entrepreneurship in the 19th Century (London: Macmillan, 1974), p.27.

3. A. H. Mackmurdo, Pressing Questions (London: H. John Lane, 1913), p.124; Charles Fay, "Co-partnership in Industry," Economic Journal, 22 (Dec. 1912), p.541.

4. Sidney Pollard, The Development of British Economy, 1914-50 (London: Edward Arnold, 1967), p.34.

5. Paul Derrick and J. F. Phipps ed., Co-ownership, Co-operation, and Control (London: Longmans, Green, 1969), p.25.

6. Conservative Research Department, Co-partnership Today (London: Conservative Political Centre, 1946), p.13.

7. Ministry of Labour, Report on Profit-sharing and Labour Co-partnership in the U.K., Cd. 544 (1920), p.13.

8. See Rodrick Floud and David McCloskey ed., The Economic History of Britain since 1700, vol.2 (Cambridge: Cambridge Univ. Press, 1980); Eric Hobsbawm, Industry and Empire (N.Y.: Penguin Books, 1971 ed.); David Landes, The Unbound Prometheus: Technical Change and Industrial Development in Western Europe from 1750 to the Present (Cambridge: Cambridge Univ. Press, 1969); David McCloskey ed. Mathematical Social Science Board Conference on the New Economic History of Britain 1840-1930 (Princeton: Princeton Univ. Press, 1971); Payne, British Entrepreneurship.

9. Hobsbawm, Industry and Empire, p.188.

10. Benjamin Browne, Selected Papers on Social and

Economic Questions (Cambridge: Cambridge University Press, 1918), p.160.

11. Hobsbawm, *Industry and Empire*, p.136.

12. Hobsbawm, *Industry and Empire*, p.215; A. L. Bowley, "The Survival of Small Firms", *Economica*, 1 (1921), pp.113-5.

13. David Schloss, *Methods of Industrial Remuneration* (London: Williams and Norgate, 1898), p.120.

14. Hugh Clegg, *The Changing System of Industrial Relations in Great Britain* (Oxford: Basil Blackwell, 1980), chapter 4; Howard Gospel, "The Development of Management Organization in Industrial Relations," in *Industrial Relations and Management Strategy* ed. K. Thurley and S. Wood (Cambridge: Cambridge Univ. Press, 1983); W. R. Garside and H. Gospel, "Employers and Managers," in *A History of British Industrial Relations 1875-1914* ed. Chris Wrigley (Amherst, Mass: Univ. of Massachussets Press, 1982).

15. Quoted in Craig Littler, *The Development of the Labour Process in Capitalist Societies* (London: Heinemann, 1982), p.86.

16. Charity Organization Society, Special Committee on Unskilled Labour, *Minutes of Evidence*, Q. 963.

17. Labour Co-partnership Association, *Report of London Co-partnership Congress*, (1926), p.8.

18. Schloss, *Methods*, p.179.

19. *Report*, Cd. 544 (1920), pp.22, 185-9.

20. E. H. Phelps Brown and M. Browne, *A Century of Pay* (London: Macmillan, 1968), pp.170, 221; Barbara Mitchell, *Abstrat of British Historical Statistics* (Cambridge: Cambridge University Press, 1971), p.344.

21. TUC, *Annual Report*, (1957), p.287.

22. Clarke, Nicholls, and Coombs, The Proof of Pudding (London: 1919), p.12.

23. Report, Cd. 7458 (1894), p.81.

24. Ben Turner, "Real Profit-sharing: A Splendid Huddersfield Example," Socialist Review, 5 (Jan. 1910).

25. D. Wallace Bell, Financial Participation (London: Industrial Participation Association, 1973), p.31.

26. Branko Pribicevic, The Shop Stewards Movement and Workers' Control (Oxford: Basil Blackwell, 1959).

27. Steve Fraser, "The New Unionism and New Economic Policy" in Work, Community, and Power ed. J. Cronin and C. Sirianni (Philadelphia: Temple Univ. Press, 1983), p.174.

28. Paul Thompson, The Edwardians (London: Granada, 1979), pp.474-5.

29. Richard Hyman, Introduction to The Frontier of Control, C. Goodrich, p.xxiv.; See also Hyman, "Workers' Control and Revolutionary Theory," Socialist Register (1974).

30. Elie Halevy, The Era of Tyrannies (Garden City, NY: Doubleday, 1965), p.180.

31. Economist, Jan. 7, 1978, p.62.

32. Conservative Research Department, Co-partnership Today, pp.38-9.

33. South Metropolitan Gas Co., Co-partnership, 1 (1904), p.101.

34. See David Broady, "The Rise and Decline of Welfare Capitalism," in Workers in Industrial America (Oxford:

Oxford University Press, 1982); Roy Hay, "Employers' Attitudes to Social Policy and the Concept of 'Social Control' 1900-1920" in _The Origins of British Social Policy_ ed. Pat Thane (London: Croom Helm, 1978); Littler, _The Development_; Jo Melling, "'Non-Commissioned Officers': British Employers and their Supervisory Workers, 1880-1920," _Social History_, 5 (May 1980); Melling, "British Employers and the Development of Industrial Welfare c.1880-1920" Disser. University of Glasgow, 1980; Melling, "Employers, Industrial Welfare, and the Struggle for Work-place Control in British Industry, 1880-1920" in _Managerial Strategies and Industrial Relations: An Historical and Comparative Study_, ed. Howard Gospel and Craig Littler (London: Heinemann, 1983); Daniel Nelson, _Managers and Workers: Origins of the New Factory System in the U.S. 1880-1920_ (Madison: Univ. of Wisconsin Press, 1975); G. Rimlinger, "Welfare Policy and Economic Development: A Comparative Historical Perspective," _Journal of Economic History_, 26 (1966).

35.
Brody, "The Rise and Decline," p.61.

36.
Littler, _The Development_, p.91.

37.
David Schloss, _Methods of Industrial Remuneration_ (London: William and Norgate, 1898), p.173.

38.
Nelson, _Managers_, p.105.

39.
Report, Cd. 544 (1920), pp.39-41.

40.
Jones, "Profit-sharing in relation," p. 329; William Ashley, "Profit-sharing," _Quarterly Review_, 219 (1913), p.524. When pension fund was provided in connection with profit-sharing schemes, the motivation behind it was more often than not paternalistic wish to inculcate thrift. Thomas Bushill set up a compulsory deposit of two thirds of the bonus to the provident funds. He did so because he believed that workers were unable to spend the bonus properly. "In the present state of the thriftness of the working classes," he insisted, "it is desirable in their own interest that the whole would not be paid out." Royal Commission on Labour, Sitting as a Whole, _Minutes of Evidence_, Cd. 7063-I (1893), Q.6138.

41.
Labour Co-partnership, March 1917, p.47.

42.
Labour Co-partnership, Oct. 1897, p.126.

43.
R. A. Church, "Profit-sharing and Labour Relations in England in the 19th century", International Review of Social History, 16(1971), p.16.

44.
Garside and Gospel, "Employers and Managers," p.108. See also Melling, "Employers, Industrial Welfare, and the Struggle"; Hay, "Employers' Attitudes"; N. Whiteside, "Industrial Welfare and Labour Regulation in Britain at the Time of the first World War," International Review of Social History, 25, part 3 (1980).

45.
H. Moorhouse, "History, Sociology, and the Quiescence of the British Working Class", Social History, 4 (1979); A. Reid, "Politics and Economics in the Formation of the British Working Class", Social History, 3 (1978); Richard Price, "Conflict and Co-operation", Social History, 9 (1984); Patrik Joyce, "Labour, Capital, and Compromise", Social History, 9 (1984).

46.
Hay, "Employers' attitude," p.115.

47.
Patrik Joyce, Work, Society and Politics (London: Methuen, 1980).

48.
Walls, Progressive Co-partnership, p.252. The journal of the South Metropolitan Gas Company insisted that "Everyone must get the idea that his own present and future interests are boun up in the company." Co-partnership, March 1921, p.28.

49.
Edward Bristow, "Profit-sharing, Socialism, and Labour Unrest," in Essays in Anti-Labour History ed. Kenneth Brown (London: Macmillan, 1974), p.262.

50.
Arnold Rogow, "The Labor Relations under the British Labor Government", American Journal of Economics and Sociology, 14 (1954/5), p.361.

51.
Quoted in Edward Walls, Progressive Co-partnership (London: Nisbet, 1921), p.280.

Selected Bibliography

Manuscripts

Cecil of Chelwood Papers. British Museum, Add. Mss.

Gas Light and Coke Company. "Minutes of Proceedings of the Court of the Directors."

Lever Brothers. "Co-partnership Trust Deed" at Unilever House, London.

"Leverhulme Correspondence" at Unilever House, London.

National Union of Gasworkers and General Labourers of Great Britain and Ireland. _Rule_ 1890 in the Webb Collections in the British Library of Political and Social Science.

South Metropolitan Gas Company. "Directors' Minute Book."

South Metropolitan Gas Company. "Proprietors' Report."

Unilever PLC. "Special Committee Minutes."

Newspapers and Journals

Amalgamated Society of Carpenters and Joiners, _Journal_

Amlgamated Engineers Journal

Anti-Socialist

Commonweal

Co-partnership, The Magazine of South Metropolitan Gas Company

Daily Herald

Daily Mail

Daily News

Democrat

East London Observer

Engineering World

Fabian News

Free Labour

Industrial Welfare

Journal of Gas Lighting

Justice

Labour Chronicle

Labour Co-partnership

Labour Elector

Liverpool Daily Post

Liverpool Echo

Liverpool Incorporated Chamber of Commerce, Monthly Journal

London Chamber of Commerce, Journal

New Statesman

Northern Daily Mail

Northern Echo

People's Press

Progress: the Magazine of Lever Brothers

Ratepayers' Chronicle and Parish Parliament

Renolds's Newspaper

Star

Times

Yorkshire Factory Times

Parliamentary Papers and Parliamentary Debates

Hansard..Parliamentary Debates, 3rd series; 5th series.

Royal Commission on Labour. Minutes of Evidence, Cd. 6708 (1892); Cd. 6894-ix (1893-4); Cd. 6894-VII (1893-4); Cd. 7093-I (1893).

Royal Commission on Trade Dispute and Trade Combinations. Minutes of Evidence, Cd. 2826 (1907).

Royal Commission on Poor Laws. Minutes of Evidence. Cd. 5066 (1910).

The Committee for the Relations between Employer and Employee. Final Report, Cd. 9153 (1918).

Board of Trade. Report on Profit-sharing and Labour Co-partnership in the U.K., Cd. 7458 (1894).

Board of Trade. Report on Profit-sharing and Labour Co-partnership in the U.K., Cd. 6496 (1912).

Ministry of Labour. _Report on Profit-sharing and Labour Co-partnership in the U.K._, Cd. 544 (1920).

Printed Documents

Charity Organization Society. Special Committee on Unskilled Labour, _Minutes of Evidence_. London: 1905.

Gas Light and Coke Company. _Report of Proceedings of the half-yearly Meetings_.

Institute of Gas Engineers. _Transactions_.

Labour Co-partnership Association. _Report of the Industrial Conference_. Newcastle: 1899.

Labour Co-partnership Association. _Report of London Co-partnership Congress_. London: 1920, 1923, 1926.

National Association for the Promotion of Social Science. _Transactions_.

National Union of Boot and Shoe Operatives. _Monthly Report_. Leicester.

National Union of Gasworkers and General Labourers in Great Britain and Ireland. _Annual Report and Balance Sheet_.

Shipconstructive and Shipwrights Association. _Report_.

Trades Union Congress. _Annual Reports_.

The Union of the Employer and the Employed. Report of the Provisional Committee. London: 1894.

United Society of Boilermakers and Iron and Steelship Builders. _Monthly Report_.

Books and Articles

Askith, M. E. _Profit-sharing: An Aid to Trade Revival_. London: Duncan Scott, 1926.

Amalgamated Society of Woodworkers. Our Society's History. Manchester, 1939.

Ashley, William. "Profit-sharing." Quarterly Review, 219 (Oct. 1913), pp.509-30.

Bartholeyns, A. O'D. "Profit-sharing between Capital and Labour," Westminster Review, 177 (1912).

Bell, D. Wallace. Financial Participation. London: Industrial Participation Association, 1973.

Booth, Charles. Life and Labour of the People in London. 2nd series, vol.3. London: Macmillan, 1903.

Bowie, James. Sharing Profits with Employees. London: Sir Isaac Pitnam, 1922.

Bristow, Edward. "Profit-sharing, Socialism, and Labour Unrest," in Essays in Anti-Labour History ed. K. Brown London: Macmillan, 1974.

Broady, David. "The Rise and Decline of Welfare Capitalism" in Workers in Industrial America. Oxford, Oxford University Press, 1982.

Brown, E. H. Phelps and Browne, M. H. A Century of Pay. London: Macmillan, 1968.

Browne, Benjamin. Selected Papers on Social and Economic Questions. Cambridge: Cambridge University Press, 1918.

Burgess, Keith. The Challenge of Labour. London: Croom Helm, 1980.

Burgess, K. The Origins of British Industrial Relations. London: Croom Helm, 1975.

Bushill, Thomas. The Relations of Employers and Employed in the Light of the Social Gospel. London: Alexander and Shepherd, 1889.

Cadbury, Edward. "Some Principles of Industrial Organization: the Case for and against Scientific Management," Sociological Review, 7 (Apr. 1914), pp.99-117.

Carpenter, Charles. Industrial Co-partnership. London: Labour Co-partnership Association, 1921.

Carter, C. J. "An Employee Co-partner on Co-partnership," Nineteenth Century, 85 (Feb. 1919), pp.227-31.

Child, John. British Management Thought. London: George

Allen and Unwin, 1969.

Church, R. A. "Profit-sharing and Labour Relations in England in the 19th century," International Review of Social History, 16 (1971).

Citrine, Walter. Men and Work: An Autobiography. London: Hutchison, 1964.

Clegg, Hugh. The Changing System of Industrial Relations in Great Britain. Oxford: Basil Blackwell, 1980.

Clarke, Nicholls, and Coombs. Profit-sharing Rules. London: 1890.

Clarke, Nicholls, and Coombs. The Proof of Pudding. London: 1919.

Clegg, H., Fox, A., and Thompson, A. F. A History of British Trade Unions since 1889. vol.1. Oxford: Oxford University Press, 1964.

Cole, G. D. H. The Case For Industrial Partnership. London: Macmillan, 1957.

Collison, W. The Apostle of Free Labour. London: Hurst and Blackett, 1913.

Conservative Research Department. Co-partnership Today. London: Conservative Political Centre, 1946.

Cronin, James. Industrial Conflict in Modern Britain. London: Croom Helm, 1980.

Cronin J. and Sirianni, C. ed. Work, Community, and Power. Philadelphia: Temple University Press, 1983.

Derrick, Paul and Phipps, J. F. ed. Co-ownership, Co-operation, and Control. London: Longmans, Green, 1969.

Dougan, David. The History of North East Shipbuilding. London: George Allen, 1968.

Edinburgh Review. "The Principles and Practices of Labour Co-partnership," 209 (Apr. 1909), pp.308-33.

Edwards, R., Gordon, D., and Reich, M. Segmented Work, Divided Workers: The Historical Transformation of Labor in the U.S. Cambridge: Cambridge University Press, 1984.

Fawcett, Henry. "Strikes, their Tendencies and Remedies," Westminster Review, 74 (July 1860), pp.1-13.

Fay, Charles. Co-partnership in Industry. Cambridge: Cambridge University Press, 1913.

Floud, R. and McCloskey, D. ed. The Economic History of Britain since 1700. vol.2. Cambridge. Cambridge University Press, 1980.

Fox, Alan. "Managerial Ideology and Labour Relations," British Journal of Industrial Relations, 4 (Nov. 1966), pp.366-78.

Furness, Christopher. The American Invasion. London: Simpkin, Marshall, Hamilton, Kent, 1902.

Furness, Christopher. Industrial Peace and Industrial Efficiency. West Hartlepool, 1908.

Garside W. R. and Gospel, H. "Employers and Managers" in A History of British Industrial Relations 1875-1914. ed. Wrigley, C. Amherst, Mass.: University of Massachussets Press, 1982.

George, W. L. Labour and Housing at Port Sunlight. London: Alston Rivers, 1909.

Gilman, Nicholas. Profit-sharing between Employer and Employee: A Study in the Evolution of the Wages System. Boston: Houghton, Mifflin, 1889.

Goodrich, Carter. The Frontier of Control. London: G. Bell, 1920.

Gospel, Howard. "The Development of Management Organization in Industrial Relations" in Industrial Relations and Management Strategy. ed. Thurley K. and Wood, S. Cambridge: Cambridge University Press, 1983.

Halevy, Elie. The Era of Tyrannies. Garden City, NY: Doubleday, 1965.

Hanson, E. H. "Profit-sharing Schemes in Great Britain," Journal of Management Studies, 2 (Oct. 1965), pp.331-50.

Hay, Roy. "Employers' Attitude to Social Policy and the Concept of "Social Control" 1900-1920" in The Origins of British Social Policy, ed. Thane, P. London: Croom Helm, 1978.

Hobsbawm, Eric. Labouring Men: Studies in the History of Labour. Garden City, NY: Doubleday, 1967.

Hobsbawm, E. Industry and Empire. NY: Penguin Books, 1971.

Hobson, John A. Ruskin: Social Reformer. Boston: Dana Estes, 1898.

Holton, Bob. British Syndicalism, 1900-1914. London: Pluto,

1976.

Holyoake, George J. The History of Co-operation. London: T. Fisher Unwin, 1908.

Hunt, N. C. Methods of Wage Payment in British Industry. London: Sir Isaac Pitman, 1959.

Jevons, William. Methods of Social Reform. London: 1883. rpt. New York, August M. Kelly, 1965.

Jones, Thomas. "Profit-sharing in Relation to Other Methods of Remunerating Labour," Accountants' Magazine, 8 (1904).

Kynaston, David. The British Working Class 1850-1914. Totowa: Rowman and Littlefield, 1976.

Labour Co-partnership Association. The Report of the Proceedings of the Industrial Remuneration Conference. London: Cassell, 1885.

Lever, William. "Prosperity-sharing vs Profit-sharing in Relation to Workshop Management." Economic Review, 11 (Jan. 1901), pp.47-64.

Lever, W. "Prosperity-sharing; Rejoinder," Economic Review, 11 (July 1901), pp.316-21.

Lever, W. The Six-hour Day ad Other Indutrial Questions. London: George Allen and Unwin, 1918.

The second Viscount Leverhulme, Viscount Leverhulme by His Son. London: George Allen and Unwin, 1927.

Littler, Craig. The Development of the Labour Process in Capitalist Societies. London: Heinemann, 1982.

Livesey, George. "The Failure of the Wages System of Payment and the Remedy--Profit-sharing." Institute of Gas Engineers, Transactions, 1892.

Livesey, G. "Another Step in Promoting the Union of Capital and Labour." IGE, Transactions, 1897.

Livesey, G. The Profit-sharing Scheme of the South Metropolitan Gas Company: The History and Results. London, 1899.

Livesey, G. "Profit-sharing: A Vindication," Economic Review, 11 (Oct. 1901), pp. 410-21.

Livesey, G. "Co-partnership." IGE, Transactiions, 1908.

Mackmurdo, A. H. Pressing Questions. London: John Lane, 1913.

Marshall, Alfred. Memorials of Alfred Marshall. ed. Pigou A. C. NY: Kelly and Macmillan, 1956.

Marx, Karl and Engels, Frederic. Articles on Britain. Moscow: Progress Publishers, 1971.

Melling, Joseph. "British Employers and the Development of Industrial Welfare." Disser. University of Glasgow, 1980.

Melling, J. "'Non-Commissioned Officers': British Employers and their Supervisory Workers, 1880-1920," Social History, 5 (1980).

Melling, J. "Employers, Industrial Welfare, and the Struggle for Work-place Control in British Industry, 1880-1920" in Managerial Strategies and Industrial Relations: An Historical and Comparative Study, ed. Gospel H. and Littler, C. London: Heinemann, 1983.

Mill, J. S. Principles of Political Economy. Collected Works vols. 2-3. Toronto: University of Toronto Press, 1965.

Morton, J. A. "Co-partnership and Profit-sharing Schemes," Socialist Review, 62 (1913).

Narashimhan, P. S. "Profit-sharing: A Review," International Labour Review, 62 (Dec. 1950), pp.469-99.

Nelson, Daniel. Managers and Workers: Origins of the New Factory System in the U.S. 1880-1920. Madison: University of Wisconsin Press, 1975.

Nelson, D. Frederick W. Taylor and the Rise of Scientific Management. Madison: University of Wisconsin Press, 1980.

Nelson, D. "The Company Union Movement," Business History Review, 56 (Autumn 1982), pp.335-79.

Nelson D. and Campbell, S. "Taylorism vs Welfare work in American Industry: H. L. Gantt and the Bancrofts," Business History Review, 46 (1972).

Nicholson, J. S. "Profit-sharing," Contemporary Review, 57 (Jan. 1890), pp.64-77.

Pease, Edward. Profit-sharing and Co-partnership: A Fraud and A Failure, Fabian Tract, 170, London: 1912.

Perks, R. "Real Profit-sharing: William Thomson and Sons of Huddersfield, 1886-1925", Business History, 24 (1982).

Pollard, Sidney. "The Economic History of British Shipbuilding, 1870-1914." Diss. University of London, 1951.

Pollard, S. The Genesis of Modern Management. London: Edward Arnold, 1963.

Pollard S. and Turner, R. "Profit-sharing and Autocracy: the Case of J. T. and J. Taylor of Batley," Business History, 18 (1976).

Poppelwell, F. "The Gas Industry" in Seasonal Trades. ed. Webb, Sidney and Freeman, A. London: Constable, 1912.

Price, Richard. Masters, Unions, and Men: Work Control in Building and the Rise of Labour 1830-1914. Cambridge: Cambridge University Press, 1980.

Price, R. "The Labour Process and Labour History," Social History, 8, (1983).

Price, R. "Conflict and Co-operation," Social History, 9 (1984).

Quelch, Harry. The Co-partnership Snare. London: Twentieth Century Press, 1912.

Ramsay, A. "Cycles of Control: Worker Participation in Sociological and Historical Perspective," Sociology, 2 (1977).

Reader, W. J. "Personality, Strategy and Structure: Some Consequences of Strong Minds" in Management Strategy and Business Development. ed. Hannah, L. London: Macmillan, 1976.

Rogow, Arnold. "Labor Relations under the British Labour Government," American Journal of Economics and Sociology, 14 (1954/5).

Ruskin, John. Unto This Last. London: George Allen, 1907.

Samuelson, Paul. "Thoughts on Profit-sharing" in Profit-sharing: A Symposium. ed. Sauermann H. and Richter R. Tubingen: J. C. B. Mohr, 1977.

Schloss, David. Methods of Industrial Remuneration. London: Williams and Norgate, 1898.

Semmel, Bernard. Imperialism and Social Reform. Garden City, NY: Doubleday, 1960.

Taylor, Sedley. "A Real 'Saviour of Society'," Nineteenth Century, 8 (Sep. 1880), pp.370-83.

Thorne, Will. My Life's Battle. London: George Newnes, 1925.

Thornton, William. On Labour. London: 1869; rpt. Shannon: Irish University Press, 1971.

Tomlinson, J. The Unequal Struggle. London: Methuen, 1982.

Turner, Ben. "Real Profit-sharing: A Splended Huddersfield Example," Socialist Review, 5 (1910).

Urwick, Lyndall. "Co-partnership and Control," The Human Facto 8 (1934).

Urwick, L. and Brech, E. F. L. The Making of Scientific Management. London: Management Publishers Trust, 1949.

Wallace, William. Prescription for Partnership. London: Sir Isaac Pitman, 1959.

Walls, Edward. Progressive Co-partnership. London: Nisbet, 192

Watson, Angus. My Life: An Autobiography. London: Ivor Nichols and Watson, 1937.

Webb, Sidney. The Works Manager Today. London: 1918; rpt. NY: Arno, 1979.

Webb, S. The Root of Labour Unrest: An Address to Employers and Managers. Fabian Tract, 196. London: 1920.

White, Joseph. "1910-1914 Reconsidered" in Social Conflict and the Political Order in Modern Britain ed. Cronin J. and Schneer, J. New Brunswick, NJ: Rutgers University Press, 198

Williams, Aneurin. Co-partnership and Profit-sharing. London: William and Norgate, Thornton Butterworth, 1913.

Williams, Trevor. A History of the British Gas Industry. Oxford: Oxford University Press, 1981.

Wilson, Charles. The History of Unilever. vol.1. London: Cassel, 1954.

Wilson, C. "Management and Policy in Large-scale Enterprise" in Essays in British Business History ed. Supple, Barry. Oxford: Clarendon, 1977.

Yarmie, Andrew. "The Captains of Industry in the Mid-Victorian Britain." Disser. University of London, 1975.

Zeitlin, Jonathan. "Trade Unionism and Job Control: A Critique of 'Rank and Filism.'" Bulletin of Society for the Study of Labour History, 46 (1983).

INDEX